"Any good journey outward requires a good and arduous journey inward. In *The Mystical Imagination*, Mark Votava carefully guides us on an inner journey of formation marked by an honest account of our truest need and our greatest contribution in the world. It awakens us to the possibility that God can in fact be expressed and experienced in our heart of hearts, pouring over into meaningful acts of love and service. This book is a true gift." **Christiana Rice**, co-author of *Altered*, Leadership Coach and Community Cohort Facilitator with Thresholds, neighborhood practitioner

"*The Mystical Imagination* is a wise and gentle plea for us all to come to attention and examine the true shape of our lives together. Mark Votava urges us to find the space to rest and reflect on how we might collectively embody in our daily lives what we say we believe about the gospel of Jesus. Drawing on the work of philosophers (Willard, Ellul), contemplatives (Merton, Weil, Nouwen), and activists (Cleveland, Sine), this book manages to be intellectually stimulating, spiritually refreshing and deeply practical all at the same time." **Michael Frost**, author, *Incarnate, The Road to Missional, Seeing God in the Ordinary*

"Communities are shaped though rhythms and rhythms are formed through practices. The values and culture of a community emerge from these rhythms and practices. In *The Mystical Imagination*, Mark Votava, explores how practices such as listening, questioning, silence, and communal dreaming form a mystical imagination which in turn forms us individually as well as communally. I highly recommend *The Mystical Imagination* to anyone who is seeking to grow a beloved community that is deeply rooted in a place, yet mindful of a reality beyond what we can see or touch. I believe our capacity to cultivate a mystical imagination determines our ability to become transforming and healing agents in our communities and our world." **Wendy McCaig**, author of *From the Sanctuary to the Streets*, Executive Director of Embrace Richmond

"A must read! Mark unpacks the beauty of entering into the embrace of the sacred mystery, where we are given permission to search, to question, imagine and be in endless wonder ... where we search for God, and God instead finds us." **Eileen Baura Suico**, Adjunct Professor of Leadership and Contemporary Culture at Fuller Theological Seminary, Co-Founder, Pastor, and Director at With, contributing writer to *The Gospel After Christendom*

"Our crowded, overly-consumed, hyper-active, digitally-addicted lifestyle is draining the life out of us. We are desperate to transcend the chaos and find a better way to live. We need a mystical imagination. Get ready to be transported into the depths of meaning as Votava breaks open the contemplative path and shows you how to live your life to the fullest." **Phileena Heuertz**, author of *Pilgrimage of a Soul: Contemplative Spirituality for the Active Life* and founding partner, Gravity, a Center for Contemplative Activism

"So much of the new locality movement is about strategy, rhetoric and technique. In contrast, Mark Votava offers a soulful path for living locally in community with others for the good of the world. He is a masterful compiler of the best wisdom of the mystical Christian tradition and writes with honesty and characteristic intensity. This is a serious book for people who want to live awake to the sacred in all of life." **Mark Scandrette**, activist, founder of ReIMAGINE and author of *FREE, Practicing the Way of Jesus* and *SOUL GRAFFITI*

"I underlined and highlighted this book like crazy. I'm chomping at the bit to reflect on all that stood out to me. Votava's book is the kind that demands further reflection. It is deep, challenging, and convicting. Indeed, the Holy Spirit used this book to expand my imagination and to help me better see the sacredness of life." **Marlena Graves**, author of *A Beautiful Disaster: Finding Hope in the Midst of Brokenness*

"*The Mystical Imagination* is an essential read for anyone sensing that following Christ just might be a whole-life adventure transforming everyday moments into our chance to join the Spirit in community as the 'body' reciprocally serves God by serving neighbor. Mark has put into words a deep longing for Shalom that woos me to invite the Holy Spirit to enliven my imagination for seeing that God is already present, at work, and graciously welcoming all to lives of rest, play, creativity, and beauty." **Dwight J. Friesen**, Associate Professor of Practical Theology at The Seattle School of Theology & Psychology, co-author of *The New Parish, Routes & Radishes*, and author of *Thy Kingdom Connected*

"In *The Mystical Imagination*, Mark Votava explores how to create a holistic counterculture that seeks to explore within a Christian context the rhythms of silence, listening, togetherness, solitude, intentionality, presence, neighborliness, hospitality, learning, and exploring. Those seeking to delve into the mystery of faith will benefit by his wisdom and guidance." **Becky Garrison**, satirist and storyteller, author of 8 books including *Roger Williams Little Book of Virtues* and *Jesus Died for This?*

"Mark's book is a deeply personal expression of his spiritual journey to a place and a people. Through solitude, listening, and reflection, he proposes a way to develop an integrated, ordinary, everyday faith in a neighborhood. With a mystical imagination, framed by rhythm and discipline, we can become a gift to our community." **Sherry Maddock**, urban farmer, co-author of *Sowing Seeds of Shalom in the Neighborhood*

"Just one look at the table of contents of this book made me eager to dive in. Mark hasn't left anything behind when it comes to contemplative spirituality. With an emphasis on not just the individual journey but also the communal one, this book is sure to be a gift for the new parish movement." **Lacy Clark Ellman**, spiritual director, author of *Pilgrim Principles: Journeying with Intention in Everyday Life*

"The vision I've caught from Mark isn't for 'a mystic on every block,' but one of Christians everywhere who are fully alive to the possibilities and responsibilities of the present moment. A wise and generous guide, Mark never takes us somewhere he hasn't already been himself. This book is an invitation to ALL Jesus followers—not just the rarified few—to explore the mysteries of God as embodied, placed, interconnected and interdependent people." **John Pattison**, co-author of *Slow Church: Cultivating Community in the Patient Way of Jesus*

"Votava invites his reader to enter into a world where one is reminded of the wonders of life. Mysticism may not be that out of reach after all. The gifts God gives us- the body, the mind, the sounds and silence around us- are, in the end, the path to God. Mark Votava's words are like drinking tea with honey, but don't be fooled. *The Mystical Imagination* is not for the faint-hearted. The work of silence, of deep reflection and of material sacrifice are, as Christ warned us, a difficult path indeed. But what a beautiful path it is, if we are to trust Mark Votava's wonderful instincts." **Jenna Smith**, author of *A Way: The Story of a Long Walk*

"Mark aptly slips on the shoes of a modern-day mystic who is both theologically sound and experientially in tune with God's presence within himself and the community (and within the parish, as he puts it). Mark does a wonderful job blending practical experience through his own personal story, stories from his community in Tacoma, and through great scholarship, in which he has woven a masterful array of quotes from a variety of authors both old and new. The essence of this book, if I could sum it up in one word, would be awareness. God is present. God is working within and without. Mark says it best: 'God's presence is always living within us and our particular context. Even in the most seemingly forsaken place, God is always present.' Mark not only tells us how to see the sacredness of life, he models it. This is a treasure worth getting and returning to again and again." **Dave Arnold**, author of *Pilgrims of the Alley* and *Building Friendships*

"Consider this book a gentle and strong invitation toward a more peaceful, human and sane way of being. Be inspired to clear space and allow the longing for God to rise up. Let the compulsive desire to pursue distraction and patterns of escapism gradually become subdued. Instead, in the welcome void, nurture patience, contemplation and authentic relationships. Words that move us toward mystery and transformation as individuals and as communities are a gift. Thank you Mark Votava for your work, forged in the trenches of real life and offered up as a hopeful guide." **Kelly Bean,** author of *How to Be a Christian Without Going to Church: The Unofficial Guide to Alternative Forms of Christian Community*

"Mark Votava's *The Mystical Imagination* is a call to nurture a deep contemplative spirituality for the 21st century. The vision is of 'an undistracted life of liberation' that may bring healing from all that keeps us diminished and fearful, and contribute towards the healing of our world. Mark makes clear that this possibility is for everyone—as he memorably calls us to become 'ordinary mystics.' He has gathered a wide and compelling collection of contemporary wisdom and experience, whilst reflecting with vulnerability on his own story, and drawing on his experience of shaping rhythms of life in the context of parish. I was moved, encouraged and challenged by this book, and love Mark's suggestion of a new paradigm for the parish: 'Dreaming, Awakening and Remembering.' The book closes with an enticing adventure back into the vital spiritual tradition of mystical love for God: 'Sometimes I imagine that Christ is the pillow or cushion beneath my head. I imagine Christ holding me as I rest my head upon him.' I warmly commend this book." **Ian Adams**, poet, photographer, retreat leader, Anglican priest, partner in Beloved Life, director of StillPoint, Spirituality Adviser for CMS and author of *Cave Refectory Road: monastic rhythms for contemporary living, Running Over Rocks: spiritual practices to transform tough times* and *Unfurling*

"Mark Votava has written a passionate call for the church to make a serious commitment to contemplative formation. Votava's own mystical imagination is fiercely incarnational, insisting that rootedness in a specific context—'in the parish,' as he says—is critical. Without being anchored in a community, we can easily chase the fantasy of loving God and humanity without involving either the true God or actual humans. Mindfulness. Honesty. Learning and unlearning. Awareness of our mortality, attentiveness to our longing. These disciplines will make the difference between going to church and being the church. A loving and prophetic call." **Susan R. Pitchford**, sociologist at the University of Washington, author of *The Sacred Gaze: Contemplation and the Healing of the Self, God in the Dark: Suffering and Desire in the Spiritual Life,* and *Following Francis: The Franciscan Way for Everyone*

The Mystical Imagination

The Mystical Imagination

Seeing the Sacredness of All of Life

MARK VOTAVA

Urban Loft Publishers | Portland, Oregon

The Mystical Imagination
Seeing the Sacredness of All of Life

Urban Loft Publishers
2034 NE 40th Avenue #414
Portland, OR 97212
www.urbanloftpublishers.com

ISBN-13: 978-0692580882

Made in the U.S.A.

Table of Contents

Foreword
by Kathy Escobar

When I think of the words "mystical" and "imagination," I smile because despite their lack of use in much of the language of contemporary Christianity, they are the exact right words to describe the best hope for the Body of Christ's future. The "kingdom of God" that Jesus talks about throughout the gospels is filled with mysticism and imagination. With radical trust that comes from a deeper knowing that is beyond knowledge and certainty. With creativity in ways that people experience transformation and deeper connection with God. With relationships that don't make sense in the world's eyes but are the truest reflection of God's heart for people.

The Kingdom of God is so full of imagination! But often, we as followers of Jesus have lost what was originally intended. Our search for knowledge, certainty and a cookie cutter system of church has robbed us of creativity and choked out many aspects of what "faith" really means.

The future of the church does not depend on more knowledge. What it desperately needs is more imagination!

Foreword

Some other words for imagination include: *creativity, resourcefulness, awareness, inventiveness, vision, imagery, originality.* These words are embedded into this book and are a reflection of what I believe we are called to participate in as followers of Jesus.

When I think of the words "mystical" and "imagination" I think of Mark Votava. He is not only a wonderful mix of theologian, spiritual guide, advocate, and friend, but he also has a prophetic voice into the future of Christianity. He sees what could be. He experiences Jesus in unlikely places. He calls people to be open to God in new ways that will stretch not only their hearts and minds but their hands and feet as well.

He is also an ordinary mystic, and I love what he says in this book about them. He offers, "Ordinary mystics are not weird, strange people who have lost contact with reality. On the contrary, they are people who live with awareness, mindfulness, love, and humility toward others, God, and the place they inhabit." This material is a wonderful call for us to be ordinary mystics as well, "a collective ... as the body of Christ in everyday life who seek God by cultivating the native passion of the soul."

This kind of soul work is not easy.

It cannot be spoon fed to us.

It cannot be imparted through just words.

We will have to participate, experience, and become learners.

The Mystical Imagination helps us learn. By challenging us to become lifelong learners "as a practice of following Christ," Mark asks us to reconsider some important rhythms and spiritual practices in our lives. Contemplative spirituality, hospitality, and incarnational, relationship-centered living are a few of the components that you will be challenged with as you read this book.

I know I was.

Mark reminded me, yet again, how living into the kingdom of God here and now requires an interesting and creative mix of intention and letting go. Of nurturing and cultivating systems but also releasing control and trusting their organic development. Of developing spiritual practices that quiet our hearts and minds at the same time we are actively engaged with our neighbors through tangible relationship. Of forgetting the status quo and leaning into deep stirrings in our soul no matter the cost. Of engaging deeply in community while also making room for solitude and silence.

In a world always looking for simple solutions, formulas and easy fixes, Mark is a different kind of voice that calls us to deep transformation and trust in the long story. This isn't popular in many circles, however, as many of us know people are leaving church in droves right now. Many are "done" with the system but far from done with being a follower of Jesus. Many may be either dissatisfied with church or left all together but still have a burning desire for authentic community. Many sitting in the pews are much less certain about what they believe but even more passionate about justice and mercy and living that out not in words but in action. We need guides for a spiritual journey that will look so much different than it did before.

That's why this book is important.

We need confirmation in our souls that our desire for less certainty, conformity, and affiliation and greater freedom, mystery, and diversity in our faith is a good thing. That ultimately we will draw closer to God and God's dreams for people, not further away. That our desire for a deeper spirituality that is centered on incarnational living is not crazy or heretical but a reflection of Jesus.

I'm grateful for Mark's voice, passion, and challenge to dream not just individually but collectively as well.

May we keep cultivating our mystical imagination together.

We need it.

The "church" needs it.

The world needs it.

Kathy Escobar, Co-Pastor of The Refuge, Spiritual Director, Author of *Faith Shift: Finding Your Way Forward When Everything You Believe is Coming Apart* and *Down We Go: Living Into the Wild Ways of Jesus*

Part 1

A Mystical Sense of Discipline: Seeking God In Everyday Life

Chapter 1

Developing Rhythms of Discipline: Continually
Seeking God as a Way of Life

> Spiritual formation, good or bad, is always profoundly social. You
> cannot keep it to yourself. Anyone who thinks of it as a merely
> private matter has misunderstood it. Anyone who says, "It's just
> between me and God," or "What I do is my own business," has
> misunderstood God as well as "me." Strictly speaking there is
> nothing "just between me and God." For all that is between me
> and God affects who I am; and that, in turn, modifies my
> relationship to everyone around me. My relationship to others also
> modifies me and deeply affects my relationship to God.[1]

Growing up, I never really knew what spiritual formation was. It
seemed to be something mysterious and difficult to talk about. Maybe
that's why there wasn't a lot of focus on it in the environments I was in.
It seemed that if you believed in God, you just went to a church
building, prayed vocal prayers, and sang songs while tolerating someone
recite a liturgy, homily, or sermon.

It seemed kind of boring to me. The only time I said "Thanks be to
God" was when the whole thing was over and I could go home to do

---

[1] Willard, *Renovation of the Heart*, 182.

something that was more interesting to me. I have never liked church the way I experienced it. The rituals, creeds, prayers, songs, homilies, sermons didn't mean a lot to me, even though I have always had an innate sense of a Creator who had created the world.

Maybe I thought that God had created the world, but wasn't present to it especially in my daily pain and struggles. The formation of a deep contemplative spirituality was something I was never really presented with. I had never heard of a mystical way of life where we engage the world with an interior listening and longing for the kingdom of God within. I had never heard of some of the great spiritual writers like Thomas Merton, Dorothy Day, or Simone Weil, who would later influence me a lot in my interior growth and formation.

Living in a Catholic family in which I was baptized and confirmed didn't help me much as I wasn't too interested in seeking God for a lot of my life. I just went along with it because that was my parents' tradition and I did not want to upset them or start any major conflict in our family. Not knowing what I believed in, I had never explored what is authentic to me. I just believed in what I saw on TV, what I heard from my family, and the things I learned through environments of school and church. But I sensed there was more to God then what I had experienced or had been taught.

So now I am much older and have seen, experienced, and felt the lack of focus on spiritual formation in the body of Christ. There seems to be a lot of current talk about community and mission, but that formation is one of the hardest things to figure out. This is so because it demands a much more interior, mystical way of life that takes work, focus, and passion to develop. This goes way beyond just going to a gathering, it encompasses all of life. It is an ongoing conversion throughout our entire lives. It is not just individual, but intentionally social too. It is disrupting to the status quo patterns we have learned from our families, schools, churches, and North American media sources.

Maybe that is why it seems so impossible. But it is not. We have just never been taught the way of deep interior rhythms, formation, and discipline to discover the life of Christ living within us. So this is what I have learned of spiritual formation as I know it in the twenty-first century world after almost two decades of research and practice. I now believe if we do not practice a healthy spiritual formation as the church, both as individuals and together, we will lack credibility and bring damage to our world through our experiments with community and mission.

An Undistracted Life: Healing the Patterns of Escapism

Everyone undergoes spiritual formation in our culture whether we realize it or not. Spiritual formation that is good and holistic is connected within a rootedness to place. It is connected with how our lives affect those we are in relationship with. It is integrated into the sanity of our souls within the body of Christ in everyday life together.

There is a mystical sense of discipline we need to develop within us as the body of Christ in the parish. We need to learn how to heal the patterns of escapism through an undistracted life of mystical discipline. We oftentimes like to escape everything that does not produce immediate, comfortable results. But that is not how rootedness in a place works. Our rootedness will most likely cause us pain and discomfort at times. There are things that are so complex in our local community that it takes years of listening and faithful presence to understand what is going on.

The mystical imagination is one where we undergo the healing of patterns of escapism and seek to live with courage from the fears that we try to escape a lot of the time. When will we become undistracted in our lives together to pursue God and heal the patterns of escapism that threaten our very existence? Elizabeth Hanson Hoffman and Christopher D. Hoffman say in their book *Staying Focused in an Age of Distraction*, "You can move forward equipped with the skills to stop squandering your valuable focus. We truly believe that your focus does become your life."[2]

Everything we do affects our relationships in the place in which we live. Nothing is just private and individualistic. God is profoundly calling us to a rootedness and a communion that cannot be escaped in everyday life together. We must face it and collaborate with the mystical imagination within us.

"Be perfect, therefore, as your heavenly Father is perfect" (Matthew 5:48). Jesus is calling us to perfection in life. This passage is in the context of loving others, friends and enemies alike. Christ is teaching us to not have a bias toward our love for friends over enemies. This has tremendous implications for the context that we live in. Our rootedness makes us face this question of love. I want to propose that this perfection has little to do with pietism, morality, and ethics per se. The major thrust of the teaching is about the perfecting of our relationships in our local context without patterns of escapism. The life of perfection to which Christ is calling us is about healing the patterns of escapism within the parish. Twentieth century mystic Thomas Merton writes, "The way of perfection is not a way of escape. We can only become saints by facing ourselves, by assuming full responsibility for our lives just as they are, with all their handicaps and limitations."[3]

We need a profound healing to take place within us as the body of Christ in our local community so that we do not destroy ourselves through our patterns of escapism. Perfection and escapism cannot co-exist within us. The mystical imagination calls out for the perfection of facing the real in life with courage and wisdom. We have to find a way to be faithfully present rather than escape our responsibilities and limitations.

---

[2] Hoffman, *Staying Focused in an Age of Distraction*, 17.

[3] Merton, *Life and Holiness*, 50-51.

We become dysfunctional when we live everyday life without a sense of mystical discipline that connects us to one another. Our limitations must be faced through an undistracted life within the mystical imagination. Christ is alive within us through the mystical imagination in the parish. We cannot escape our spiritual formation any longer. Social psychologist Christena Cleveland writes, "Individualistic American Christians are less likely to see more extrinsic and social faith practices as valuable. As a result, collective faith practices are less valued and in some cases, not even considered legitimate Christianity."[4]

Maybe we need to move from the freedom of escape to the liberation in being alive. We use our freedom as Americans to escape many things that do not suit our agendas. We think of free will as the freedom to live individualistic lives disconnected from a local community, to live individualistically, to pursue a private spirituality that is rootless. But our freedom to pursue all kinds of escapism is really no freedom at all. It is an illusion of our own making.

We need to pursue a liberation to be alive through the mystical imagination in the place we live as the body of Christ in everyday life. This liberation to be alive is undistracted, disciplined, and rooted. Katheen Norris notes, "We can no more escape from other people than we can escape from ourselves."[5] In our liberation we are free to seek God in the local community that we inhabit. We are liberated with a mystical discipline of discovery, listening, and embodiment. Our lives become undistracted.

We become local practitioners in the midst of our life together. We become the people who care for a place and lay our lives down for its well being. We cannot escape what is annoying or inconvenient any longer. We cannot run from our confusion as the body of Christ in the parish. The mystical imagination will always embrace the liberation to

[4] Cleveland, *Disunity in Christ*, 146.

[5] Norris, *The Cloister Walk*, 379.

be alive and rooted through the practice of a mystical sense of discipline.

The mystical imagination is not built on chance or fate. The mystical imagination is a metaphor of our communion with God. This is a communion that will be creative, passionate, alive, evolving, unpredictable, and rooted. The mystical imagination does not practice patterns of escapism, but embraces truthfulness in our lives together. "We are unwilling, it seems to me, to leave anything in our lives to chance except the way we live out our lives in communion with the One who gave us life in the first place. It seems odd to me," observes contemplative Robert Benson.[6]

It seems odd to me also that we are intentional about so many things in life—our families, our shopping, our entertainments, our social life, our careers, our sexuality, our appetites, our comfort and security—except our communion with our Creator. We have almost no imagination for the mystical in everyday life. We settle for the cliché of our concept of predestination that says "everything has a purpose and if it's meant to be it will happen." So we end up paying very little attention to pursuing God within the framework of the mystical imagination. We say, "It just isn't a part of the real world." It is secondary to the "real world" of what we can see right in front of us all of the time through images on screens and mass amounts of entertainment. We need a mystical imagination that redefines what the "real world" is to us as the body of Christ in the parish.

We need a mystical sense of discipline that helps us to engage God and one another through our local context. We need an undistracted life of liberation. God needs to be pursued with everything that lives within us. This will not happen by chance. So let us forget about chance and learn the life of the mystical imagination with some discipline and no distractions. This is the path of becoming saints in our local community through our relationships in all the commonality and diversity that

---

6 Benson, *In Constant Prayer*, 78-79.

abide there. French Sociologist Jacques Ellul states, "Above all, I must not become aware of reality, so images create a substitute reality. Artificial images, passing themselves off for truth, obliterate and erase the reality of my life and my society. They allow me to enter an image-filled reality that is much more thrilling."[7]

We are not very interested in the truth of our reality, so we settle instead for the reality of the "real world" presented to us through images that captivate our imaginations. We become anything but human and create a world around the images offered by the media, internet, advertisements, and shopping malls. We have become hyper-distracted and our imaginations have been murdered by the images of the "real world" that we have created out of patterns of escapism around us. We need the liberation of the mystical imagination to give push-back to the "real world" we have created. The mystical imagination has the power to liberate the life of Christ within us in ways that will counter the "real world" matrix in our culture.

The mystical imagination is interested in our liberation from these images that are killing our lives together. We cannot live our lives together distracted by escape mechanisms any longer. We cannot be the body of Christ together in everyday life if we are distracted and leave everything up to chance. Nothing will ever happen with chance. It is an illusion of our own making. Debbie Blue writes:

> I sometimes think it's just amazing we don't go really way crazier living within the fabrications that structure our world. And how does all that false structure ever manage to contain the chaos that it so misrepresents? Or maybe we're really already just so crazy we don't ever notice it anymore. We see but we don't perceive, hear but don't understand (and all that). We just turn right, turn left, stop, go, wear this, eat here, watch that and we're really all insane, blind to some truth or some chaos swirling all around us. But we look pretty normal.[8]

[7] Ellul, *The Humiliation of the Word*, 128.

[8] Blue, *Sensual Orthodoxy*, 65.

God has given us agency as human beings to be in communion with one another and creation. It is about time we stop escaping reality and start living into something that represents a holistic counterculture. The body of Christ needs to be based on something that is truthful, authentic, and relevant. There is no good news in the "real world" of our illusions. It is based on escapism, untruthfulness, dishonesty, and distraction. The mystical imagination will put us in a place of awareness where we wake up to what is authentic and begin to experience liberation. This will not happen by chance. The Spirit is wanting our collaboration with the mystical imagination as God leads us to become alive in everyday life together.

"Ask and it will be given to you; seek and you will find; knock and the door will be opened to you. For everyone who asks receives; he who seeks finds; and to him who knocks, the door will be opened" (Matthew 6:7). If we seek the mystical imagination within us we will find life. The door will be opened to live an undistracted life of discipline if we truly want it. We will receive the strength for healing our patterns of escapism if we seek it. We will start to understand the mystical imagination within us if we desire it.

We are the only ones who are keeping us from all of this. We need to allow our desires to be shaped by the longings within us. The mystical imagination of embracing the real will not be denied to anyone who is seeking it. When we seek Christ in this way a whole paradigm will be opened up that leaves our individualistic ways to find something more interdependent in our local community. Maggie Jackson states:

> Yet increasingly, we are shaped by distraction. The seduction of alternative virtual universes, the addictive allure of multitasking people and things, our near-religious allegiance to a constant state of motion: these are markers of a land of distraction, in which our old conceptions of space, time, and place have been shattered. This is why we are less and less able to see, hear, and comprehend what's relevant and permanent, why so many of us feel that we can barely keep our heads above water, and our days are marked by perpetual loose ends. What's more, the waning of our powers of

attention is occurring at such a rate and in so many areas of life, that the erosion is reaching critical mass. We are on the verge of losing our capacity as a society for deep, sustained focus.[9]

For some reason we think that there is life in our distractions. Distractions are the American way. Distractions are the norm. Distractions are predictable. Distractions are controlled. We love to escape our lives and responsibilities to one another for the thrill of distractions. Distractions, we think, are the ultimate path to our "happiness." But the truth is that distractions always lead us to illusion.

Distractions take away our imaginations for something countercultural. Distractions try to scare the mystical imagination with images of the "real world" promoted by the narratives of individualism and narcissism. Distractions are a technique to escape reality. Distractions are addictive and irrelevant to true life. When will we as the body of Christ in everyday life be tired of being seduced by our distractions?

Christ understood and practiced a mystical sense of discipline. He was not drawn into the distractions around him. His intense focus in his locality enabled him to live with intentionality. He never escaped reality in life. He always faced reality in truthfulness. Christ is the ultimate example of the embodiment of the mystical imagination. Jesus was the most disciplined person who ever walked the face of the earth. He was always aware and mindful of the subsidiaries going on around him. We are all called to follow Christ in this way by becoming disciplined and focused in our everyday lives together.

My friend Ben does media fasts every so often. He does not engage with the internet, email, recorded music, TV, movies, or magazines for a period of time. Ben says that it helps him to listen to others and God more holistically. He finds more time to spend with others without any distractions. Sometimes he cooks, practices meditation, does yoga, journals, writes music, takes walks, and has a chance to reflect in

---

[9] Jackson, *Distracted*, 14.

silence. He says that creating spaces in life where we can practice the discipline of being undistracted, mindful, and listening to the simple miracles of God all around us in everyday life is essential if we are to share life with others.

What would happen if we all found a way to practice being undistracted in everyday life as the body of Christ in the place we live? Listening to others and God would begin to manifest itself in the graces of compassion and love within us into our local community. We would see more of God's simple miracles in everyday life if we would dare to become undistracted and face each other in the reality of our context. As Henri J.M. Nouwen writes in his book *Clowning In Rome*, "Discipline implies that something very specific and concrete will need to be chosen."[10]

The Spirit is leading us into healing the patterns of our escapism that we hold onto so tightly by creating an undistracted revolution within us through the mystical imagination.

Finding Rhythms: The Beginnings of Faithful Presence

When our Downtown Neighborhood Fellowship first asked people to move into the neighborhood of Downtown Tacoma many people couldn't right away, so we encouraged them to participate in rhythms that were small steps that would make the transition easier over time. We encouraged a rhythm of spending an hour once a week in a coffee shop. or going for a walk in the neighborhood. or spending time with friends in the neighborhood doing something fun like a movie or going to a public space like a park. These rhythms became important to us because even small rhythms of presence in the neighborhood can become the seeds of imagination that grow with unlimited potential and possibility.

---

[10] Nouwen, *Clowning in Rome*, 73.

It is important to develop some kind of rhythms in the parish. Rhythms foster rootedness and faithful presence and they are symbolic in the sense of helping us to remember God's presence within us and the place we live. Margaret Feinberg asks, "Will you develop rhythms in your life that foster spiritual vitality and a greater awareness of God?"[11] All of life has rhythms to it. We need to have locally based rhythms that help us to share life and cultivate the mystical imagination in us as the body of Christ in everyday life. Rhythms of silence, listening, togetherness, eating, laughing, planning, communicating, serving, reading, walking, shopping, sleeping, playing, relaxing, working, meditating, reflecting, resting, socializing, and exercising all have a place in our lives together in the place we inhabit.

When we create rhythms of faithful presence in our lives together; we are reminded again and again of God's presence with us, in us, and through us. We mystically become connected to the long history of our place at the creation of the world. There is so much we do not understand about creation, the earth, land, and our particular place that we inhabit together. Our rhythms help us to remember and honor the place that we walk on. The mystical imagination helps us to value our world in many multifaceted ways.

"And surely I am with you always, to the very end of the age" (Matthew 28:20). God's presence is always living within us and our particular context. Even in the most seemingly forsaken place, God is always present. God is intertwined into our world. God is intertwined into our locality. God is intertwined in our relationships. God will never leave us abandoned and alone even though we can often feel like this is happening.

Our rhythms bring awareness of God's presence within and around us. The more rooted practices and rhythms that we develop, whatever they may be, the more we will be connected to the mystical imagination within us. We need to become creative and intentional with exploring

---

[11] Feinberg, *Wonderstruck*, 56.

unlimited possibilities of rhythms that can be experimented with in our local community.

Rhythms are always relational and contextual. I cannot tell you what rhythms will work for you and you cannot tell me what rhythms will work for me. That's why it is dangerous to have a centralized hub of power telling you what to do outside of the particular context. This will not work and will result in colonialism and exploitation which doesn't represent the beauty of the gospel. New Monastic Simon Cross says, "We might conceive of all lives having rhythms. In this context, a rhythm of life is again all about intentionality. We choose to do certain things at certain times, to accept certain parts of life as necessary, and to incorporate ways of being into our way of life."[12]

Intentionality, spirituality and locality need to find a way to fit together in everyday life for rhythms to actually develop and have some sustainability. In the name of God, we can cultivate a rhythm of fragmentation and speed that is not rooted in place and is unconsciously violent. This is obviously not a good representation of the body of Christ and will do much damage. But we can also create rhythms that are helpful, beautiful, relational, convivial, rooted, peaceable, loving, and for the common good. I hope we will chose to orientate our rhythms around the latter. If this does not happen, it is questionable what kind of a future we will leave our children.

There is no escaping rhythms in the parish if we are to be the body of Christ in everyday life. Life can be so beautiful when we pursue all of life as local, sacred, networked, and convivial with rhythms that support this life-giving nature. This is where relational revelations happen within the context of the mystical imagination in the place we inhabit together.

This mystical sense of discipline will cultivate relational rhythms, both with others and with God that will over time begin to create a holistic

---

[12] Cross, *Totally Devoted*, 61.

counterculture. There is nothing more beautiful and powerful than a community of people who pursue rhythms together in a particular place for the survival, sanity, and sustainability of their souls as the body of Christ in everyday life. The mystical imagination longs for such things.

There is no more subversive act than the simple rhythm of walking in the neighborhood. It is so enjoyable to hear the sounds, and to breathe the air, to feel the wind, to be amazed at the colors and textures of buildings, to watch the cracks on the sidewalks, to greet neighbors who pass by, to smell the food of restaurants, to look into the windows of stores, to touch the trees in the park, to notice the beauty of art displays, to gaze at the waterfront, to notice the sky, and to watch the birds. This has shaped me tremendously and given me a higher regard for the place I inhabit.

I am beginning to be shaped by the place where I live more than I could have realized ten years ago. I am beginning to see everything that makes up this place as sacred and beautiful and hopeful. It is part of the mystical imagination that is developing in me. It is a miracle of God taking place in me. In an often hopeless world of fragmentation, we need to see the world and our particular place in it as beautiful again through the mystical imagination.

Rhythms help us to listen. The mystical imagination cultivates listening. Listening helps us to become more aware of others in our parish. Listening helps us to honor the place that we live. The earth, land, and place becomes sacred to us as we cultivate a rhythm of finding ways to listen. God is the Creator of the earth and we need rhythms with which to honor its creation. As Macrina Wiederkehr writes, "Indigenous peoples often have an innate awareness of the need to honor the natural place and rhythm of their inner beings. They seem able to pick up signals drawing them into a stance of obedient listening."[13]

---

[13] Wiederkehr, *Seven Sacred Pauses*, 22.

I propose that we need to learn from indigenous people such as the Native Americans who are highly in touch with the earth, their land, and the place where they live. They listen more than we do. They live more simply and experience life less dualistically. They seem to understand the ecology of life, how all of life is connected, and they live more holistically. They have rhythms that are relational and contextual to the good of the place they inhabit. We might think that there is nothing to learn from these people, but that will be our great mistake. We need some rhythms that will help us to develop an honoring way of life toward our place.

Rhythms are ways of seeking God in a specific local community as the body of Christ in everyday life. There is such a need today for creative ways to seek God. It is hard to seek God apart from the body of Christ in everyday life and apart from a commitment to a particular place. It is hard to seek God when we're disconnected from culture and others. Celia Wolf-Devine states, "we need to develop certain habits that facilitate God's work in us."[14] Has seeking God totally disappeared in our time? The less we commit to our context, each other, culture and creativity, the less we tend to know of seeking God. I want to encourage a different context to seeking God today in our everyday lives together.

I want to encourage rhythms of silence, listening, togetherness, solitude, intentionality, presence, neighborliness, hospitality, learning, and exploring. Through a sense of mystical discipline and rhythms of locality, we could start to create a holistic counterculture together in the most difficult of contexts. We were made to practice rhythms of seeking God through the mystical imagination in the parish. There is no more challenging and peaceful way to live out our lives together as the body of Christ in everyday life.

There is a freedom, not to escape, but to find rhythms that cultivate the mystical imagination in the parish. There is a balanced, holistic

---

[14] Wolf-Devine, *The Heart Transformed*, 9.

discipline that needs to be sought out in our local community. A mystical sense of discipline will liberate our imaginations to value one another as humans and connect us to our particular place that we inhabit without abuse. "We need to find freedom," states Lynne M. Baab, "by embracing healthy discipline."[15]

There is a reconciliation that happens with healthy discipline. We live more holistically when we become rooted in a particular place over time. All healthy spirituality happens within the disciplined rhythms of the mystical imagination in the parish. To live as a countercultural people, we need to find creative ways to explore rhythms in our local community. This is where the mystical imagination begins to find its life in us.

Our culture wants to take these healthy rhythms out of our lives together. Our culture wants us to dance without this kind of rhythm. Our culture wants the narrative of individualism to dictate the lives we live. Our culture is not very open to its counterculture and will do almost anything to stop it. Christine Sine of Mustard Seed Associates says:

> Finding God's pace in a world that constantly leaves us gasping for breath isn't easy. What kind of a rhythm is best for our lives? Most of us can't or don't want to totally disconnect from the high-speed world in which we live. On the other hand, we don't want to settle for that agonizing rhythm that leaves us gasping for air when life gets tough. What most of us are looking for is a rhythm that both paces us through the everyday and sustains us through the mountain passes—a life with a measured beat and a sense of balance.[16]

We are always being threatened with the opinions of our culture. Our culture can be mean at times. Our culture wants to turn us into machines for the global economy. Our culture is not friendly to the

[15] Baab, *Sabbath Keeping*, 99.

[16] Sine, *GodSpace*, 32.

mystical imagination. Our culture loves church buildings or meetings that promote services with little hospitality toward one another in everyday life. Our culture loves endless talk about the gospel with no action and life to it. Our culture is not easily fooled and is very smart.

Without courage, intelligence, practice, rhythms, perseverance, love, humility, and listening, we will not be able to create a holistic counterculture in our local context. The mainstream culture is too clever to allow this to happen. The mainstream culture wants to keep us from having a rhythm of sharing life together through living in proximity and rooting in the parish. The mainstream culture will do anything to keep us from being in holistic relationships with one another in everyday life. The narrative of individualism in our culture is too strong for that to go down while it lives oftentimes unconsciously in our imaginations. We must seek out freedom and liberation from all of this.

Radical Obedience as a Lifestyle of Worship: Developing a Personal Practice

The mystical imagination cultivates a lifestyle of worship through a radical obedience to Christ. This is the foundation of our personal practice in the parish. This radical obedience is manifested by being rooted in the parish. It is manifested in listening, loving, communion, silence, humility, grace, simplicity, longing, reflection, learning, hospitality, empathy, faithful presence, vulnerability, authenticity, solidarity, solitude, rest, proximity, shared life, and togetherness. A lifestyle of worship is not about singing songs, although that is not a bad thing, but is about living out together the songs that spring from the longings we experience for God's *shalom* in the place we live. We need to re-imagine how we can practice radical obedience as a lifestyle of worship in our local context.

> Therefore, I urge you, brothers, in view of God's mercy, to offer your bodies as living sacrifices, holy and pleasing to God—this is your spiritual act of worship. Do not conform any longer to the pattern of this world, but be transformed by the renewing of your

mind. Then you will be able to test and approve what God's will is—his good, pleasing and perfect will" (Romans 12:1-2).

Can we know God's will outside of a local, relational context where we share life with others? Can we know God's will without a lifestyle of worship and obedience? Can we live into a lifestyle of worship without being rooted in the parish? These are very challenging questions that we need to struggle with if we want to live into an authentic faith and be a part of the body of Christ in everyday life. Jamie Arpin-Ricci states in his book *The Cost of Community:*

> ... yet too often we settle into the status quo of nominal obedience, emphasizing our articulated beliefs rather than focusing on our living and active faith. When challenged, we often cite our sinful imperfection and dependence on grace as a way to minimize or dismiss the indictment of our compromises.[17]

So many people seem to dismiss the potential of radical obedience as a lifestyle of worship because they do not realize that Christ lives within them. We sometimes just like to focus on our sin and ignore the divine image of God within us, and say, "I'm just a sinner," as if we could not be anything more than that. Why do we rarely focus on Christ living within us calling us to authenticity? Is it because we don't understand, are apathetic, or is it something more? I don't understand how we can live with this view that dismisses the promises of God to us. Natalie Smith writes, "Obedience is not a popular concept in our world today."[18]

We do not have to live according to sin and shame! So much of Scripture points this out. "Do not offer the parts of your body to sin, as instruments of wickedness, but rather offer yourselves to God, as those who have been brought from death to life; and offer the parts of your body to him as instruments of righteousness." (Romans 6:13). We are created in the image of God and our bodies have this divine essence

---

[17] Arpin-Ricci, *The Cost of Community*, 202.

[18] Smith, *Stand On Your Own*, 112.

living within us because we are created by God. We have the potential to reflect the image of God to others.

The Father, the Son, and the Spirit live inside of our bodies to give us life, wisdom, and strength. How can we not see that this is so important to understand as the body of Christ in everyday life? We will do great damage if we do not understand this because apart from love most of our relationships will turn exploitive and manipulative. And who wants that? People in our culture have seen in us too much of the sin and not a lot of the divine essence of love and compassion. The mystical imagination cultivates the image of God within us as the body of Christ in the parish.

We need to work out our salvation through a radical obedience in the parish with others as the body of Christ in everyday life. We need a radical obedience as a lifestyle of worship to create a holistic counterculture. Only people who worship God with their whole lives will be able to embody love. We need to re-imagine what worship is in our time. We need to broaden our paradigm of worship and make it more inclusive to all of life in a particular place such as: caring, loving, neighborliness, compassion, hospitality, listening, contemplation, reflection, resting, silence, solitude, humility, simplicity, generosity, faithful presence, vulnerability, and friendship. All of life can be worship and this is what we are called to as the body of Christ in the parish.

A holistic counterculture is really a culture of worship, a culture of radical obedience, and listening. The mystical imagination is always integrated with a holistic worship that is grounded in the place where we live. As Norman Wirzba says, "We have divorced worship too much from our everyday lives and placed it in a purely spiritual realm, not realizing that in doing so we have rendered it abstract and anemic, cut off from the flows and patterns of daily life."[19]

---

[19] Wirzba, *Living the Sabbath*, 159.

A lifestyle of worship cannot be separated from this way of life. It calls for a radical attention to the particulars of relationships and context.

A radical obedience as a lifestyle of worship opens us up to awareness, mindfulness, love, compassion, humility, listening, contemplation, empathy, and grace. This is the kind of spirit that the mystical imagination longs for. My dear friend Eileen Baura Suico says, "Worship happens anywhere and everywhere … Worship draws our attention to God, and at the same time, enables God to be encountered in the world."[20]

We start to understand things on deeper levels through a radical obedience in the parish. We begin to think about and reflect on deeper meanings of everyday life than what we had known.

We start to value people as if they mattered. Consumerism and entertainment become less interesting to us. We desire more time in silence and solitude. We start to have some imagination for an alternative to our status quo lifestyle. Our lives are not necessarily all about what we do, but about the spirit we bring to the things that we do. Do we bring a spirit of encouragement and inspiration to the things we do? Do we bring a spirit of joy and celebration? Do we bring a spirit of love and humility? The locality that we inhabit needs a spirit of life, hope, peace, love, celebration, and imagination from the people who live there. The body of Christ in everyday life is called to bring this kind of spirit to our parish. Michael Frost and Alan Hirsch encourage us to look at worship in this way:

> Nowhere does Jesus call us to worship him in the Gospels; what is clear is that he does demand obedience. Understood from a Hebraic perspective, obedience is the worship we should render him. When we merely approve of Jesus, take his side as if we can agree intellectually with what he is saying, we can easily domesticate his demands, making them into mere sayings and

---

[20] Suico, "With," 277.

aphorisms of a wise man. They are far more dangerous and demanding than that.[21]

Christ calls us to worship him through a radical obedience as the body of Christ in the parish. Obedience to Christ is worship. At the heart of radical obedience are our longings and dreams of seeking God in the midst of everyday life. We desire that God would live within us through the mystical imagination. Christ wants us to develop a lifestyle of worship through radical obedience. Christ is dangerous to the status quo lifestyle. Christ is dangerous to our boxes of safety and comfort. Christ is dangerous to us because our dualities that we hold will not survive. Christ is the destroyer of fabricated religious illusions in his name. We do not know what Christ will do through us until we allow this mystery to live in our bodies without being oppressed.

I remember when I first heard the word "obedience" as referring to what we were supposed to be striving after within Christianity. A friend of mine in college was talking a lot about it and it intrigued me. I started learning about an obedience by grace. I had always thought that grace was only for forgiveness. This obedience by grace opened up the possibilities for me to see that I can live for God with creativity, passion, humility, love, and intelligence. I could reflect God's image within me. I could follow the light, eat the bread of life, and live in union with Christ. I didn't understand all of this, but these ideas from Scripture began to captivate my imagination.

Maybe I didn't have to be just a "sinner." Maybe I could actually live a beautiful life and seek God in obedience by grace. I wanted to follow, eat, live, listen, and drink in this obedience. What did all of this mean? I really didn't know, but I was open to exploring the potential and the possibilities that a radical obedience of grace would hold for me. Today, about twenty years later, I am learning to understand this radical obedience of grace, this lifestyle of worship, this mystical imagination through the body of Christ in the parish. I am not just a "sinner," I am

---

[21] Frost and Hirsch, *ReJesus*, 155.

more than that. I am created in the image of God. I am an expression of love. I have a mystical imagination. Joseph R. Myers says in his book *Organic Community*:

> A theology of God as creator of organic order, however, allows for collaboration with him. We are privileged to participate with him in the forming of our future. He invites our ideas, our energy, our creativity, our perspective. He gives up a measure of control to facilitate relationship with us and to demonstrate his love.[22]

A theology of "God as creator of organic order" connects a lot to the theology of place. It invites us into participation and collaboration with God, others, and the place itself. What it manifests is a theology of "God as creator of organic order" within that particular place because we are empowered to develop a personal practice of love, grace, hospitality, humility, and creativity alongside God. In other words, we are beginning to practice a mystical imagination. A radical obedience as a lifestyle of worship has so much to do with both a theology of "God as creator of organic order" and a theology of place.

When we begin to live into a radical obedience as a lifestyle of worship, we begin to see God's grace from a different angle. We begin to be strengthened by a beautiful, not oppressive, power that is of God that allows us to create our futures together into the place that we inhabit. If we are in a place long enough, we can shape our futures together and bring a tremendous amount of beauty into the world in the process. To integrate a theology of "God as creator of organic order," a theology of place, and a radical obedience as a lifestyle of worship as lived out together as the body of Christ in everyday life would be a miraculous gift of God to us all. I believe that this was what the early church was founded on. They understood this and embodied it in their lives together.

---

[22] Myers, *Organic Community*, 130-131.

Developing Rhythms of Discipline

Chapter 2

The Embodiment of Mystery: Embracing the Wisdom of Seeing

Living In Our Bodies: Integrating Incarnational Embodiment

Our bodies are meant to be lived in. They connect us to the ecology of life in a neighborhood. All of life is connected and our bodies are part of the overall body of Christ in a particular place. Nothing can escape the body. It is how we experience our lives together in all our commonality and diversity. The mystical imagination connects us to an embodied incarnational spirituality in our bodies. Our locality and our bodies need one another. The body longs for God in a particular place. Associate Professor of Philosophy at Geneva College, Esther Lightcap Meek, states, "The primary phenomenon of human persons is the lived body."[1] The lived body is how we experience our salvation together as the body of Christ in the parish.

There is no life outside of the lived body. There is no truth outside of the lived body. If our bodies are not lived in, we are dead even though we are still breathing and walking. The body is sacred, unique, beautiful, mystical, powerful, intuitive, intelligent, and is the holder of

---

[1] Meek, *Loving To Know*, 413.

all imagination. We need our bodies desperately in order to live and experience sanity. We need to see the body as being created in the image of God. The body can be used for good purposes and compassionate work within our everyday lives in the parish.

The lived body is meant to embody our redemption throughout our days. Our bodies are a gift from God, and it is a mistake to take them for granted. Our bodies identify intuitively with the ecology of life. They have an intuitive power beyond what we can sometimes understand. They are relational and interdependent. We need a mystical sense of discipline to live in our bodies in everyday life. This is such a subversive, countercultural practice for our time. Henri J. M. Nouwen writes, "A new spirituality is being born in you. Not body denying or body indulging but truly incarnational. You have to trust that this spirituality can find shape within you, and that it can find articulation through you."[2]

The body is extremely sacred in every dimension of life in the parish. The body is not "sinful" as some tend to think. But it is oftentimes perceived as "sinful" when we constantly misuse it through an individualistic lifestyle. The body is created by God to be used for intentional purposes of love, grace, humility, shared life, compassion, kindness, solidarity, nonviolence, and creativity. Craig G. Bartholomew says in his book *Where Mortals Dwell*, "Recovery of place requires a new view of the body."[3]

The body is meant for life, is the receiver of life, is the expression of life, and the proof of life. There is no substitute for the lived body that is connected and rooted in place. We have become a displaced, disembodied, dislocated society that rejects the potential and limitations of the body. Our potential is in the exploration of incarnational embodiment together. Our limitations protect us from exploitation and colonialism.

[2] Nouwen, *The Inner Voice of Love*, 32.

[3] Bartholomew, *Where Mortals Dwell*, 179.

The lived body is leading us by the Spirit in the place we live. The lived body longs for the mystical imagination to be alive in us. "Just as you used to offer the parts of your body in slavery to impurity and to ever-increasing wickedness, so now offer them in slavery to righteousness leading to holiness" (Romans 6:19). When we become a slave in our bodies to righteousness this means becoming committed to valuing people and committing to a particular place to create community. How can we be relational in any other way? Righteousness and holiness have a lot to do with people, God, and place as experienced in the lived body.

Living in a place and living in our body are so interrelated that we cannot elevate one over the other. They need to be practiced together through an incarnational embodiment of the mystical imagination. North Americans seem to live outside of their bodies a lot of the time. We are fragmented and scrambling for some peace and sanity in the midst of rejecting the proper use of the lived body. We are used to creating any kind of life we want at the expense of other people. We become subtly, unconsciously violent through our individualism. We need to learn how to recover the lived body in our postmodern culture as the body of Christ in the parish. It is not very easy and will take some work on our part. But it is definitely possible. Stephanie Paulsell states, "It is through our bodies that we participate in God's activity in the world. And it is through daily bodily acts ... that we might live more fully into the sacredness of our bodies and the bodies of others."[4]

Do we understand what it means to live in a particular place? Do we understand how to become an expression of love in the place that we live? Do we understand how to seek God in our local community with passion and intelligence? Have we forgotten how to listen to the mystical imagination as the body of Christ in everyday life? We cannot dismiss these questions anymore just because we are American and pretend to have all the answers in our propositional clichés.

---

[4] Paulsell, "Honoring the Body," 15.

The Embodiment of Mystery

Some things that I have done to practice living in my body are: exercising, eating meals with others, slowing down, listening, reading, reflecting, walking in the neighborhood, gardening, cooking, hospitality, writing, meditation, silence, solitude, resting, working locally, living locally, shopping locally, partnering, collaborating, meaningful conversation, relaxing, laughing, contemplation, being faithfully present, and artistic expression.

I once took a local songwriting class in which I had to write songs and play them publicly in front of others in the class. I was so intimidated and afraid because I didn't think I had a good voice. I was new at playing the guitar. I didn't want to write songs about the typical romantic themes we all hear so often. So I wrote a song about the disturbing draw of progress in our culture. It was about how we are always haunted by the ideology of always needing more at the expense of everything else that's important in life.

I was not sure how this would go down. I hadn't played many songs before, but this experience caused me to become aware of living in my body. After I played the song, I felt as though my entire body was connected and whole. My voice was connected with my mind, with my hands, with my arms, with my legs, with my eyes, with my emotions, with my friends, with my place. The time I took writing the words, creating the music and playing the song connected me with the people in my neighborhood in a very mystical way. I could not fully understand what was happening in me, but I believe the simple act of living in my body through creating a piece of art for the good of others and the place I live cultivated the mystical imagination within me that day. The mystical imagination always works in very ordinary and mysterious ways.

The lived body is the medium of all relational revelations in our lives together as the body of Christ in the parish. When we live in our bodies we are truly alive in a holistic way as the mystical imagination becomes our reality in all we do. There is no separation between the mystical imagination and the lived body. All truth is lived and rooted in the wisdom of our bodies. As contemplative Martin Laird says, "The body is a great reservoir of wisdom."[5] We cannot experience the wisdom path that Christ wants to teach us without living in our bodies. The incarnational embodied life is powerful and beautiful. It is a miracle and a gift of God. The body contains so much wisdom if we would only allow ourselves to live in the context of what we have been given by God.

The wisdom of the lived body is needed to be in relationship with others, God, and our place. When we dismiss the body, we dismiss our spirituality. We dismiss all wisdom in life. We dismiss our very humanity. We dismiss all of our potential. We dismiss all that is beautiful and good within us. We dismiss the conviviality among us. To come to a place of new understanding of the body is crucial for a change deep within us as the body of Christ in everyday life in the parish. To create a sustainable shared life together we will have to recover the lived body. To live in our bodies, to love in our bodies, to be silent in our bodies, to be passionate in our bodies for the good and beauty of the place we inhabit is what the mystical imagination longs for. Lauren F. Winner writes, "What I want is to pay more attention— and more explicitly theological attention—to my body and the things it does every day and the connections between the work of my body and the daily service of God."[6]

Christ lived in his body, he became a servant in his body, he loved others in his body, he lived in humility in his body, he lived locally in his body, he listened in his body, he cared for the earth in his body, and he communed with the Father in his body. The lived body is a spiritual practice that we need to take seriously as the body of Christ in everyday life together. To ignore the body is to ignore the mystical imagination. It is to ignore God. It is to ignore Christianity in its most authentic form. It is to ignore life.

---

[5] Laird, *Into the Silent Land*, 45.

[6] Winner, *Mudhouse Sabbath*, 75.

The body is our teacher of wisdom, reality, and truth. It cannot be displaced any longer within the body of Christ. The body is all we've got in this life to experience the goodness of God. Without the body we are dead. Without the body we do not exist. Any Christian spirituality that does not regard the lived body as sacred is false and misleading. The sacredness of the body is our greatest hope. The sacredness of the body opens us up to the mystical imagination within us.

How can we experience the world without our bodies? How can we see the beauty in everyday life without our bodies? How can we be known and loved by others without our bodies? Philosopher Dallas Willard writes:

> The body is the focal point of our presence in the physical and social world. In union with it we come into existence, and we become the person we shall forever be. It is our primary energy source or "strength." And it is the point through which we are stimulated by the world beyond ourselves and where we find and are found by others.[7]

The wisdom of the lived body is the only way we can actually live our lives holistically together as the body of Christ in the place we live. To live in our bodies is to exist properly in our world, in our locality. When we live in our bodies, we become the body of Christ together in the parish. We begin to create a holistic counterculture and begin to find some sanity. Our smiles are not so broken anymore and we begin to cope with our pain better.

When we were born, we came into existence in a body. As we grew, we came to understand the world through normative patterns and clues. We experienced our understanding through guidance from others and living in our bodies. As we got older and more "sophisticated," we became independent and forgot about the body.

---

[7] Willard, *Renovation of the Heart*, 35.

We separated the sacred from the body, the economic from the body, the local from the body, the relational from the body, the environment from the body, and the material from the body. Now we need to dig ourselves out of a hole and learn to live in our bodies again as a sign of life. This is one of the most important things for us to understand as the body of Christ in the parish. We need to recover the importance of living in our bodies, refusing to separate the body from all of life's dimensions. The mystical imagination always honors the body.

Living Into the Mystical Nature of Christianity: Becoming Ordinary Mystics

In recent decades, our spirituality has become too rationalistic, too embedded in the modernity of our culture. In the midst of all this, we have lost sight of the mystery of the gospel, the mystery of the body of Christ, the mystery of God's ordinary miracles among us, and the mystery of the human being. Our Christianity has a mystical nature rooted in the imagination. When you take away that mystical nature, you have a distorted spirituality that is void of substance and life. You have a skeleton instead of a body. Tony Campolo and Mary Albert Darling write, "One of the marks of mystical Christianity is a growing awareness of the wonders of our everyday, ordinary experiences, which leads to a greater sense of how precious the ordinary really is."[8]

Retrieving the mystical nature of Christianity could bring a lot of life back to the body of Christ in the parish. Christianity was meant to have a mystical nature in everyday life. This is how we commune with God together. The mystical nature of Christianity is our very life and strength. It comes to us in all kinds of ordinary ways through the relational context we live in. It lives by the mystical imagination within us. Evelyn Underhill states, "True mysticism is never self-seeking … The true mystic claims no promises and makes no demands."[9]

---

[8] Campolo and Darling, *The God of Intimacy and Action*, 6.

[9] Underhill, *Mysticism*, 92.

We are uncomfortable sometimes with the mystical nature of Christianity because it pushes us to live in our bodies. It pushes us to become selfless and lose our ego identities. It opens up the imagination to see alternatives to the American status quo culture. We might become frightened because Christ will disturb and haunt every agenda with unpredictability. The ego shuns the mystical imagination. It hates the mystical imagination that seeks to destroy all our illusions we have created. There is no escaping the mystical nature of Christianity. It is the only way we can follow Christ in this postmodern age. It should shake us up in a way because we will truly lose our lives to it.

There is so much mystery to the mystical nature of the gospel. Mystery is what lives within the imagination. This mystery is lived out by the body of Christ in the parish. "… God has chosen to make known among the Gentiles the glorious riches of this mystery, which is Christ in you, the hope of glory" (Colossians 1:27). The mystical imagination is alive among us in the mystery that lives within our relationships in the place we inhabit together in everyday life. To become blinded to the reality of the mysteries so close to us, that are trying to speak to us, trying to pull us out of the status quo is a distortion of our identity. We have become less than human without a sense of mystery. The mystical nature of Christianity puts the mystery back into our lives together as the body of Christ in the place we live.

Jonathan S. Campbell and Jennifer Campbell say, "We are all mystics."[10] To have an identity rooted in being ordinary mystics rooted in a local community where relational revelations have the possibility to flourish can be unusual. But this is who we are as the body of Christ. Ordinary mystics are people who live their everyday lives grounded in communion with God. Ordinary mystics are practical and have ever growing imaginations for togetherness, humility, love, grace, simplicity, and locality. Ordinary mystics live in their bodies, not outside of them. And we are all ordinary mystics deep within, if we would only listen to the mystical imagination within us. Margaret Silf states:

---

[10] Campbell, *The Way of Jesus*, 133.

In each of us there is a potential mystic and a potential prophet. The mystic intuits what is really going on beneath the surface of things, notices the divine amid the ordinary, and sees others with God's eyes. The prophet addresses what the mystic sees, challenging all that is threatening to undermine humanity's journey towards life-in-all-its-fullness, and encouraging all that is nourishing and empowering that journey.[11]

Ordinary mystics are not weird, strange people who have no contact with reality. On the contrary, they are people who live with awareness, mindfulness, love, and humility toward others, God, and the place they inhabit. We are called to be a collective of ordinary mystics as the body of Christ in everyday life who seek God by cultivating the native passion of the soul. Our native passion within our bodies is a longing for God, for the beautiful, for reconciled relationships. We are called to be a church of ordinary mystics who embody the gospel in mystery and wonder within the parish. Without the mystical nature of Christianity none of this is possible. We will be doing Christianity without following Christ. And the results will be sad and tragic for the culture around us.

God cannot be figured out. God cannot be boxed into a concept, a proposition or an agenda. God is mysterious and calls for our participation in all of life as the body of Christ in the neighborhood. God is the destroyer of all our illusions and the Creator of the mystical imagination. Irish philosopher Peter Rollins states in his book *The Fidelity of Betrayal*, "God is not a problem to be solved but rather a mystery to participate in."[12] God speaks to us through participation, collaboration, and embodiment. If we are not listening ordinary mystics who live into God's mysteries, we will never know true wisdom within us. God's nature is mystery and cannot be reduced to anything else.

We cannot control the mystical nature of Christianity. God will not allow it. The mysteries are too real, quiet, and unpredictable. It takes a

---

[11] Silf, *Companions of Christ*, 88.

[12] Rollins, *The Fidelity of Betrayal*, 115.

whole lifetime to begin to understand God's mysteries within us. We need to have a conversion to mystery by which we dedicate our entire lives to the body of Christ in the parish. This conversion to mystery could change everything about the way we experience life. It would certainly manifest a lot of beauty in the world as we know it. And it would help us get along better in life. The mystical imagination longs for this conversion to mystery. Thomas Merton writes:

> Hence the folly of a mysticism which does not turn outward to the "other," but remains enclosed within itself. Such mysticism is simply an escape from reality: it barricades itself from the real and feeds upon itself.[13]

The mystical imagination is both inward and outward. We experience life within that becomes our very identity, but this life within is manifested relationally in our lives together to figure out how to love, how to show humility, how to show grace and compassion for others in our world. There is a deep mystery to this paradox. We focus inward by focusing outward. We focus outward by focusing inward. The mystical imagination works in all kinds of paradoxes of mystery. That is why it is important to have a conversion to mystery because without this we will not be able to create a holistic counterculture as the body of Christ in the parish. Susan Rakoczy writes:

> Mysticism flows from the deep desire of the human person to surrender to the Mystery of total Love. Only Love explains mysticism. True mysticism is never self-seeking, never exhibitionist and self-centered, for one loses one's life in order to gain real Life.[14]

Only God can teach us what it means to seek life within ourselves. Only God knows what we need in order to seek beauty together as the body of Christ in the parish. We need to be okay with these mysteries and not get so freaked out by them. We need to become more aware

---

[13] Merton, *The New Man*, 34.

[14] Rakoczy, *Great Mystics and Social Justice*, 102.

and mindful of the realities within and around us all the time. God is kind, good, beautiful, present, but very mysterious.

In my own experience, I have always intuitively been interested in the mystery of life. As I grew up, I remembering playing outside and seeing the creation around me: birds, trees, dirt, grass, hills, trails, mountains, the sky, stars, sun, rain, squirrels, rabbits, and bugs among other things. All these things fascinated me. There were so many colors, textures, and shapes. I loved walking the streets in my neighborhood, exploring trails in the woods or looking into the sky to feel the air that I was breathing. All of this was what I was born into, not really understanding anything about its mysteries.

As I got older, I found more mystery in food, sexuality, my body, education, friendships, exercising, traveling, sleeping, movie narratives, visual art, music, dancing, and celebration. I was fascinated by all of this too. When I was in high school and college, I started to lose this sense of mystery because life handed me some unexpected hardships that I wasn't prepared to handle. I slowly became depressed, hopeless, and afraid. It took me a while to recover this sense of mystery.

As I grew in my spirituality and became more rooted relationally in place, I slowly recovered the mystery in life through my understanding of God, the body of Christ, and the mystical nature of Christianity. I am still learning to understand mystery more, and what that means to me in community with others; sometimes I am not so sure, but my own experience is constantly confirming that mystery is essential to life.

The mystery of the gospel integrates us within the context of wonder. Without wonder there is not much to live for, and we end up becoming machines in a system (empire) that has little mystery to it. This empire wants to root out of us the mystical nature of Christianity. It will take everything within us to not let this happen anymore. Michael Frost notes, "Wonder invites us to an uncertain place, a place filled with mystery and experience but not necessarily with certainty and definition."[15]

Wonder lives within the mystical imagination. Wonder is the friend of mystery. They work together to build the body of Christ in everyday life in the parish. Mystery and wonder are characteristics of ordinary mystics in our postmodern age. Mystery and wonder will cause us to become more aware and mindful of God's ordinary, relational miracles in us and around us in the place we inhabit. Mystery and wonder are never certain and cannot be contained and managed by our systems of rationality. Mystery and wonder open us up to the mystical imagination. They create a longing for a mystical sense of discipline within us. They encourage us along the path to following Christ in the place we live. John Main says in his book *The Way of Unknowing:*

> We can hardly dare to imagine what a society would be like where everybody was on the road to the realization that being is mystery, that each of us possess an infinite capacity, an infinite potential for expansion of the spirit into the mystery of God. And yet we should dare to imagine that: it is possible for a society to exist where compassion takes precedence over judgment, where mercy and forgiveness are the regular currency. But compassion, mercy, forgiveness and love all depend upon that discovery of ourselves and others to be more than machines. This discovery will mean seeing society not as some anonymous body that needs servicing but as a community of persons committed to maturity, to growth, to understanding, to love. But that society cannot be, unless men and women can be found who will undertake the pilgrimage to the bedrock of their own being, who will be prepared to undertake the discipline of discovering their own infinite depths, their infinite capacity for love, for understanding: for God …[16]

This is what the mystical imagination needs for us to live into a holistic countercultural with beauty, mystery, and wonder. Compassion, mercy, forgiveness, and love will be embodied in our everyday lives together.

---

[15] Frost, *Seeing God in the Ordinary,* 174.

[16] Main, *The Way of Unknowing,* 74.

We will become "a community of persons" committed to place, growth, understanding, wisdom, and discipline. We will become ordinary mystics in the parish who value the mystery and wonder of life.

Seeing with a Sense of Clarity: Re-imagining Wisdom for Our Time

We need the mystical imagination to see with a sense of clarity. Our seeing is so cluttered with fragmentation, distraction, disembodiment, and default ways of knowing. We have oftentimes become so focused on things that don't matter that our seeing has turned to blindness. We have lost sight of wisdom. Most of the time we don't even know what is happening; this goes on unconsciously within us.

The mystical imagination calls us to an awakening toward something more holistic and life-giving. The mystical imagination teaches us to see with the eyes of an ordinary mystic. We become more mindful and aware. We become more loving and full of grace. We develop more of a longing for the God of mystery. We become people of wonder and grace. We become passionate about our faithful presence in the place we live. Elaine A. Heath asks the question, "… what would it mean to read our world with a hermeneutic of love?"[17]

Seeing with a sense of clarity puts us into a posture of receiving wisdom and listening. It gives us an imagination for the body of Christ in everyday life in the parish. As we practice love more and more, God slowly reveals to us the mysterious, beautiful ways of deep wisdom. But these revelations do not come fast, they come very slowly. We cannot force them, but we must live with an openness to the point where we can listen whenever we discover something of their nature. This is the purpose of our lives here on earth in the place we live. We should always be longing to discover the relational revelations within us and around us. There is nothing like an intuitive discovery of relational wisdom in the place we care about and inhabit.

---

[17] Heath, *The Mystic Way of Evangelism*, 119.

"The eye is the lamp of the body. If your eyes are good, your whole body will be full of light" (Mathew 6:22). Seeing with a sense of clarity is light to our bodies. We will have greater clarity if we become aware of the beauty in the world around us. Beauty, light, body, place, love, humility, grace, simplicity, and faithful presence all integrate into creating a sense of clarity within us as we follow Christ together through the mystical imagination.

The mysterious God is revealed slowly in unpredictable ways through all of this process of cultivating clarity and direction within us. Our eyes and bodies need to be open to an imaginative light within us. There is so much potential and clarity that awaits to be discovered if we would only seek to find this wisdom and listen in the midst of our confusion. This is a difficult discipline so we need to allow the mystical imagination to guide us in our discipleship to become expressions of love in the world. Henri J. M. Nouwen writes:

> Discipleship, however, calls for discipline. Indeed, discipleship and discipline share the same linguistic root (from *discere*, which means "to learn from"), and the two should never be separated. Whereas discipline without discipleship leads to rigid formalism, discipleship without discipline ends in sentimental romanticism.[18]

Discipleship and discipline as well as mystery and wonder are huge aspects of the mystical imagination in everyday life. Without discipleship there is no discipline. Without discipline there is no discipleship. (Again, another paradox of the mystical nature of Christianity within place.) Discipleship and discipline are the tools that we need in order to see with greater clarity.

As time passes, we will struggle through conflicts and frustrations. Without an active practice of discipleship and discipline we will not have enough strength to continue on in the parish. We will give up and cave in to the narratives in our society that say, "When things get hard, just move on and leave, and seek out something better for yourself."

---

[18] Nouwen, *Spiritual Formation*, 18.

But wherever we go our troubles will always follow us. We cannot run away from them even though our culture tells us that we can. The mystical imagination helps us discern with greater clarity such false narratives. Dallas Willard thinks about discipline this way:

> Discipline is in fact a natural part of the structure of the human soul, and almost nothing of any significance in education, culture, or other attainments is achieved without it. Everything from learning a language to weight-lifting depends upon it, and its availability in the human makeup is what makes the individual human being responsible for the kind of person he or she becomes. Animals may be trained, but they are incapable of discipline in the sense that is essential to human life.[19]

Having a sense of discipline is important to seeing with a sense of clarity in the parish. This sense of discipline is crucial for the mystical imagination to thrive within us. Discipline is what our souls long for. Sometimes we do not even realize this and spend huge parts of our lives without any discipline. Our souls are not alive within us when we allow this to happen, and we usually don't see so well either.

Human beings are made in the image of God to practice discipline, which means to practice living within our limitations and in our bodies. It also means living within our responsibilities by being faithfully present to others in the place we live. If we want to live a beautiful, fruitful life we need to practice a mystical sense of discipline. It is essential. There is no getting around it.

We cannot be lazy, unintentional, comfortable, and apathetic anymore. We cannot just talk about our spirituality without having a disciplined, embodied practice. This will not work in our postmodern culture. We have to live with more courage than that to have anything of beauty to offer our place. When we see with a sense of clarity, this will help us to have courage within the mystical imagination. One of the most

---

[19] Willard, *The Great Omission*, 150-151.

influential Catholics in American history, Dorothy Day, states, "The only purpose for which we were made was to become saints."[20]

Do we really believe that we are all called to be ordinary mystics and saints as the body of Christ in the twenty-first century? I believe we were made to see with that kind of clarity. We were made to have that kind of power. To dance the dance of the prisoner set free, the exile finding their authenticity, to subvert the empire among us. We could follow the disciples as they followed Christ. We could enter into the stories of the people in the book of Acts who lived for Christ by becoming a part of this beautiful narrative in history. We could be like one of the "sinners" Jesus hung out with and ate with in the gospel stories. There is no end to the possibilities that we could experience in our lifetime if we lived into our callings as saints. This should be our sole passion in everyday life.

Saints are the ones who live with a sense of clarity through their practice of discipline and discipleship. Saints are ordinary radicals who live into a mystical imagination. Shane Claiborne says, "Some of God's most precious saints are quiet people, gentle prophets, secret saints that live in the shadows."[21] Saints usually go unnoticed and unrecognized; but the world is a better place because of the beauty and love they bring into the world. They usually act like they don't know much or have little imagination or don't know what to say, but this is not true. They are some of the wisest, most imaginative visionaries of our time.

My friend Melody is one of the greatest examples of what it means to be a saint that I know of. She is so kind, gentle, loving, imaginative, passionate, quiet, and such a servant to everyone around her. Her gentle, passionate voice always teaches me of the nature of God. I always think, God's voice must be like that.

---

[20] Day, *On Pilgrimage*, 195.

[21] Claiborne, *Follow Me to Freedom*, 76.

It is such an unusual paradox for me to see someone's passionate, gentle, and quiet life and voice becoming so influential and powerful in small, local ways. But Melody is one of the people in my life who has shown me the mysterious nature of God in this way. I wonder if Jesus was like this.

Melody is always showing me examples of grace and love. She does small acts in our neighborhood that not very many people take notice of except those who might look very closely. Melody loves the mystical imagination within the shared life of our community. She loves silence, solitude, contemplation, and meditation as well as hospitality, cooking, caring, loving, and sharing life with others. I have heard her say these symbolize revolutionary practices to her.

She exemplifies what a saint in our postmodern culture is. She is not up for canonization by the Catholic Church, but she is a saint in my eyes and in the eyes of others in our neighborhood. She is a saint because she is an ordinary woman who shares life with her neighbors and lives within the mystical imagination among us.

Discipline is liberation! What a different paradigm to live by. Sometimes we might not like discipline because it takes away time from other things we like more. The mystical imagination links discipleship, discipline, and liberation. We could have the freedom and liberation to follow Christ in the parish together. Our everyday lives could become an ongoing discovery of liberation through the mystical imagination. Anne Lamott writes:

> It is not now and never was in anybody's best interest for you to be a seeker. It's actually in everybody's worst interest. It's not convenient for the family. It may make them feel superficial and expendable. You may end up looking nutty and unfocused, which does not reflect well on them ... Your little search for meaning may keep you from going far at your school or your company as you might otherwise have gone, if you had had a single-minded devotion to getting ahead. Success shows the world what you're

made of, and that your parents were right to all but destroy you to foster this excellence.[22]

We can come to a place of seeing with a sense of clarity, with a sense of wisdom through a lot of practice and experimentation. When we are disciplined within ourselves, we are constantly being shaped because discipline fosters listening. God is always shaping us. Our life is about constantly allowing God to shape us and define our meaning in the here-and-now. The mystical imagination is always working to shape us and cause us to listen to its revelations. Practicing discipline within the mystical imagination is one of our greatest hopes for the body of Christ in everyday life. We will become people of greater clarity when this kind of a lifestyle has been cultivated. We will experience our salvation together in everyday life through a liberation of the individualistic status quo.

The mystical imagination creates longings within us that can be created by none of our clever techniques. Our longings are connected to our clarity. Our longings and clarity work together to create in us an imagination for a holistic counterculture in the parish. As Annemarie S. Kidder notes, "We long for eyes to see ourselves, others, and our God more clearly."[23]

Our eyes are full of light, possibility, and beauty when we see with a longing for something more than what we have known. We need to cultivate countercultural eyes that long for what is beautiful and relational as the body of Christ in the parish. It is hard to see ourselves, others, and God clearly; we need to have a discipline that longs for such particular eyes. The holistic counterculture of the mystical imagination longs for eyes to see with a sense of clarity. Everything else is secondary to this pursuit of the mystical imagination. Susan Cain writes in her book *Quiet*, "Figure out what you are meant to contribute to the world and make sure you contribute it."[24]

---

[22] Lamott, *Stitches*, 24-25.

[23] Kidder, *The Power of Solitude*, 2.

[24] Cain, *Quiet*, 264.

Chapter 3

Creative Insecurity: Learning to Live Life

Becoming a Lifelong Learner: The Gift of Literacy

We all need to be seeking God in such a way that makes us passionate about becoming lifelong learners in everyday life. If we do not take on a posture of becoming lifelong learners, through the study of books and relational context, we will not have the wisdom necessary to create any kind of a counterculture among us in the parish. One of the greatest gifts of God is the ability to read. How neglected is the gift of literacy for those of us who can read. It is much easier to watch a movie, TV, or surf the internet. But books are a gift from God.

There is so much I have learned from mentors, dead and alive, who have written about their wisdom. I think about Dorothy Day, Thomas Merton, Alexia Salvatierra, Christina Cleveland, Martin Luther King Jr., Karen Wilk, Christine Pohl, Lillian Daniel, Jon Huckins, Kelly Bean, Peter Bock, Kathy Escobar, Wendy McCaig, Lisa Sharon Harper, Ivan Illich, Mary Jo Leddy, Christine Sine, Rachel Held Evans, Paul Sparks, Letty Russell, Pam Hogeweide, Walter Brueggemann, Margaret Silf, John Perkins, Marva Dawn, Paulo Freire, Eileen Baura Suico, Tim Soerens, Marshall McLuhan, Margaret Wheatley, Bill McKibben, Jacques Ellul, Paula D' Arcy, Lauren

Winner, Rene Girard, Phileena Heuetz, Gustavo Gutierrez, Erin S. Lane, Lacy Clark Ellman, Robert Lupton, Cynthia Bourgeault, Noel Castellanos, Sue Monk Kidd, Soren Kierkegaard, Julie Clawson, Marshall Rosenberg, Jean Vanier, Sharon Daloz Parks, Thich Nhat Hanh, Wendell Berry, Martin Laird, Anne Lamott, Daniel Kemmis, Elizabath Newman, Brene Brown, Thomas Keating, Mother Teresa, Christopher Heuertz, Joan Chittister, Vandana Shiva, Parker Palmer, Evelyn Underhill, Tony Kriz, Kathleen Norris, Debbie Blue, Mark Van Steenwyk, Beatrice Bruteau, Mae Elise Cannon, Enuma Okoro, Jamie Arpin-Ricci, Richard Rohr, Brenda Salter McNeil, Joanna Macy, Annie Dillard, John McKnight, Esther Lightcap Meek, Carl McColman, Henri Nouwen, Simone Weil, Michael Frost, John Pattison, Tom Sine, Macrina Wiederkehr, Lynne Baab, Shane Claiborne, Charlene Spretnak, Esther De Waal, Barbara Brown Taylor, Brian McLaren, Peter Rollins, Jonathan Wilson-Hartgrove, Paula Huston, Dianna Butler Bass, Mark Scandrette, Chris Smith, Ilia Delio, Dwight Friesen, and many others.

There is so much wisdom out there if we will read and learn from others in this way. As we learn this deeper wisdom, we have an opportunity as the body of Christ to bring an expression of beauty into our world in the parish. Some of the greatest moments of my life have been reading subversive texts that help me to have an expansive imagination for something more than what I have known. I long and live for this kind of stuff. "In terms of emphasis, learning is the spiritual practice that receives the greatest attention in the Gospels," states James C. Wilhoit. "Jesus is continually teaching and calling his disciples to greater understanding."[1]

What if becoming a lifelong learner became important to us? What if we saw learning as a practice of following Christ? Christ values our desire and personal practice to become lifelong learners in the parish. But before we learn from Christ, there are a lot of things we need to unlearn. We need to unlearn our individualism, consumerism,

---

[1] Wilhoit, *Spiritual Formation as if the Church Mattered*, 142.

fragmentation, disconnectedness, and division among us. We need to unlearn unhealthy ways of being in relationship with others. We need to unlearn our illusions about the "real world" that we live in. Lifelong learners need to be open to unlearning the engraved conventional individualism of our time.

Christ is always teaching us about life in the parish. Christ is teaching us how to be the subversive body of Christ in everyday life in the midst of the empire. We need to live within the mystical imagination to become lifelong learners in all aspects of life. Michael Frost and Alan Hirsch write, "So much of what we think we know needs to be unlearned."[2]

Learning is not just about reading books; it is also about learning from the subsidiary relational contexts we find ourselves in as the body of Christ in everyday life. We need this subsidiary relational awareness as well as the practice of reading and studying good books that expand our imaginations in the parish. We cannot become lifelong learners without learning through the relational context and the studying of texts from other voices outside of our locality. This brings a better perspective and balance to our lives together. The subsidiaries of relational awareness are the things in our context that are going on around us all the time without us necessarily being aware of them. They are the unconscious realities that we need to recognize through an embodied practice that is integrated and focused.

My friend Paul constantly shows me what it means to be a lifelong learner. He has very little college education and was not very excited about high school. And yet he devours books of all kinds. This is his lifestyle. I have never met someone who reads so much.

He says that he doesn't understand how others can live their lives without reading. His library is huge. He has thousands of books that are marked up and which he quotes from in order to inspire others to

---

[2] Frost and Hirsch, *The Shaping of Things to Come*, 194.

adopt a more integrated personal practice in the parish. He has become a lifelong learner for the purpose of loving others in our neighborhood.

Paul is a very passionate man. He loves studying about the technological society, culture, leadership, philosophy, theology, sociology, epistemology, and many other things. He loves coaching others to help them to be in relationship with a particular place. He loves his friends and understands that he has to unlearn so many religious things that were taught to him in the name of God.

Not only is Paul passionate about reading books and learning in this way; he also loves to learn from others through a subsidiary relational awareness and presence. He lives with a mystical imagination that keeps opening up more possibilities in his life for creativity, communion, and compassion. I have grown so much over the years through getting to know Paul because he has shown me what it means to be a lifelong learner in everyday life. I am grateful for our friendship. He has introduced me to many subversive authors that I probably would not have known about if it were not for him.

God is calling us to this gift of reading, if we are able. This discipline of reading has the power to revolutionize the body of Christ in the parish. Reading will help us with discipleship, relationship, community, and our commitment to place. "Few of us," writes Debra K. Farrington, "give much thought to spending more time reading and studying as a discipline."[3] We need to devote more time to the discipline of reading.

The discipline of reading cultivates the mystical imagination within us in mysterious ways. Our imaginations become bigger than our egos. The imagination communicates vision for an embodied practice of beauty through our bodies in the parish. As we begin to become lifelong learners, we start to become more aware of the mystical imagination within us. Every book that we read has the potential to become a building block to our interior life as a part our personal

---

[3] Farrington, *Living Faith Day by Day*, 127.

practice in the parish both collectively and individually. Our motives change, our intentionality intensifies, our loves deepens, our humility is more engrained within us, and we experience everyday life in a holistic way.

The ability to read may not be true for everyone, but for those who can read it is such a precious gift that oftentimes is co-opted by the empire through consumerism and certain kinds of entertainment. It is common for truly visionary people to be readers. I have read biographies of people such as Dorothy Day and Thomas Merton that point out that they were ferocious readers. They had a healthy discipline of reading in their lives and this contributed to their passion, their relationships, and their life's work.

I would propose that becoming a lifelong learner in everyday life is more important than a college education. We can live into a holistic counterculture without having a college education. It can be helpful, but it is not necessary to be a lifelong learner. If college education does not make us lifelong learners, it is not of much value. But if it can inspire us to become lifelong learners than it is indeed valuable to us.

We live in a society that pretty much says everyone needs to go to college to be somebody. But I don't believe this is true, because a lot of us go to college and then rarely ever read a book outside of our college experience. We live lives more interested in entertainment, the internet, and our careers than in becoming a lifelong learner. Usually most learning stops after school is finished. The mystical imagination pushes us toward the discipline of becoming lifelong learners. Within the mystical imagination learning never stops and a hunger for it grows. The great Southern novelist Walker Percy says, "… only about two percent of Americans regularly read books."[4]

We need to increasingly live with a mystical sense of discipline toward reading more, learning more, and loving more. The holistic

---

[4] Percy, *Signposts in a Strange Land*, 170.

counterculture is calling us beyond the two percent status quo. Without having a love for reading, we will have trouble getting along as the body of Christ in everyday life. Reading and studying are the tools we need to embrace the mystical imagination in our locality together. We need to be an informed, discerning, faithful presence as the body of Christ in the parish. We most likely will not become this without having a passion for reading.

"Take my yoke upon you and learn from me" (Matthew 11:29). We can learn from Christ through the Scriptures, but we can also learn from Christ through reading the wisdom of all kinds of authors. Christ speaks to us in all kinds of ways in the world through the diverse books we read as we develop into lifelong learners. He speaks to us through books on theology, spirituality, psychology, sociology, technology, anthropology, agriculture, economics, leadership, art, culture, biography, philosophy, mysticism, fiction, poetry, and history. He speaks to us through all kinds of people of diverse race, nationality, age, and socio-economic status. He speaks to us in long books and shorter books. He speaks to us through female authors and male authors.

Christ uses all kinds of things to cultivate the mystical imagination within us in our local context. We need to take this challenge to become lifelong learners seriously if we are going to be the body of Christ together in everyday life. We are missing out if we do not have an imagination for this. Gordon MacDonald writes, "But all of us need to have at least one good book going at all times, more if possible."[5]

To always be reading a book that helps our imagination develop is a good piece of wisdom for us to practice. The body of Christ should be made up of lifelong learners who are excited about reading and studying all kinds of texts. Lifelong learners are the most well-informed, innovative, reflective, beautiful people in the place they inhabit. Our culture needs beauty discovered in it through those who

---

[5] MacDonald, *Ordering Your Private World*, 114.

use their lifetime to learn and not just live an unintentional life with no real focus.

The lifelong learner is subversive, influential, courageous, and passionate. The lifelong learner takes many risks, lives with intentionality, and practices action/reflection as a way of life. The lifelong learner hungers to discover beauty in the parish. The lifelong learner gives his or her whole being to understanding everyday life in all its complexities and contexts. The mystical imagination is made up of lifelong learners.

We lose a lot of capacity for an expanding, growing imagination when we do not read. Our imaginations suffer because of it. The empire does not want us to read. It is a subversion of the empire to have a disciplined reading practice in the parish. The body of Christ is called into this subversion in everyday life. Donald S. Whitney states, "You have too much to lose by not reading, and too much to gain by disciplined reading."[6]

We have indeed a lot to gain. We gain wisdom, understanding, imagination, intelligence, humility, strength, sight, and passion. We live in union with the mystical imagination. The world of books becomes our delight. Books become our friends that help us on the journey of life. The books we read become one of the mediums we use to experience God in our everyday lives together. The texts may have a mystery to them that is hard to understand, but they empower and create our imaginations in mysterious, ordinary ways.

Our imaginations can be cared for by becoming lifelong learners in all aspects of our lives. When we read a book, we begin to develop our true selves and see with greater clarity. We are opening up to discovery. We are learning from a different perspective. We are becoming new again. It is like a fresh breeze on a hot summer day.

---

[6] Whitney, *Spiritual Disciplines for the Christian Life*, 232.

Living By Faith: Freedom and Insecurity

"For in the gospel a righteousness from God is revealed, a righteousness that is by faith from first to last, just as it written: 'The righteous will live by faith'" (Romans 1:17). The righteous, those who live in reconciled relationship with others, will live by faith as the body of Christ in everyday life in the parish. This is truly what social justice means. Righteousness and justice start within us through the mystical imagination. We are all called to live by faith in our local community with others. We cannot ignore this.

Faith doesn't always make sense to us as we live in a rationalistic and pragmatic mode with very little mystery. If we let the intuitive mystical imagination live within us, we will have greater clarity and intentionality as the body of Christ in the place we live. Living by faith oftentimes requires risk, courage, and creativity which lead us to freedom within. Richard Rohr states, "God is clearly into freedom, imagination, and creativity."[7] Living by faith will bring us freedom from the systems of the empire, but we will also experience an insecurity because our ego will be bothered by this freedom. Our ego wants to be secure through what is rational, concrete, and safe. Our ego wants to control and manipulate our environment. Living by faith will not allow the ego to do this.

The ego wants us to live more like robots and machines than as human beings. The ego ignores all the mystery to our human potential. The ego has virtually no imagination for life beyond the status quo. Living by faith calls us away from the ego and into a relational context of mystery and wonder as the body of Christ in the parish. Living by faith makes us insecure, but this is our greatest freedom. It is good to be insecure, uncomfortable, and shaken from the status quo, and to live into a mystical imagination for something more. Subversive French writer Jacques Ellul says:

---

[7] Rohr, *Immortal Diamond*, 89.

What people want when they talk about freedom is not being subject to others, being able to have their own dreams or go where they want to go. Hardly more. They definitely do not want to have to take charge of their own lives and be responsible for what they do. This means that they do not really want freedom. In effect freedom can give us everything except security by demanding that we be. Security is always inevitably bought at the cost of freedom.[8]

Freedom and security do not mix well. Security is slavery to the empire around us. Security is most often too comfortable in the status quo. We need to long for freedom, liberation from this kind of security that makes us numb and machinelike. Freedom promotes the shattering into pieces of all status quo obstacles in our pursuit of creating a holistic counterculture as the body of Christ in the parish. Do we really want this kind of freedom? Freedom in our country is oftentimes related to independence, bloodshed, and war. What I want to propose is a freedom related to love, humility, communion, connection, interdependence, and integration. This kind of freedom lives within the mystical imagination.

Freedom represents a responsibility to place. When we have security we do not have freedom, and we do not live by faith. Security makes us abusive, exploitive, and oftentimes unloving. We cannot sacrifice our freedom any longer in order to feel secure. The body of Christ needs to live in freedom, we need to live by faith, we need to live in our bodies in everyday life in the parish.

Living by the mystical imagination, living by faith, and inhabiting a place over a long period of time can be difficult. We will feel the blow of the empire at times, but the mystical imagination will help us to persevere in our difficulties. Living by faith can lead us to some dark places within ourselves. And we will struggle to find some freedom at times. But this is a part of God's process of teaching us what we cannot currently understand. These times teach us to live by faith. We begin to

---

[8] Ellul, *The Subversion of Christianity*, 168.

understand more what this means. Twentieth-century mystic Thomas Merton says:

> But when the time comes to enter the darkness in which we are naked and helpless and alone; in which we see the insufficiency of our greatest strength and the hollowness of our strongest virtues; in which we have nothing of our own to rely on, and nothing in our nature to support us, and nothing in the world to guide us or give us light—then we find out whether or not we live by faith.[9]

Will we abandon God when we feel the darkness of being alone, rejected, misunderstood, and powerless? Will we live by faith in these times? Will we run away and hide from others and from God? Or will we show love and humility through our pain? Will we allow ourselves to be insecure and afraid for awhile waiting for a better season of recognized beauty? When we are cold and it is raining, when we are wet and shivering, will we turn away from living by faith? Will our imagination die in these times?

The mystical imagination is not so perplexed by these times. It is not a time to fear. The mystical imagination sees these times as a season in which we will experience God in ways that are less familiar to us. The body of Christ will struggle at times to be a holistic counterculture in the process of sharing life and learning to love. This is no easy task and goes against almost all of the structures of our culture. Our freedom will sometimes lead us to these times, but we have the imagination to persevere. Jean Vanier in his book *Becoming Human* notes:

> A lack of freedom equals fear—fear of reality, fear of others; lack of freedom means clinging to illusions and prejudices. It is imposing a vision on reality or wanting to change reality through force instead of forming a new vision of reality. Lack of freedom means thinking that you alone have the truth and that others are wrong or stupid. It means being controlled by prejudice.[10]

---

[9] Merton, *New Seeds of Contemplation*, 258.

[10] Vanier, *Becoming Human*, 116.

Our lives together as the body of Christ are not always easy. We shouldn't expect it. This is not reality. But if we are serous about our discipleship and discipline, we will work through things relationally with others in our context. This will only happen if we live by faith. It is a miracle and gift when we can live this way. We can live this way! We can live by the mystical imagination in the parish. New Monastic activist Shane Claiborne states, "In fact, if our lives are easy, we must be doing something wrong."[11] Our lives together are not supposed to be always easy. We are probably not really sharing life holistically if everything is always easy.

We will have tension, we will have failure, and we will also struggle at times to find freedom. However, through all of this our faith and our imagination will help us to remain together. Living by faith together, being committed to the parish, will sometimes tear us apart inside. We will not always understand the struggle within, but we must have the mystical imagination to trust God.

This is the very process of discipleship and discipline we most need. It doesn't always feel good and it doesn't always make us feel secure, but it is sometimes how we must live relationally. There is nothing easy about discipline, about discipleship, about following Christ. There is nothing easy about conflict. There is nothing easy about relationships. There is nothing easy about our spirituality. There is nothing easy about living by faith. There is nothing easy about freedom. But as E. F. Schumacher says in his book *Small Is Beautiful*, "The denial of freedom, of course, is a denial of responsibility."[12]

If we deny freedom and choose instead to live by security, we choose irresponsibility. Our spirituality is cultivated by the responsibility of faithful presence. We need to be characterized by our responsibility to others, to God, to the mystical imagination. The body of Christ needs to have the mystical imagination to live by faith in this way in the

---

[11] Claiborne, *The Irresistible Revolution*, 136.

[12] Schumacher, *Small is Beautiful*, 243.

parish. We need to deny a comfortable security that makes us complacent and apathetic toward one another and our culture. If we pursue freedom together, we will see relational revelations happening within and around us.

Our freedom will give us the awareness of Christ among us, in our neighborhood, in our bodies. Our freedom will show us things we could never understand about God's mysteries in any other way. Our freedom is the reality we are called to live in as the body of Christ in the parish. Our freedom and our sense of responsibility call out to us from the streets in our neighborhood. Will we listen to these cries and become responsible followers of Christ in our postmodern culture? The cries will not stop. They will go on and on. Living by faith helps us to better understand these cries and leads us to the responsibility that is implicated in the place we inhabit. Co-founder of the Catholic Worker Movement Dorothy Day says:

> It is cheering to remember that Jesus Christ wandered this earth with no place to lay His head. And when we consider our fly-by-night existence, our uncertainty, we remember (with pride at sharing the honor) that the disciples supped by the seashore and wandered through cornfields picking the ears from the stalks wherewith to make their frugal means.[13]

Our Downtown Neighborhood Fellowship has had to find the freedom to live by faith and get along in everyday life. This has not been the easiest thing to do all the time. When we tend to get upset by something someone has done, we have to choose to live by faith. By this I mean we have to take responsibility for our feelings. We have to find what we are feeling and needing without blaming or judging the other. We have to communicate by making a request without demanding in a respectful way that does not blame. We have to forgive or else we will live in resentment. We do not live by faith when we fight with one another and lose a sense of perspective on love, grace, gentleness, and humility. We lose our freedom when we live by our

---

[13] Day, "Day After Day," 52.

own agendas at the expense of others. We lose our freedom when we give up on the place we inhabit. We lose our freedom when we do not take responsibility for our feelings and blame and judge others instead of love.

Downtown Tacoma has been a place of hope for us. So many of us have hoped for this place. We have been rooted here for some time now and are beginning to see beautiful things happen. As we have developed a relational network of care in our neighborhood over the last ten years, we are in the beginning stages of creating a holistic counterculture among us. Sometimes we feel our loneliness and pain in the process, but we are learning to embrace the mystical imagination as the body of Christ in the place we live no matter how difficult it gets.

I have heard it said that in order for the body of Christ to have any influence in a place we have to stay there a minimum of ten years, and even after that nothing is guaranteed. We can't control the process, but we can take some responsibility for a faithful presence in everyday life. Living by faith has been a challenge for us in Downtown Tacoma, but we are learning to experience more freedom through practicing love. Each day we are unlearning so many things that we thought we understood about the gospel. The mystical imagination is teaching us. We are learning a righteousness and justice that God is revealing to us through the way we relate to one another in love.

So much of seeking God today is done individualistically. It's detached from everyday life in the parish. But is this really even seeking after God? How can we seek God apart from the body of Christ? We must learn that the mystical imagination is about seeking God together through living by faith in a particular locality. This is how we create community among us. Community is done together by faith. Tim Keel writes, "We must relearn what it means for us to seek God."[14]

---

[14] Keel, *Intuitive Leadership*, 259.

This is a practice of living by faith around which we need to have more wisdom if we are to survive. Seeking God is the purpose of the body of Christ in the parish. If we are not seeking God together, then what are we doing? When we seek God together in everyday life, we become a beautiful expression of life to one another. The mystical imagination calls us to experiment with "relearning" what it means to seek God together in everyday life. This relearning could be the practice or experiment we need in order to listen to the mysteries within us, within our neighborhood. Our lives are to be about seeking God through living relationally and in solidarity with others.

Living by faith is uncertain. We do not always known exactly how God is leading us. The mystical imagination is very intuitive. Living by faith is a way of life that needs to be practiced with diligence and perseverance. This is our freedom and our liberation. Sometimes we will not understand God's leading and guidance, but trusting in the process is what living by faith is about. We have to do the best we can even when we do not understand. The mystical imagination within will help us. Influential writer Brian D. McLaren says:

> In a real way, faith is about constructing a model of reality. This is why faith must always be growing, and why the disciple must always be teachable, open to correction, ready to admit "I'm wrong," and ready to think again. This is because none of us is so naïve as to believe that he or she has the whole cosmic theological equation figured out. Nobody's model is perfect. We are constantly in the process of critiquing our model, adjusting it, recalibrating it.[15]

The mystical imagination is always about our spiritual formation as we listen to the context of life in the parish. The mystical imagination helps us to seek God together in this way. The mystical imagination helps us to live into a beautiful reality full of potential. We need to be open, ready, and teachable in everyday life as we live by faith. God is

---

[15] McLaren, *More Ready than You Realize*, 120.

hidden, but always revealed through the particulars of the place where we live.

Thinking Often of Death: Realizing the Life Within Us

Death is often not a popular topic of discussion these days. We live in denial of death. That is the last thing we want to think about. But I want to propose that this is an important practice for us as the body of Christ in the parish. Thinking about death often gives us a perspective on our limitations and mortality. The ego does not like the thought of death. It denies this reality at all costs. Twentieth-century visionary Ivan Illich states, "A person who has tried to establish the habit of virtuous action, so that living the right way becomes second nature, incorporates in his action the knowledge of death."[16]

Thinking of death often causes us to have an imagination that is beyond just ourselves. Death puts things in perspective. The mystical imagination thinks of death often. When we think about death, we are making a way for life in our bodies. This becomes who we are in our true selves. The "knowledge of death" inspires the mystical imagination to come alive within us. This helps us to live justly among others. We are less prone to use God to exploit others and the place we inhabit.

Our virtues are cultivated when we think of death often as the body of Christ in the parish. We become more loving, more graceful, more peaceful, and live with more humility when we practice this. Death is what reminds us that we are human and we have a Creator. Death and humility are closely linked. If we are often thinking of our mortality we will naturally practice a sense of humility in everyday life. We will be reminded over and over again to live by faith within our bodies. We will be reminded that people are important, that place is important, that the earth is important, and that our lives are important.

---

[16] Illich, *The Rivers North of the Future*, 165.

Men and women become like robots, like machines when they forget about death. When we ignore death we become less than human. We can easily become disembodied in our technological society. Marshall McLuhan says in his book *War and Peace in the Global Village*, "Man is not only a robot in his private reflexes but in his civilized behavior and in all his responses to the extensions of his body which we call technology."[17]

This technological society that we live in is making it hard for us to be embodied in the parish. This is making it hard for us to think often about death in everyday life together. Technology masks the reality of death. A lot of the time we want to live by the extensions of our bodies and are not too interested in the reality of death anymore. Sometimes we think we can transcend death through our technology. But we can't. We need to learn to face this as the body of Christ in the place where we live.

We are not robots, but human beings who have a life to live out together. Robots cannot experience the miracles of God. Robots are not alive in the here-and-now. Robots cannot experience the mystical imagination. Robots cannot be a part of the body of Christ. Robots cannot share life with anyone. Robots operate by a false reality. Our ever-increasing technologies will never transcend death. This is not possible. Thinking about death often reminds us of this truth.

"For to me, to live is Christ and to die is gain" (Philippians 1:21). Death roots us in ambiguity, powerlessness, uncertainty, questions, brokenness, and limitations. It teaches us that we don't have it all figured out. We don't have all the answers. Thinking of death often helps us to have a mystical imagination as the body of Christ in the parish. Ursula King states, "... when we learn to face death with full

---

[17] McLuhan, *War and Peace in the Global Village*, 19.

awareness we can discover new wonder, wisdom, and gratitude for what life has given us."[18]

Thinking of death often can help us to become centered in wisdom, gratitude, and new wonder. It helps us to know ourselves better. It helps us to live in reality. Thinking of death often helps us to embrace the importance of place, the importance of relationships, the importance of our context. Thinking of death often does not displace us, but places us within a particular local context. Thinking of death is related to our priorities because we reflect on our lives a lot more through this practice.

Thinking of death often has been a Benedictine monastic practice for hundreds of years. Macrina Wiederkehr notes, "In the rule of St. Benedict we are asked to keep death daily before our eyes."[19] That can sound kind of morbid, but it's actually liberating for our souls. When we are not afraid of our mortality we become more human. I think this happens because we start living more honestly and authentically. It strengthens us to have a better perspective to live relationally in the place where we live.

We consider the words we speak more carefully. We become more sensitive to our locality. We have solidarity with our environment. We see the beauty in life. We long for the collective good. The Benedictines have a lot of wisdom to share with us after so many years of practice. Thinking of death often cultivates the mystical imagination within us in everyday life as the body of Christ. This is a powerful practice if we can handle looking into what is real within ourselves. The mystical imagination does not fear keeping death before us in our everyday lives together in the parish. Sara Miles states:

> ... we are all going to die. That these busy lives, full of eating and drinking and buying and talking on our cell phones, are going

---

[18] King, *The Search for Spirituality,* 101.

[19] Wiederkehr, *Seven Sacred Pauses,* 117.

down to the dust. That despite the lies of the culture, the fantasy that money or objects will keep us alive, we mortals are just mortal and connected to one another through that raw, fleshy fact.[20]

We are only alive if we can face death in everyday life. We are only alive if we use our life to live. The status quo does not like to face death. It wants to pretend that there is no reality of death for us. We are too strong and healthy for that. We are too independent. We are too young to be thinking about that. This is only what people do when they are senior citizens. How do we truly know that we are alive? Longtime Benedictine David Steindl-Rast says:

> The fact that you are not dead yet is not sufficient proof that you are alive. It takes more than that. It takes courage—above all, the courage to face death. Only one who is alive can die. Aliveness is measured by the ability to die. One who is fully alive is fully able to die. In peak moments of aliveness we are reconciled with death. Deep down within us something tells us that we would die the moment our life reached fulfillment. It is fear of death that prevents us from coming fully alive.[21]

The mystical imagination does not fear facing death in order to embrace life. We are not guaranteed to live another day. We do not know how long our lives will last. Each of our days is a gift from God. The mystical imagination teaches us to value our days while we live in our bodies in the place we inhabit. Thinking of death often prevents us from being disembodied, disillusioned, and dislocated. Thinking of death often gives us courage to face the unique challenges of life together.

It is a strengthening practice for us as the body of Christ in everyday life. This practice makes us more vulnerable to our neighbors. Thinking of death often is a redemptive practice that opens up the mystical imagination within us. Life will come to us in unusual ways when we

---

[20] Miles, *City of God*, 139.

[21] Steindl-Rast, *Gratefulness, the Heart of Prayer*, 191.

think about death often. We will begin to see that all of life is a gift from God.

When I was younger, death was something I was very afraid to think about. Sometimes I would lie in my bed wondering what would happen to me. It just seemed completely incomprehensible to even face the reality of death. This scarred me so much I would avoid it. Now that I am older, there is still a lot of mystery about death, but I am not as afraid to reflect on what this means to me. I know that one day I will stop breathing and my heart will give out. My body will be cremated or buried in the ground and I will live on into the mystery of life after death. This is a hard reality to face sometimes, but God is helping me to face it. God willing, I will live for another 50 years or so. The world will go on without me.

There was one time that I dreamt my mom had died. I was probably under 10 years old. As I remember it, I woke up scared and afraid. It was the worst nightmare. I could not understand how I would live without having my mom to take care of me. My mom stayed at home and did not work when I was younger, so I had spent more time with her than with my dad. She was always there for me. After I woke up, it took me a while to realize that my mom was just in the other room. It was just a dream! I was so relieved to realize that she was alive and had not abandoned me.

This was kind of a traumatic experience for me. I don't even think I ever told my mom about it, but it was one of the only dreams I vividly remembered as a kid. Since then, I have come to grips with the reality of death through a lot of personal work and reflection. I know my mom will someday die, my friends will someday die, and I will someday face death. I am not as terrified of it as I used to be, and cultivating the mystical imagination within myself is helping me to see with some greater clarity.

This last year one of my friends died of cancer. He was around 77 years old and had been living at one of the Tacoma Catholic Worker houses in our neighborhood for the past 22 years. His name was Alfredo and he was a Mexican who could never quite receive his citizenship as an immigrant in the United States. So the Catholic Worker took care of him for over two decades providing him with friendship, hospitality, housing, and arranging for hospice care in the months before he died.

Last summer, we noticed something was wrong with Alfredo's health as his blood pressure went up and at times he kept falling as he tried to walk. So we took him to the hospital. Following some testing, the doctors told us that Alfredo has had cancer for a while and it had spread throughout his body. They gave him three months to live. There was nothing more they could do.

We called Alfredo *El Presidente* of the Tacoma Catholic Worker. He was so much a part of our lives that we were all saddened and shocked to learn that he was going to die so soon. After finding out the news, Alfredo wanted to paint the front porch before he died to honor the place he had lived for so long. He was going to see that it got done. He worked on it constantly for several weeks with the help of others, even though he didn't have much strength some days. After about a month it was finished!

Some days Alfredo was very open with us, wanting to be around others and sharing his food as a sign of appreciation. Other times he would be in his room resting, watching TV or sitting in a chair slumped with his head down in despair. It was very sad to watch him slowly die. As the next few months passed, his body grew more frail and weaker by the day. Alfredo ended up living longer than expected. He died after about six months following his diagnosis.

One day he fell for the last time. We called the hospice nurse who told us that he would surely die before the day was over. So we called many of our friends who loved Alfredo. In the next several hours, they gathered around Alfredo's bedside to say goodbye to their dear friend. He died at around 5:00 that evening as we watched him stop breathing.

There were many people around him that evening and he died in a peaceful way. The day before he was up making his own food and using the bathroom himself. And now he was gone. It was hard to believe. We brought in a bowl of water with some towels as we washed his arms, legs, chest, and head in a way to honor our friend. We all said goodbye before they took his body away.

I had never seen someone die before. This was one of the most mysterious, powerful, difficult things I had ever seen. Here was a community of people coming around someone with whom they had no biological connection as he lay dying. He was held in love by so many who cared for him in everyday life for so many years. He was not alone when he died, and to me it was beautiful that he should be surrounded by such love. Alfredo had no family, so we were the only family he had. Many of us said that this is how we would like to die, peacefully and surrounded by the people we love most.

After reflecting on this night when Alfredo died, I keep death before me in a clearer way. Every time I enter Guadalupe House and walk up the steps to the porch, I remember Alfredo. I am sure I will remember this for the rest of my life as I experience more family and friends die before it's my turn. I am learning not to fear thinking of death often, and I'm learning to accept facing the pain of loss I will experience when others pass on.

Kathleen Norris says, "To acknowledge our mortality need not be depressing, if it encourages us to enjoy the beauty of life while it is still fresh and new."[22] Thinking of death often can inspire us to see life with more beauty and imagination, a new angle, a new perspective, a new possibility. Our paradigms begin to shift about what is important to us. We begin to live as the body of Christ in everyday life in the parish. We become more connected to one another. The mystical imagination is cultivated in us as we practice this new perspective on death.

---

[22] Norris, *Acadia and Me*, 89.

Creating Insecurity

Our mortality could be our greatest strength if we will see our pursuit of God as our very sanity and survival in everyday life. Our mortality could inspire the mystical imagination within us in multiple ways. It could show us so much about the mysteries of life, the mysteries of grace, the mysteries of love. It could bring us together as the body of Christ in everyday life. Our mortality could help us to live in our bodies. Our mortality could bring us into a state of peace as we live out our lives together. Carolyn Weber says, "Thus, in order to live wisely, we must embrace the mystery and meaning of death. By exploring facets of death, we define life."[23] Thinking of death often could be one of the practices that saves the body of Christ from irrelevance in everyday life. We need to take this practice seriously if we are to be the body of Christ together. We cannot escape our mortality, so we must embrace it through the mystical imagination.

---

[23] Weber, *Holy is the Day,* 175.

Part 2

A Prophetic Practice: Contemplative Spirituality

Chapter 4

The Value of Awareness and Mindfulness:
Recovering from Our Dualistic Thinking

Awareness: Becoming Present to God

God is calling us to awareness as the body of Christ in the parish. We are being drawn into an awareness of place, conviviality, mystery, integration, neighborliness, love, humility, and beauty. Awareness is subversive. Awareness is prophetic. Awareness has an intuitive sense of imagination. The practice of contemplation cultivates the mystical imagination of awareness. Contemplation is about listening deeply without words, with a keen sense of mystery that cultivates awareness.

We are enabled to embrace a conscious awareness of God's presence through practicing contemplation as the body of Christ in our local community. We will become aware of so much in everyday life that would otherwise go unnoticed by practicing contemplative spirituality. God is longing for our participation in this form of listening. We do not need language, words, or techniques to practice this. All we need is the desire, passion, willingness, and commitment to cultivate the mystical imagination in this way.

There is no listening without a contemplative posture in everyday life. There is no awareness without this contemplative posture as the body of Christ in the parish. We humiliate ourselves when we live without a sense of awareness. Christians are called to an awareness of God's presence and beauty in the place where we live. It is about everyday awareness in our local context, our local community. Carl Arico writes, "Awareness of God's presence enables us to see all things as relating to God. We see the world with fresh eyes and ears."[1]

We see our local community through the mystical imagination of awareness. We see with an awareness of God's presence in our everyday lives together. We see the importance of the practice of contemplation to cultivate this awareness, this listening. Everything is a gift from God. We see the beauty of this, the truth of this, the reality of this. There is an ecology to God in the place we live. Everything is from God and connected to God. And God is connected to the place we inhabit and the relationships we enter into as gift. Our awareness could liberate the mystical imagination to this ecology.

God is present in our life now. God is planting seeds of life through the air we breathe. The body of Christ in the parish should long for an awareness of this. There is no stopping this reality breaking through to our souls. Contemplation helps us to listen to these mysteries. Our awareness will come alive as we practice being present to God in our local community. We will find life in the place we inhabit together. Cynthia Bourgeault writes, "The reality is that God is always present, and we're the ones who are absent!"[2]

We need to dance into this present awareness. We need to become aware of the presence of God in our everyday lives, in ourselves, our locality, our relationships. God is not somewhere out there up in the sky, untouchable to the world around us. God is present to us in this present moment, in all the particulars of everyday life together. This

---

[1] Arico, *A Taste of Silence*, 22.

[2] Bourgeault, *Centering Prayer and Inner Awakening*, 157.

gives us the hopeful strength that we are not alone in our awareness as the body of Christ in the parish. The mystical imagination teaches us of this. James Finely, a student of Thomas Merton, says in his book *The Contemplative Heart:*

> It is true that as we pull back even the least little bit from our contemplatively realized oneness with the mystery we seek we cannot help but notice in our reflective awareness how the stream of gifted wakefulness is pooling ever deeper within ourselves. It's true that as we step back even further, we cannot help but see how we, in the midst of all our craziness and fragmentation, are being transformed into one who is learning to realize the ever more expansive nature of the way and fulfillment it embodies. Rightly received, this knowledge of ourselves as one on the way heightens our sense of humble gratitude for all that has been received thus far, accompanied by an openness to all that lies ahead. As soon, however, as we turn to possess, on our own terms, this path along which we are being dispossessed of our illusions of possessiveness, we become confused. We begin to lose our way, until, discovering how we have once again slipped into delusions of possessiveness, we humbly let go. And in this renewed stance of letting go, we realize ourselves to be once again caught in the updraft of grace.[3]

This self-awareness of being the body of Christ in our local community creates the potential for us to see relational revelations through our seeds of contemplation. The mystical imagination cultivates a oneness with the mystery of our locality. Our awareness is a gift from God. We live in the mystery of God, the mystery of place. God shapes us through our awareness. It is through this listening awareness that we come to understand the gift of our lives together. We cannot possess this ourselves with our own agendas. It is only possessed by God in mystery. We need to participate in this mystery as the body of Christ. Just when we think we possess it, we've lost everything that is a gift to us.

---

[3] Finley, *The Contemplative Heart*, 208.

Our awareness reveals the reality of God's omnipresence. God has not abandoned our neighborhood, but lives and works within it more than we sometimes realize. Our awareness helps us to see and understand God's work and presence among us. "We rarely think of the air we breathe, yet it is in us and around us all the time," states Thomas Keating. "In similar fashion, the presence of God penetrates us, is all around us, is always embracing us. Our awareness, unfortunately, is not awake to that dimension of reality."[4]

If we had an awakened awareness to this "dimension of reality," it would change everything about us as the body of Christ in everyday life together in the parish. God is the present reality that we are called to recognize, become aware of, and attentive to. This practice is both subversive and prophetic. With a contemplative posture, we begin to understand the importance of this reality within the place we inhabit together. Our awareness will teach us many things about ourselves, others, and God. We need the courage to face this "dimension of reality" together. Our very sanity depends on such things. We need one another, God, and the place we inhabit more than we sometimes realize.

My own understanding of awareness has been difficult in many ways. I used to think that I was separated from God in everyday life, that God had little or no connection to the place where I live, to the relationships I have, or to the things I do. Church seemed to be more about a building and less about a community. But I soon realized that maybe I had it all wrong. I discovered that something was missing within me that could open up my soul to a different way of awareness. I didn't yet have an awareness of God's presence living within me and in the parish as the body of Christ in everyday life. I didn't have a steady practice of contemplation. But the lonelier I became, the more I pursued God through a form of contemplation that I didn't really understand at the time.

---

[4] Keating, *Open Heart Open Mind*, 44-45.

Other than on Sunday, I was usually on my own with my faith. I had to figure out growth, formation, and discipleship on my own. I had no one there to help me or mentor me. I was living by myself in an apartment, working as a school teacher. I was frustrated and didn't know what to do, so I started to read books for self-mentorship. I started practicing what I would later come to understand as contemplative spirituality to develop some growth, formation, and intentionality in my life. I really didn't know what I was doing; I just followed the longings of my soul.

Sometimes I would lie in my bed and cry. I would think about things that mattered to me. I would dream of things I wasn't experiencing or seeing in everyday life. This was all beyond any words or language that I was able to express to anyone. I didn't understand what was going on and how God was shaping me.

Through many years of practice, and then becoming a part of the Downtown Neighborhood Fellowship, I received some guidance and developed a lot of awareness and a better understanding of the mystical imagination. I started to have an awareness for new paradigms of communion with God, formation, the body of Christ, and the importance of a theology of place. Now after many years, I believe that an awareness of God's presence in a particular local community is so important for experiencing the body of Christ in everyday life, and that a practice of contemplation beyond language and words is essential to this.

God is always present with us, we just are not always aware of it. There is no coming in and out of God's presence. To say differently is a distortion of reality. We are always living in the presence of God. God lives around us, within us, through us. God is our Creator and the sustainer of our very existence as the body of Christ in everyday life in the parish. Richard Rohr says, "We cannot attain the presence of God because we're already totally in the presence of God. What's absent is awareness. Little do we realize that God is maintaining us in existence with every breath we take."[5]

Every breath is given to us by God. God helps us to live and move. God helps us to be the body of Christ together. The mystical imagination helps us to live in the awareness of these realities. Our contemplation always confirms this. We need to be wildly alive in our practice of awareness. Our awareness could start a revolution of love within us in everyday life. Our awareness could change everything that we do and are. Our awareness could cultivate the mystery of place in our spirituality. Our awareness could bring all kinds of gifts to our relationships. Our awareness cultivates our resting in the reality of God's ongoing presence with us in every moment of our lives together. There is no longer any need to try to achieve or attain God's presence. Awareness makes that obsolete.

There is nowhere we can be but in the presence of God. We cannot be outside of this reality. We just need to cultivate an awareness of this reality. Our Creator transcends all our boxes. We may prefer to confine God's presence to certain "religious" occasions. But God lives, plays, works, and speaks within the particulars of our local context in everyday life all the time. William Shannon states:

> Unfortunately so many of us do not actualize this capability: we are not aware that we are in the presence of God. We are, as I say, victims of spiritual apartheid. We have the notion that generally we are apart from God, except for important moments. As if you could be any place else—except in the presence of God. The really gigantic fear would be trying to place yourselves outside the presence of God. If you could do it—which actually you can't—it would mean immediate annihilation for you. It wouldn't mean you would die. It would mean that you would entirely cease to be.[6]

---

[5] Rohr, *Everything Belongs*, 29.

[6] Shannon, *Silence on Fire*, 29-30.

We need to cultivate this awareness that as the body of Christ in everyday life together we do not and cannot live apart from God. Through the parish, God is mystically incarnate among us and through us as we live out our lives together. God is alive in our neighborhood. The mystical imagination sees these things and helps us to better understand them. We need to strive to live with a deep understanding of an awareness of God's presence through the relational context we find ourselves in.

"Surely the Lord is in this place, and I was not aware of it" (Genesis 28:16). Jacob had some struggles with an awareness of God's presence in everyday life. Jacob thought that he was on his own, but God revealed to him the reality of this ongoing presence in the place Jacob would inhabit. The Creator was calling him to become a community of people who would become rooted in place with an awareness of God's presence. We oftentimes act like Jacob before he had an awareness of God's presence in everyday life. As a result, we oftentimes struggle around in our blindness. God is calling the body of Christ to become more aware of this reality. Through practicing contemplation, which helps us to listen, we will cultivate a mystical imagination of this awareness among us.

Subverting the Sacred/Secular Divide: Centering Ourselves

Our lives together cannot be divided by sacred/secular categories anymore. I want to propose that all of life is sacred. The body of Christ needs to live into this sacredness of life in the parish. There is a sacredness to place. We will subvert the sacred/secular divide if we understand this. Our practice of contemplation cultivates this subversion within us. We become more aware of how this division is damaging our lives together. It's not healthy to think and live dualistically. The only way to sanity and peace is through embracing the sacredness of all of life. That's what Jesus did. He saw everything as sacred. Thomas Merton notes, "The world is a sacred vessel which must not be tampered with or grabbed after."[7]

Embracing the sacredness of life, the sacredness of the earth, the sacredness of our world, the sacredness of our relationships, will dissolve all dualistic thinking among us. God is the reference point of all authenticity so there can be no fragmentations anymore. The mystical imagination subverts the sacred/secular divide which is destroying the body of Christ in everyday life.

We cannot go along anymore living individualistic lives apart from the body of Christ in everyday life in the parish. It is sad and confusing to me that many churches today seem to promote dualistic thinking. Why don't they want to subvert this sacred/secular divide? Maybe they think it costs too much to actually have to live out the gospel with others and be the body of Christ together. "If we are out of our mind, it is for the sake of God; if we are in our right mind, it is for you. For Christ's love compels us" (2 Corinthians 5: 13-14).

There is no sacred/secular divide when the body of Christ is living, abiding, and trusting in the divine presence within them and around them in the place they inhabit together. The mystical imagination shows us that Christ is part of everything in our context in a mysterious way. We have to have the eyes to see it. The secular realm does not exist. We cannot live as if it does. It is an illusion of our own making. Secular perceptions will dissolve among us when we learn to see all of life as sacred. There is a whole divine ecology that displays itself to us locally all the time. The body of Christ lives within this divine ecology in the parish.

God has placed the sacredness of life within us. Nothing escapes this manifestation. The neighborhood is sacred even when we have trouble seeing it. The neighborhood is filled with God's goodness and beauty. It is the sacred space where we become the body of Christ together in

---

[7] Merton, *Mystics and Zen Masters*, 76.

everyday life. Every day God is destroying the illusions of the sacred/secular divide in us as we live out the gospel. There can be no more tolerance for this division. We have to become fed up with it and seek a better way in the parish or we will become blinded by the illusion of the secular which takes away the radical nature of the gospel and leaves us in our comfort and security. The illusion of the secular wants to capture our imaginations, but the mystical imagination will not tolerate this.

God's incarnation in us is an ongoing reality in our world through the lives we lead as the body of Christ in the parish. It is through the small, particular, local, relational things of life that we become the hands and feet of Christ in everyday life. The incarnation and a theology of place are linked together in mysterious ways. They are one of the only hopes for the world as we know it. We experience salvation when the incarnation and a theology of place touch each other in our souls as the body of Christ working together. This is where the sacred/secular divide no longer exists. Everything becomes sacred through the incarnation as Christ lives both within us and in the material world we inhabit. Norvene Vest says:

> Incarnation as a theological principle means not just that God once took actual, temporal, material form, but that God can be found everywhere, all the time, within everything. God is not contained within but revealed through the material. Outward form is not unimportant, for the material form has been created by God for a specific purpose. We are invited to look with awe at each person and thing, for in some mysterious way, Christ shines forth from each. The world in which we live is a medium for the divine revelation. There is a continuous and creative interpretation of the spiritual and the material in all of created reality.[8]

God is revealed through the material world we live in. We need to recover a material theology in our local community. The material life is sacred. It is how we experience our salvation, our relationships, our place. Our neighborhood is the medium of relational revelations. It

---

[8] Vest, *No Moment Too Small*, 18-19.

teaches us about the illusion of the secular and that all of life is sacred. All our relationships are sacred. Everything we do is sacred. All our ordinary experiences are sacred. Nothing escapes sacredness. It takes imagination to experience all of life as sacred. Wendell Berry says in his book *The Way of Ignorance:*

> When Jesus speaks of having life more abundantly, this, I think, is the life He means: a life that is not reducible by division, category, or degree, but is one thing, heavenly and earthly, spiritual and material, divided only insofar as it is embodied in distinct creatures.[9]

To experience an abundant life as the body of Christ is to discover our way out of this sacred/secular divide. It is to see all of life as a miracle or gift of God. These categories of sacred/secular cannot exist when the incarnation and a theology of place live within us as the body of Christ. We enter into a holistic spirituality when the sacred/secular division disappears and is forgotten. It seems that all great people of faith experienced a conversion to seeing all of life as sacred. They refused to believe in the notion of the secular. It had no relevance for them. Likewise, we cannot let our lives be lived within the confines of the sacred/secular divide. We want out. We will protest against the idea of the secular. We live in Christ in the sacred, in the material, in our locality, in the abundance of our spirituality. There is no turning back. We forget the illusion of the secular and embrace all of life as sacred.

The sacred infuses everything we are. The sacred is friendly, beautiful, good, and trustworthy. There is an abundance to the sacredness of life. Sacredness can only be experienced in the tangible, material world of the place in which we live. It does not exist anywhere else. The body of Christ needs to embrace this call to an awareness of the sacredness of all of life. Our neighborhood, our relationships and the work we do in common are all sacred. Everything is sacred. I want to repeat that: Everything is sacred! There is no escaping the sacredness of life. The mystical imagination will free us from the sacred/secular divide.

---

[9] Berry, *The Way of Ignorance*, 136.

Our contemplation will help us to understand, listen and become aware of the illusions of this sacred/secular divide. Over time we develop strength to subvert this divide. Parker J. Palmer says, "The divided life is a wounded life, and the soul keeps calling us to heal the wound."[10] When we live in the sacred/secular divide we are unconsciously blinding ourselves. We live in a woundedness that will not go away. We become okay with it and think it is normal. But this woundedness is not okay, and we do not have to bear its scars anymore.

Jesus is healing this wound in us as the body of Christ in the parish. Our soul cries out for liberation from the cage of the secular, from the illusion of the secular, from the religion of the secular. This stamp of the secular is so commonplace we will have to unlearn almost everything we know about ourselves, the body of Christ, and God. Unlearning the illusion of the secular and practicing all of life as sacred will reorient our entire lives to the radical nature of the gospel. Our souls will call us away from our woundedness and into an integration of life which experiences everything as sacred. We become the body of Christ that experiences our salvation together through the sacredness of everyday life in all things. Healing this wound of the sacred/secular divide takes courage and practice. A contemplative spirituality is important to cultivate the mystical imagination that gives us the courage to live without this division. We come to experience all of life as sacred through the mystical imagination. Anne D. LeClaire writes, "Paying attention. Being in the moment of life. Honoring its sacred nature. In fact, realizing the inaffable, sacred nature of everything. Having reverence. If this is not the center of spirituality, then what is?"[11]

Our Downtown Neighborhood Fellowship has struggled over the years to embrace all of life as sacred. We had a big divide in the way we used language. There was a divide in theological ("sacred") language around certain people and normal ("secular") language around others. Over

---

[10] Palmer, *A Hidden Wholeness*, 20.

[11] LeClaire, *Listen Below the Noise*, 201-202.

time, we all began to see that we cannot divide our language any more than we can divide our bodies. We began to see how weird this was becoming. We knew that if we were going to stick around our neighborhood for any period of time, we were going to have to stop dividing our language into neat little compartments and start to practice all of language as sacred.

We still value theological language. But what seemed to happen was the theological language that we thought was more "sacred" became less relevant to us in our relational context. We began to embrace the normal ("secular") language as sacred in everyday life. And this seemed to feel right. We cannot manipulate and exploit others so easily through normal language. We can only communicate at work in normal language. We can only work through conflict together with normal language. We can only create friendships with normal language. We can only communicate love with normal language. We can only express our pain to God with normal language.

Through much practice of listening to our lives with a contemplative posture we began to ignore the sacred/secular division in our language. Now that we understand better the sacredness of ordinary language, we are developing a sacredness of respecting others for who they are and not pressuring our friends to believe what we perceive to be a correct theology. Our relationships have the freedom to practice hospitality and love right where someone is at without getting all weird about our differences. Our sacred normal language is helping us to cultivate an accepting posture in our relationships. We think this is the foundation of cultivating over time long-term relational revelations in our neighborhood. If we still lived in the sacred/secular divide we would have stopped listening and written off lots of people. Thank God we haven't gone that route!

Our neighborhood is filled with divine possibilities. There are revelations waiting to happen all around us. There are divine altars in the ordinary things of everyday life if we could just listen and see. Our contemplation cultivates the mystical imagination to listen in this way. Barbara Brown Taylor states:

> Human beings may separate things into many piles as we wish— separating spirit from flesh, sacred from secular, church from world. But we should not be surprised when God does not recognize the distinctions we make between the two. Earth is so thick with divine possibility that it is a wonder we can walk anywhere without cracking our shins on altars.[12]

We cannot at the same time fragment our lives and hope to live into a holistic counterculture. A holistic counterculture experiences all of life filled with divine altars and relational revelations in everyday life in the place we inhabit together. There is potential all around us all the time. God completely ignores and refuses to recognize all our self-made categories of life. God did not create the sacred/secular divide. We did. We must therefore be willing to destroy what we have created and live into something much more holistic.

All of life is sacred. All of life is worth living. All of life is calling us to a radical expression of the gospel in the parish. What would happen if we experienced all of life together as sacred in a particular place? I think we would experience a great amount of wisdom and liberation.

Mindfulness: Experiencing an Authentic Liberation

Jesus practiced a mindfulness in all that he did. I would say that Jesus was the most mindful person who ever lived. Mindfulness is the fruit of a contemplative spirituality that helps us to listen, cultivating awareness and compassion for those around us. Mindfulness is about a wisdom that Jesus teaches us as the body of Christ. In order to be sane we need to practice mindfulness. Without it we become selfish, individualistic people who do not care about much in life. This is not what the body of Christ is called to in everyday life together. We need to be a mindful

---

[12] Taylor, *An Altar in the World*, 15.

community that practices the teachings of Christ. This is what the mystical imagination is made up of.

Mindfulness is about being in touch with reality, experiencing it and letting it shape us. All truth is mindful of reality. Mindfulness helps us to experience the truth of who we are. Mindfulness helps us to experience our place in a proper context. We learn to care, show compassion, and gratitude. Mindfulness guides us into all relational revelations in the place we inhabit. There is no greater teacher than Jesus on the practice of mindfulness. He was an expression of mindfulness during his life in his local context. Jesus had a mystical imagination that cultivated mindfulness.

There is a gift in mindfulness that allows us to see the many possibilities before us as the body of Christ in the parish. The possibilities of love, compassion, grace, and humility live in little seeds within us. They need to be cultivated through the mystical imagination. We can dedicate ourselves in ways we never thought possible to the practice of mindfulness through contemplation. Macrina Weiderkehr says, "We all have the potential to give ourselves wholeheartedly to whatever it is we must do. This is the gift of mindfulness."[13]

It takes a lifetime to cultivate our gifts' full potential. Mindfulness is a liberator of the gifts that lie within us all. When we become mindful, we experience our salvation working itself out within us in everyday life together. We are drawn into the mystical imagination and shaped in the process. This gift of mindfulness can lead us to beautiful places relationally in our local community. Our relationships become more holistic. Everyone can practice a mindfulness as the body of Christ in everyday life in the parish. Jesus practiced mindfulness and we are called to imitate him in our local context. Ilia Delio states, "Compassion is growth in consciousness. It is a way of being for others that flows from a mindful connectedness and our awareness of unity."[14]

---

[13] Wiederkehr, *Seven Sacred Pauses*, 25.

[14] Ilia Delio, *Compassion*, 64.

"So then, just as you received Christ Jesus as Lord, continue to live in him, rooted and built up in him, strengthened in the faith as you were taught" (Colossians 2:6-7). Our mindfulness is rooted in Christ. We live into the gospel through mindfulness. We become strengthened in our faith together as the body of Christ through our mindfulness in everyday life. A contemplative spirituality lives in mindfulness. It's always listening to the mysteries of life within oneself and in the world. The mystical imagination lives with a mindfulness that is not dualistic.

Mindfulness is a training of sorts that pushes us beyond the status quo. It helps us to live deeply. It will shape us in mysterious ways as it works to form us as the body of Christ in the parish. We receive life as a gift through our mindfulness. Mindfulness helps us to embrace the mystical imagination within when we are shaken up and experience losses in life. Gunilla Norris says:

> Practicing mindfulness is much like physical training. The long-distance runner must deal with hills as well as valleys. The hills are hard. And they make one strong. If we can welcome them, and know that they will be followed by valleys, we will be learning something about steadfastness. We may find strength to continue by taking the long view: recognizing that bliss and pain are part of each other, that both together are more than either is separately.[15]

Life will be hard at times. There will be difficulties and hardships. This is guaranteed. So we need a steady presence of mindfulness through our lives together as the body of Christ in the parish to help strengthen us. Mindfulness is the gift that will sustain us. Our contemplation facilitates this gift. We develop a contemplative spirituality with a mystical imagination as we practice mindfulness. Our listening becomes more integrative. Our compassion becomes deeper. Mindfulness is the miracle that guides us in the place we inhabit, and the facilitator of relational revelations in our local context. Mindfulness keeps us abiding in Christ in everyday life. The mystical imagination

---

[15] Norris, *Inviting Silence*, 71.

needs mindfulness. Thich Nhat Hanh says that "each of us has the capacity of being mindful, everyone has the seed of mindfulness in himself or herself. If we know how to water this seed, it will grow, and we will become alive again, capable of enjoying all the wonders of life."[16]

We have the ability and the capacity to practice a robust form of mindfulness as an expression of the gospel in our everyday context. We are not intended to be mindless creatures doing only what benefits us at the expense of others. The gospel calls out for more from us. The gospel calls us to a mindfulness as the body of Christ in the parish. We must water the seeds of mindfulness within us all. We must cultivate the wonders of the mystical imagination. We must cultivate the wonders of a life of mindfulness. These wonders are calling out to us from the heart of the gospel to give us all life in the place we inhabit. It is the call to share life together through practicing mindfulness.

Mindfulness is unpredictable and uncertain. It will cause us to embrace some courage and let go of some comfort. We need a mindfulness of grace that will sustain us in our local context. The seeds of relational revelations are constantly being shown to us through our mindfulness. Our spirituality is most mature when we practice mindfulness together in everyday life as the body of Christ.

Wisdom is rooted in mindfulness of the teachings of Jesus. Wisdom is rooted in the body of Christ in the parish. Jesus was the great wisdom teacher. He exemplified mindfulness in everything he did in the local context in which he lived. Mindfulness is what the Sermon on the Mount and all of his parables and miracles and all of his relationships were all about. His death and resurrection were his ultimate acts of mindfulness. Christ and all the saints after him built their lives on mindfulness.

---

[16] Nhat Hanh, *Touching Peace*, 102.

Our contemplation integrates us into this gift of mindfulness. The mystical imagination cultivates this gift of the wisdom of mindfulness. Mindfulness is at the heart of the gospel of Christ and exemplifies the wisdom of gospel truth. We cannot dismiss this as only some "Eastern thing." We need to really look at what Jesus taught through Middle Eastern eyes. We have Americanized Jesus too much. This is not the cultural context that Jesus lived in.

The mystical imagination creates and our contemplation develops an "ecology of the mind" within us. Our mind starts to think in different interconnected paradigms that we had not known before. We start to understand how everything we do is connected to the relational context of the place in which we live. We cannot separate our mind from our relationships or from our local context. This ecology creates a mindfulness that begins to drastically reshape us. We begin to see with greater clarity. Our inner and outer worlds become one. Gus Gordon says:

> When we are confronted with our inner world, we will be astonished at our restlessness, at the variety of conflicting emotions, at the stream of unconscious thoughts and images that seize control of our minds. We, therefore, need to develop an "ecology of the mind," so that we can begin to approach reality as we most truly are and see what's before us clearly and precisely so we can approach life with care and mindfulness.[17]

Our interior life, our inner world, is brought to life through mindfulness. We begin to experience our relationships differently. We begin to care for the body of Christ in the place we live. We begin to change the world through changing ourselves. As we change ourselves through the mystical imagination, through Christ living in us, we begin to practice mindfulness.

As our Downtown Neighborhood Fellowship has practiced contemplation together, we have started to become more mindful of

---

[17] Gordon, *Solitude and Compassion*, 45.

the poor and marginalized in our neighborhood. When we first moved to Downtown Tacoma, we did not know a lot about poverty and homelessness. But as the years have gone by, we have developed a lot of relationships and more familiarity with those in poverty. At first we did not really want to think about the prisoners who were released on the streets with nowhere to go, the hungry who had nothing to eat, the cold and lonely, the mentally ill, the ones with hygiene needs, the homeless, the disabled veteran, and the unemployed. This was quite overwhelming for us to think about.

There are hundreds of homeless people living in extreme poverty in our neighborhood. We see them almost everywhere we go. They cannot be ignored. This has been difficult for us. We do not always know what to do, but through our practice of mindfulness, we are asking questions that challenge us to be more hospitable to the poor, the lonely, the mentally ill, and the oppressed.

So we have been taking some steps to become more mindful of the poor in our neighborhood. I became a part of the Tacoma Catholic Worker and moved into one of their houses in our neighborhood where I live in solidarity with the poor, oppressed, and marginalized. My friends Paul and Liz, for a time, moved into a renovated warehouse right next to the Tacoma Avenue Shelter where 150 homeless stay each night. They now have a close proximity to a major shelter in our neighborhood, and they interact with the homeless who walk down Court E, the street they live on, on a regular basis. My friends Danny and Nichole are asking questions about their new friend Shelton who frequently visits them at their local business. They sometimes give him water or coffee and are seeking to be his friend as he struggles with mental illness.

My friend Molly has practiced a generous hospitality to our friend Darrell at her neighborhood bakery. Darrell is in his 70s. He lives close by and is mentally ill. He often buys coffee and pastries at the bakery. At times he sing songs in the bakery. Sometimes it feels awkward having Darrell around, but the bakery provides him with a place where he isn't so lonely. He passed away recently. It is kind of weird not to have Darrell around the neighborhood anymore. He usually came into the bakery a couple of times a day. Life is different without him. But we remember the gift Darrell was to us.

My friend Holly changed jobs recently and now works for a non-profit organization that works with the poor in the neighborhood. My friend Gary also became a part of the Tacoma Catholic Worker and moved into one of their houses in our neighborhood in order to live with the poor and oppressed where he loves working with the immigrants who are held in the ICE detention center nearby. He also likes to visit and mentor men who are incarcerated in prison. My friends Nick and Nora have been doing a lot of justice work for the marginalized in our neighborhood for many years now. Many of us have studied Shane Claiborne's book, *The Irresistible Revolution*, and that has raised a lot of questions and challenges for us. Our mindfulness is teaching us to ask: How do we live in a local context that has a lot of poverty? This is real to our experience and it saddens us to see so much poverty around us.

The Value of Awareness and Mindfulness

Chapter 5

The Kingdom of God Within Us: Sustainability for Our Work In the World

Creating a Longing for God: Our Sanity and Survival

A contemplative spirituality creates a longing for God within us. This longing is what keeps us alive. This longing keeps us sane in the midst of our everyday lives. Our humanity cannot be authentic without it, because without it, we have nothing much. All of Christ's followers throughout history have cultivated a longing for God through some form of contemplative practice. Longing and listening are greatly intertwined and cannot be separated. When we are longing for God, we are listening to our lives. Mirabai Starr states:

> Longing may be our legacy, but wholeness is our birthright. It lies at the heart of the disappointments and delights of everyday life. In weeding the garden and burning the toast. In falling asleep alone or enfolded in the arms of another. In reading poetry instead of watching the news. In missing the grandmother you adored and becoming the father you never had. In weeping for the suffering of the oppressed, the degradation of the planet.[1]

---

[1] Starr, *God of Love*, 61-62.

The Psalms teach us this type of longing for God. "Show me your ways, O Lord, teach me your paths; guide me in your truth and teach me, for you are God my Savior, and my hope is in you all day long" (Psalm 25:4-5). The mystical imagination always creates in us a longing for God. Yet where has this longing gone? Have we never developed it? Our spirituality is more than propositional statements, but is in fact characteristic of a passionate longing for God combined with a deep listening as human beings. Adrienne Von Speyr emphasizes listening this way as she states:

> A listening that does not stop up its ears, that is not simply escape and evasion, not simply hope that one will be able to interpret this call differently from the way it was meant. But rather one must listen to it in nakedness. Everything else is excluded and set aside: the demand for consolation or insight or reason or vision. This is contemplation in nakedness, which wants nothing else but God.[2]

We need to develop and cultivate our longing for God. This is how we seek God as the body of Christ in the parish. We need to listen to our longing for God. We need to listen for its absence. In our listening, we might discover that there is more mystery to our lives and to God than we had realized. God will not be boxed in. Our longing will reveal to us the illusions of the status quo and call us to the radical nature of the gospel. Our contemplation will create a longing for God within us in everyday life. "The time comes when we realize that this longing is itself the presence of God's longing in us," states Thelma Hall.[3]

When we listen deeply, we will start to live into a holistic counterculture. We will become the body of Christ together. Longing cannot be forgotten or ignored. We need a hospitable posture toward our longing. As we seek God, creating a longing within ourselves, we will experience our salvation embodied through the relational context we inhabit.

---

[2] Von Speyr, *Light and Images*, 75.

[3] Hall, *Too Deep for Words*, 42.

A contemplative spirituality goes way beyond words. The mystical imagination is beyond words. Our longing for God is beyond words. Words have limits. Our bodies communicate a communion with God beyond all language. Our communion has a longing to it that is very mysterious and cannot be completely understood or explained. Emilie Griffin writes, "In contemplation we learn to move beyond words ... and listen."[4] Words sometimes get in the way of us listening to our lives together.

When we "move beyond words," that is where we start to be in touch with our longing for God. Our attention goes beyond words to longing. We begin to listen. We begin to explore our interior life with more intentionality and intensity. We desperately need an intensity to our seeking after God today. Why are we so slow in seeking, listening, longing after God? We need to become the body of Christ in everyday life together that seeks, listens, and longs after God in this way. We can do this best through the local community we inhabit together.

Longing does not and cannot live in boxes. It does not even recognize boxes. Longing lives in the unknown. Longing only understands embodiment, not abstraction. Longing is mysterious and powerful. It can liberate us in ways we will not completely understand. As we explore a contemplative spirituality, we will experience a constant unraveling and rebuilding of our faith in God. Our faith will evolve and change. Our longings will challenge our present safe and possibly wrong perceptions of God. Those perceptions could be destroyed altogether. God is too mysterious for our perceptions. Thomas Merton says, "In the end the contemplative suffers the anguish of realizing that he no longer knows what God is."[5]

As we grow in our faith, the older we get and the more mature we become, it seems the less we understand of all who God is. We begin to see how mysterious God is. We begin to see that God does not live in

---

[4] Griffin, *Doors into Prayer*, 73.

[5] Merton, *New Seeds of Contemplation*, 13.

propositions. God does not live in words. God does not live in our theology. God is too mysterious to figure out. Maybe we need to stop saying that we "know" God. Do we really know God? Does anyone really understand the mysteries of God? Our longings teach us to seek this mysterious God that we will never completely know or understand. We can listen as the body of Christ to our longings for God in the parish. Longing is not about knowing everything or understanding everything, but about listening through our limitations. Simone Weil, a twentieth century mystic who refused to get baptized so she could identify with the outsider, says, "To long for God and to renounce all the rest, that alone can save us."[6]

Longing for God is manifested in living as the body of Christ in everyday life in the parish. We cannot turn our longings into an individual pursuit of God that does not take seriously place, others, and the body of Christ. This alone could save us from our irrelevance, our individualism, fragmentation, and isolation. The mystical imagination has a longing for God that it cannot live without. It is dead without this longing. And if the mystical imagination dies, so will the body of Christ. Our longing for God will always lead us to renounce what is not of the mystical imagination. Our contemplation will lead us to renounce those things that will not contribute to working out our salvation together.

Over the years, I have developed a longing for God at great expense. My family has not understood my passion. They have wanted me to pursue an upward mobility of money, career, prestige, and possessions. I have not wanted these things for myself, because I know what they would do to my soul, to my growth, to my formation. They would kill my imagination. They would kill my longing for God. They would distract me from all I want in life.

What I want is an authentic spirituality in which I can seek God holistically by being a part of the body of Christ in everyday life in the

---

[6] Weil, *Waiting for God*, 128.

place where I live. Nothing else matters to me. I don't care too much for money, prestige, or possessions. I want to live with the poor. I want to practice a contemplative spirituality. I want to share life with others in my neighborhood. I want to belong in community. These are the things I most want. My longings lead me to such things. But it seems our culture does not want to see its counterculture grow. So I have taken some bumps and bruises along the way.

It has not been easy all the time. It has taken a life of discipline to create, and a mystical imagination to sustain. Sometimes I think I want to quit, but my longings will not allow me to. They have become too developed within me over the years to ever forget about. I cannot ignore my longing for God. I cannot ignore my neighbors who need love. I cannot ignore the place I inhabit. I cannot ignore my imagination. My parents are probably still upset with such an "irresponsible" son who has renounced many things in life, but that is a boundary I will have to live with. I need to live the life God has called me to in my own authentic way.

I remember growing up as a Catholic. My parents took us to church almost every Sunday. I did not like church that much and never really thought about God. But I remember one Sunday morning a thought crossed my mind: "What if some ordinary person had given their entire life to God? What would that look like?" Then I had a second thought: "That would never happen." I could not imagine anyone ever giving their life to God. Why would anyone want to do that? But now I realize that I am becoming that person who has given his entire life to God.

For a long time now, God has been cultivating a longing within me for a holistic counterculture. I want to influence the body of Christ in our postmodern culture to do something different in the world. This is my longing, this is my passion, this is what is authentic for me. I want to embody love and compassion within my life far more than money, prestige, power, or possessions.

Our longing for God is the truest thing about us. In this we find our identity as the body of Christ in everyday life in the place where we live. It is who we are. We cannot detach ourselves from this longing. We were intended to live in, to abide in, and to trust in this longing. Thomas Keating says, "God wants to share with us even in this life the maximum amount of divine life that we can possibly contain."[7]

How much life and longing can we possibly experience in our bodies? I think that we can experience more of God's life within us than we realize. Our bodies were created for longing, for experiencing God's life as much as we possibly can in the here-and-now of our everyday lives together. Longing is earthy, on-the-ground, and opens up our inner worlds to us. We begin to sense what is beautiful. We become intuitive. We begin to listen to the mysteries in and around us. We learn to speak the new language of love and compassion as we live in community with one another.

To live is to experience an ongoing longing for God. Our longing evolves throughout our entire lives as the body of Christ. Sometimes it creates a deep ache inside of us that becomes difficult to bear. But our discipleship and longing for God are intertwined and dance together in our everyday lives despite the ache. Phileena Heuertz, co-founder of The Gravity Center, a center for contemplative activism, states, "It's difficult to sit in the ache of longing, so sometimes we avoid it. But when we embrace that gut-level discontent, we are moving and growing."[8]

The Realization of Christ Within Us: Fully Alive, Fully Human

When we practice a contemplation spirituality, we begin to have an ongoing epiphany of Christ within us. This is not just an abstract theological concept, but a living reality. We begin to uncover the buried treasures within us that have gone untapped for many years. We start to

---

[7] Keating, *Invitation to Love*, 5.

[8] Heuertz, *Pilgrimage of a Soul*, 65.

understand that there is much more within our bodies than blood, bones, arteries, and organs. We start to understand that Christ lives within our very bodies in some mysterious way. So much of Scripture points to this.

I cannot imagine an authentic Christianity where followers of Christ do not embody this. Christ in us is the greatest truth we can hold onto. Without this truth the mystical imagination cannot become fully alive within us. Christ within us is our very strength in everyday life together. Christ within us is how the Holy Spirit makes us fully alive and fully human. Contemplation creates a pathway in our souls so we can see this more clearly. We develop a conviction around nurturing the life of Christ within us. We allow our bodies to communicate the life of Christ beyond any use of words, as an embodied practice in everyday life. We speak a new language of love, grace, and compassion through our lives. "I have been crucified with Christ and I no longer live, but Christ lives in me" (Galatians 2:20). Christ lives within our everyday lives together in the place we inhabit. The mystical imagination reveals the truth of Christ living within us. MaryKate Morse states, "We do not create or introduce the kingdom. The kingdom of God is within."[9]

We are meant to live our lives through Christ living in us. Our contemplation gives us a greater sense of clarity around this revelation. We cannot ignore it. Our spirituality is not about morality per se, but about Christ living in us through contemplative awareness. Christ in us makes all of life sacred because the kingdom of God lives within us. Christ living in us helps us to live in our bodies. Christ living in us creates mindfulness and an awareness of our lives together in the parish.

Our souls cry out for Christ to become alive within us, to experience beauty, goodness, peace, love, grace, and kindness. Our bodies were created for nothing else. We are to be an expression of Christ's life in

---

[9] Morse, *Making Room for Leadership*, 28.

this world. This is the kingdom of God within. We cannot be an embodied expression of love if Christ is not living out the kingdom of God within us. Steven Chase says:

> The Christian understanding that God is present and lives within, at the core of the soul, is suggested in numerous passages in Scripture. It is the basis of how we live our lives and how we are in relation with others as we cherish the image of the living God within them.[10]

When we realize that Christ is living in us, we can honor the image of God within others. The Christ in me connects with the Christ in you in some mysterious way. This opens up all kinds of pathways to love, compassion, honesty, and vulnerability in everyday life as we seek to be human together in community. We start to understand that love is all that matters as we learn to see and celebrate the image of God in others.

Our contemplation cultivates a listening spirit within us that brings us to a deeper consciousness of Christ living in us. This consciousness brings about an interior revolution that slowly liberates us from within. Our Christ-consciousness begins to cultivate the mystical imagination within and among us. We realize that this life is not outside of ourselves, but within ourselves. Christ is a part of our very existence and the core of who we are. Christ constantly draws out all that is beautiful, truthful, and good within us. Our entire lives are sacred and Christ lives within our sacredness.

Christ is no longer experienced as an object outside of ourselves, but is experienced as a living person within us. Our everyday lives develop an intentional, intense, relaxed focus on this realization of Christ living within us. It is an ongoing experiential conversion to be taught and guided by this mysterious life within us all throughout our existence in the place we live. The body of Christ lives with an awareness of this life within us. It is the bread we eat and the wine we drink.

---

[10] Chase, *The Tree of Life*, 155.

Christ lives in us in our everyday life together. We experience the joys and the sorrows, the sadness and the pain of Christ who lives within us. Christ's pain is deep, and we need courage to allow ourselves to feel this pain. I believe Christ's pain is connected to all that we have abandoned locally—our neighbors, our local economy, our local creativity, and our locally embodied lives together.

Christ experiences joy when we are reconciled with all that is local. We need to allow this joy to live within us. The life of Christ within us cannot be reduced to a technique, a program, or an institution. We must allow this life within us to shatter all our cherished techniques, programs, and institutions. We cannot box Christ in any longer. Jesus wants to get out of our boxes, he does not like our boxes because he is beyond them. Christ wants to be embodied fully in authenticity within our bodies within the place we live.

Christ's life within us is the source of our passion. Our lives need to be lived with a passion and longing for the divine mysteries living within us in everyday life as the body of Christ in the parish. To become passionate about this we need to cultivate this life within. Our practice of contemplation will help us to realize the radical nature of Christ living within us. Jeff Imbach says, "Thinking of God's life within us as the source of our passion is wonderfully radical."[11]

Christ's life within us is indeed radical. It will shake us up out of the status quo and disturb our comfortable theologies of safe religion. Christ wants to be free to live passionately in our human bodies. Christ wants to live through his body on earth in everyday life in the parish.

Our passion for Christ living within us will cultivate the mystical imagination that will do away with the status quo. Passionate lives and status quo living do not fit together and will never fit together. We must live as passionately as Christ who lives within us. The mystical imagination longs for this to be embodied in our lives together. We

---

[11] Imbach, *The River Within*, 66.

cannot comprehend this completely, but we must constantly trust the mystery of this life within us. Carl McColman states, "A God you cannot comprehend is a God you cannot manipulate."[12]

Our Downtown Neighborhood Fellowship has done many things to cultivate our passion for a contemplative realization of Christ living within us. We have oftentimes used our neighborhood's built environment to help us to remember important themes in our lives together, to remember the One who lives within us and the place we love so dearly.

One morning some of us got together to walk around our neighborhood to specific spots that helped remind us of Christ living in us and our hopes for our lives together. At each spot, we reflected on a theme and shared hopes, longings and memories to cultivate our mystical imagination together.

We started out at the Nurture Healing Center where the theme was healing and rejuvenation. Then we walked to the Spanish Steps where the Elks Building is located. The theme there was restoration and rebuilding. As we walked to the next spot, I sensed we were all becoming more open to the life of Christ within us. It seemed that God was cultivating our realization of the mystery of life within us and connecting this to our life together in this place.

Then we walked to the water fountain by the Broadway Center where the theme was abundance. We went over to the Urban Grace building where the theme was remembering the past. We then went to Wright Park where the theme was reclaiming what was. Then we went to the Clock Tower on Tacoma Ave. where the theme was powerlessness. Lastly, we walked over to the Guadalupe Village (Tacoma Catholic Worker) where the theme was living into an alternative imagination. The more we walked, the more I sensed that a mystical imagination was becoming more alive within us.

---

[12] McColman, *The Big Book of Christian Mysticism*, 77.

As we spent time together that morning cultivating our realization of Christ living within us, within our place, within our imaginations, our shared life together was strengthened. This experience brought us together in a way that is hard to completely explain. Our love grew for each other, for our neighborhood, and for God. This is part of our shared history together that will be remembered for a long time. I hope that we will have many more experiences that will build onto this one.

Sustainability and Strength: Persevering Through All That Life Brings Us

We need to have a practice of contemplative spirituality within us in order to cultivate the mystical imagination in the parish. This brings about sustainability and strength to persevere through all that life brings us. Life can be difficult. If we do not have a practice of contemplation we will not last long in our neighborhood. The temptation to move on is too great. Most of us have the chance every year to leave and go "somewhere better," where all our "American dreams" will come true. The body of Christ should not succumb to such themes. Everyday relational life is too important to become fragmented all over again.

We need strength from God to persevere through all things. We will not give up on love, humility, grace, and each other. All the systems in life, including the church, are trying to pull us apart, trying to tell us we do not need each other that much. "Forget about interdependence," they say, "and embrace the individualistic, independent life." For them this is all there is or ever will be. But our contemplation communicates to us something different. We are open to more of a sustainable shared life together.

Our contemplation helps us find strength in an individualistic postmodern culture. The mystical imagination gives us strength to embody love in hard times when it would be easy to give up. It cultivates a sustainability among us to never give up. We will love no matter what. We will hold on no matter what. We will persevere no matter what. This is the call of our lives.

"May our Lord Jesus Christ himself and God our Father, who loved us and by his grace gave us eternal encouragement and good hope, encourage your hearts and strengthen you" (2 Thessalonians 2:16-17). Our practice of contemplation is the tool that infuses God's strength and sustainability into our lives. We can be shaped for all that we go through. Jesus is our sustainability and perseverance in order to be the church in the place we inhabit. The mystical imagination wants the body of Christ to persevere in love and compassion. There is no other way. God is empowering us through a contemplative spirituality to persevere through anything. One of the most influential writers on spirituality in the twentieth century, Thomas Merton, notes, "Contemplation lifts us beyond the sphere of our natural powers."[13]

There is little we can do without a contemplative spirituality. Our communion with God is based on such things. We need contemplation for sustainability as the body of Christ rooted in the parish. Contemplation brings a peaceable way into our relational context. We are able to touch a strength that is hard to find outside of a contemplative posture. The discovery of such things in our journey is a source of liberation to our neglected souls.

It is hard to live out a Christian spirituality in North America. It is hard to be authentic. It is hard to build community in such a mobile, technological, wealthy country. Place, locality, and neighborhood are the most overlooked aspects in our practice of Christianity. Not very many people think this is essential to being the body of Christ anymore. But those who practice a contemplative spirituality open up another possibility in everyday life. Our contemplation is intertwined with God's will on earth through the place where we live. Our contemplative spirituality teaches us that human lives in a local context are valuable. All lasting relationships take place in local contexts of face-to-face daily interaction. We cannot overlook this anymore.

---

[13] Merton, *New Seeds of Contemplation*, 240.

Our contemplation helps us to persevere relationally. To give love, grace, compassion, mindfulness, and authenticity require a strength beyond what we can come up with ourselves. For there to be some sustainability we need Christ's strength to live in us. We need to trust in our God if we are to live locally and love our neighbors in the place where we live. There is no way around this. Without abiding in Christ, we will slowly over time turn colonial, individualistic, and lack an authentic motivation. The mystical imagination trusts in Christ's strength within.

Contemplation helps us to embody the teachings of Jesus to love one another. There is a deep sustainability that is cultivated through a contemplative spirituality. It will become harder to be content with living in our illusions. Phileena Heuertz and Darren Prince say, "Contemplation helps us to faithfully live into our calling in a way that sustains us for the long haul."[14]

Long-term sustainability is the fruit of a contemplative spirituality in the parish. The more we practice it, the more able we are to persevere. We are all called to a practice of contemplation as the body of Christ. We cannot be the body of Christ without it. The mystical imagination needs it. Our calling becomes clearer when we practice a contemplative spirituality together. We become one with our place through our contemplative practice. Richard Rohr in his book *A Lever And A Place To Stand* says, "Contemplation is no fantasy, no make-believe, no daydream, but the flowering of patience and steady perseverance."[15]

Contemplation will lead us to a consistent perseverance. Nothing will move us from our call to be the body of Christ together in everyday life. We will be able to respond to pain and difficulties with more courage. A sustainable perseverance will strengthen us through the mystical imagination. Our practice of contemplation will bring some sanity to our fragmented lives. This is the only source of our sustainability as a

---

[14] Heuertz and Prince, "Devotional," 122.

[15] Rohr, *A Lever and a Place to Stand*, 105.

community in the parish. A contemplative spirituality gives us the patience necessary to persevere in all things that life can bring us. We will learn to find our strength in God.

There will be seasons of good times and bad times, lonely times and the not so lonely times, dark times and lighter times, frustrating times and joyful times. Without the practice of contemplation we will soon find ourselves giving up on the body of Christ altogether. We will become disillusioned, as so many have, thinking it isn't worth the risk. The thought goes: "It isn't worth the risk to love and care for a place. We have our own lives to live. And this is no longer our definition of life."

Contemplation does not lead us to fantasy, make-believe or daydreams. Instead it leads us to an authentic reality within the place we live. We cannot tolerate the illusions of our uprooted culture that is always telling us to find something better somewhere else if things get difficult. The mystical imagination ignores such talk and embraces contemplation as a way of life. Our very beings become expressions of contemplation as we learn to love our neighbors in the parish. This is our very communion with Christ.

Contemplation leads us to be the body of Christ in everyday life together. The mystical imagination will sustain us through all of life. Christ is our strength in all things and we will look nowhere else for our strength. Henri J. M. Nouwen says in his wonderful book *The Wounded Healer:*

> The contemplative is not needy or greedy for human contacts, but is guided by a vision of what he has seen beyond the trivial concerns of a possessive world. He does not bounce up and down with the fashions of the moment, because he is in contact with what is basic, central and ultimate. He does not allow anybody to worship idols, and he constantly invites his fellow man to ask real, often painful and upsetting questions, to look behind the surface of smooth behavior, and to take away all the obstacles that prevent him from getting to the heart of the matter. The contemplative critic takes away the illusionary mask of the manipulative world

and has the courage to show what the true situation is. He knows that he is considered by many as a fool, a madman, a danger to society and a threat to mankind. But he is not afraid to die, since his vision makes him transcend the difference between life and death and makes him free to do what has to be done here and now, notwithstanding the risks involved."[16]

Our contemplation causes us to be at peace with being misunderstood, ignored and forgotten by the wealthy and the powerful of this world. We don't need anyone's approval. We have a calling of love to live out in the parish. And this is what we persevere in. We are not bothered as much by people and institutions outside of ourselves. We look within ourselves and find the kingdom of God through contemplation. The mystical imagination is within ourselves. We can change our world and our neighborhood only by changing ourselves. This is the call of our lives together.

Our Downtown Neighborhood Fellowship has often facilitated times where we can express our longings, hopes, and desires through writing. Our expressions become the communion we hold onto as our source of strength and sustainability to get us through all the seasons of life together. Our communion helps us to remember Christ in all things.

Here is one example of this:

We are longing for more honesty. We see you in our midst in ordinary ways. We are hoping for something beautiful. We open our eyes to you. We see you all around us. You are good to us in all kinds of ways. We want to learn to love more and more. Wake us up and lead us into some kind of peaceful revolution. We open our eyes to revelation. We are desiring authenticity. We need your grace to hold our lives. We are vulnerable and afraid. We need some strength in our weakness.

Open your love to us. We will not be arrogant anymore. Show us our true selves. We need to carry our burdens to you. You are

---

[16] Nouwen, *The Wounded Healer*, 45.

moving through the wind. We will not push back anymore. We will risk our entire lives to find something that we cannot always understand presently. We cry over our failures. Our lives are beautiful together. Our days are filled with peace and life.

We will see something together. This is what we are living for. Our eyes are open and longing. Give us some sanity and peace. We need your hands to keep us going. Let us sense your grace and love. Let us live in freedom. We want to be a culture of love and grace. We desire to be kind and patient. We want to remember your love. All our days are wrapped up in you. Our lives are being shaped by our environment. There is nowhere else for us to go. This way of life is our source of belonging. Create unity and love among us as we become an expression of beauty in the place we inhabit.

Chapter 6

Seeds of Ordinary Revelation: Uncovering the True Self

Discovering the True Self: Unmasking the illusion of the False Self

Our practice of contemplation will show us our true self, who we really are in the beauty of our humanity. The true self integrates our body, soul, and spirit together within a relational context in the place we inhabit. The true self is what the gospel is calling us to embody. It can see beyond the status quo lifestyle. It longs for authenticity. Contemplation calls the true self to come alive in us. The mystical imagination is an expression of our true self. Susan R. Pitchford writes:

> Why is all this work on the self, on finding my true self, not selfish? Isn't going on a discovery that's all about Me just a little narcissistic? The answer is no, precisely the opposite. Discovering the true self is essential because the false self cannot love. It's too consumed with its own needs. This doesn't mean that people who haven't gone in search of their true self are incapable of love, far from it. But real love comes from the truest part of ourselves.[1]

---

[1] Pitchford, *The Sacred Gaze*, 124.

Through contemplation, we are empowered to discover the true self as we live out our lives in the parish. We are no longer prisoners of the status quo. The mystical imagination liberates our bodies. Our true self is enabled to think, explore, question, experiment, live, practice, and embody our spirituality in our local cultural context.

We are no longer afraid to live out the radical nature of the gospel. We are not afraid to love, to be known by others, to be honest and vulnerable, to be human. Our true self insists that we look inside and explore who we authentically are. Our true self will teach us wisdom, and to abide, trust, and hope in the divine. Brenda Salter McNeil states, "Worship is therefore to be your true self—the person that God created you to be—without pretense."[2]

Our true self manifests the kingdom of God within us. We can search everywhere outside ourselves for the kingdom of God, but the mystical imagination inspires us to look within for the kingdom of God. "The kingdom of God does not come with your careful observation, nor will people say, 'Here it is,' or 'There it is,' because the kingdom of God is within you" (Luke 17:20-21).

Christ is teaching us of the relationship between the interior life and the kingdom of God. They cannot be separated. The interior life of contemplation connects us to our true self. This connection manifests the kingdom of God within us. This is true, authentic contemplative spirituality in the parish. The kingdom of God needs to come alive in us as the body of Christ in everyday life together. Discovering our true self is the lifelong process of searching for our own identity as an authentic human being. "The search for identity," states Susan Hope, "is just that—a search, a journey which takes a lifetime."[3]

Our true self will help us to live an authentic contemplative spirituality. Christ is calling us to become our true self in the place we inhabit

---

[2] McNeil, *A Credible Witness*, 102.

[3] Hope, *Mission-Shaped Spirituality*, 17.

together. Christ is calling us to a life of communion through contemplation, to listen beyond words to the kingdom of God within. The mystical imagination is calling us to a discovery of the true self. This should be our lifelong pursuit as the body of Christ in the parish. We cannot find the kingdom of God anywhere else, but in human bodies working together for the peace of the world.

Our true self manifests beauty throughout our world. Our true self is a gift to the place where we live as the body of Christ in the parish. When we pay attention to our true self, we begin an inner healing process as our humanity manifests an abundance of relational gifts. Parker J. Palmer says, "Whatever we do to care for true self is, in the long run, a gift to the world."[4] We live in a liberation that cannot be faked. We live in the liberation of authenticity and love.

We learn to care for others instead of hate them. We learn to have grace for others instead of judgment. We learn to demonstrate humility instead of selfishness. The true self doesn't have to be defensive; it has the freedom to listen. The true self doesn't feel threatened by differences; it is loving, kind, and accepting. The true self follows Christ in its own authentic way. The true self has a courageous mystical imagination. The true self is a gift to the place we inhabit as the body of Christ in everyday life. Holly Gerth notes, "And here's the thing: we get only one you. There never has been and never will be, another you in this world. That's why I feel so passionately about you being who you are and embracing it. We don't need a copy of someone else – we need the one and only, original you."[5]

The false self wants us to live in our illusions and fragmented selves. The true self wants us to be in harmony with ourselves, with others, and with God. The true self wants us to be connected to the place we inhabit. Our contemplation connects us to what is authentic within us.

---

[4] Palmer, *A Hidden Wholeness*, 39.

[5] Gerth, *You're Already Amazing*, 180.

The true self brings a new consciousness to our union with Christ. M. Basil Pennington writes:

> In our old consciousness, where we identified ourselves as that false self made up of what we have, what we do, and what others think of us, we were in a state of constant and complete self-alienation. We were not at home with ourselves at all. As we turn within and begin to know our true self, this split begins to be healed. We are coming home. Yet the split is totally healed only when we are ourselves in pure consciousness and no longer see ourselves as an object apart from the knowing subject. This self-knowledge comes to fullness when we experience ourselves as one with God in God and God is known in pure consciousness rather than by some subject-object knowledge.[6]

Our contemplation brings awareness of our union with God as the true self lives fully in all of its potential. The true self embraces the life of God within. It does not live outside of this reality. The mystical imagination lives in union with God in the parish. James Martin says in his book *Becoming Who You Are*, "Everyone's true self is a unique creation of God's, and the way to sanctity is to become the unique self that God wishes us to be."[7]

Our true self is unique. We do not need to conform to the status quo anymore. We need to live into our uniqueness. If we were all our true selves, the body of Christ would be a shaper of beauty in the place we inhabit together.

The false self destroys the body of Christ. It wants us to go to church instead of be the church together in a particular place. The way of discipleship and of discipline is to discover our true self. Our sanity depends on us discovering our true self as the body of Christ in everyday life. The true self is the essence of authenticity. It is how we become expressions of love in the world, and how we live in our bodies

---

[6] Pennington, *Centered Living*, 96.

[7] Martin, *Becoming Who You Are*, 73.

in the parish. Alice Fryling notes, "Listening to the true self may be a countercultural experience."[8]

When I first got involved in the Downtown Neighborhood Fellowship (when it was under a different name) some years ago, the words that identified what it was were: "God for unique humans." We created environments that allowed humans to be unique, to be their true selves.

I remember when we would practice contemplation together to cultivate our true selves. There were times when we would be together pursuing a sense of listening and silence. We would think about our relational context, the place where we live, and practice an imaginative awareness in our souls.

I remember listening one time when I was not feeling so good. I couldn't sense anything happening within or around me. I could feel my breathing. I could feel my heartbeat. I could sense my body. But that was about it. I wanted to experience more. But I could only identify with the ordinary moment at hand. It was not flashy or spectacular or exciting. It was just what it was: an ordinary moment in time. These have become sacred to me, and to all of us in our neighborhood, because they show us our true self in unexpected ways.

I have come to see that I do not have to be like someone else. God has made me a unique human who wants to live out the gospel in the unique way in which God is leading. I do not always understand these leadings or longings, but I trust that God is cultivating my true self in authenticity.

Those of us in the Downtown Neighborhood Fellowship have become more at home in our true selves through much practice together. We have exposed the false self to discover something better in the parish. We have learned the importance of contemplation and its relationship

[8] Fryling, *Seeking God Together*, 117.

to the discovery of the true self. After all these years, we are still living as unique humans.

We already are our true self; we just don't live it out. It is not how our culture has taught us to live. We have been taught to live out of our false self. But the process of life is to unlearn the false self and discover the true self as the body of Christ in everyday life together. We need to have a new consciousness of the true self. We need a conversion to living more holistically out of our true self.

We will not be able to live authentically in the parish without a connection to our true self. Living locally in community will not work if the true self is denied. Richard Rohr says in his book *Falling Upward*, "Life is a matter of becoming fully and consciously who we already are, but it is a self we largely do not know."[9] We need to have a familiar connection to our true self if we are to become who we already are. The mystical imagination leads us to be who we are as fully alive and fully human.

Openness, Receptivity, and Patience: The Dangers of Expectations and Control

The contemplative way of life is mysterious. God communicates in ways that we do not expect. And so we need to understand the dangers of expectations within a contemplative spirituality and in trying to control the process of the mystical imagination.

We will constantly be upset or disillusioned if we put too much weight on seeking to rationalize it all. We cannot live solely by our intellect. We cannot figure out God. We cannot figure out the mystical imagination. We are all too often limited in our understanding of life. To embody contemplation, we must begin right where we are in the place we inhabit with openness, receptivity, and patience. There is nowhere else to start. Kathryn J. Hermes says:

---

[9] Rohr, *Falling Upward*, 97.

To become a contemplative, one must simply start to contemplate. I say simply because to begin to contemplate one must be able to honestly begin where one is; just start, and nothing more. No expectations. No achievements. No stories to tell of wisdom gained. One simply must just begin. And after fifty years of contemplating God everyday, one must begin the first day of the fifty-first year in the same way.[10]

These are the words that could speak to us at any time if we are listening and aware. So much revelation comes to us in the ordinary moments of everyday life. We do not expect such ordinariness to reveal truth to us, but it does so constantly. We need to learn openness and receptivity as we live as the body of Christ in the parish.

We cannot force our growth. We cannot force our discipline. These are good things to strive for, but ultimately God gives us revelation and understanding in ways that will take time. We only begin as a gardener preparing the soil of our lives for the seeds of openness and receptivity within us. Our contemplation helps us to listen and to lay down our expectations toward God. The mystical imagination understands such things.

To some degree, struggle will always be a part of our life. We may struggle with our rationality as we practice a contemplative spirituality. Rationality can cloud our ways of understanding and following Christ. We can try to rationalize that within ourselves we will not struggle, but we will. We will always struggle to embody our practice of contemplation as the body of Christ in the parish. This is a sign of growth and maturity. Martin Laird in his book *A Sunlit Absence* writes, "Spiritual progress is learning to confront struggle in a new way so that we don't struggle with the fact that life is fraught with struggle. But the practice of contemplation will expose us to many things we would rather not see but need to see if we are going to grow."[11]

---

[10] Hermes, *Beginning Contemplative Prayer*, 39.

[11] Laird, *A Sunlit Absence*, 133.

Maturity as followers of Christ will not come without struggle. Struggle is a part of growing into a more holistic spirituality. Our expectations will try to push our struggle away from us. But we need to embrace the struggle. Our contemplation teaches us to be content with the struggle to commune with God, to relate to others, and to commit to place. This is the way of the mystical imagination. Our expectations and our ways of controlling our communion with God will try to keep us from embracing the shaping aspect of our struggle. We cannot allow struggle to cause us to quit our contemplative practice. If we quit, we will slowly lose ourselves to fragmentation.

Contemplation is not a technique or a means of control. It is not a program, an activity or a method. Contemplation cannot demand or expect anything from God. If we attempt these things, we will start to lose sight of God altogether and our everyday lives will become unhealthy. Contemplation will always develop an inner posture of listening, openness, receptivity, and patience. This is the attitude or outlook in which we abide.

Contemplation embraces all of life holistically in every dimension. It is a part of our sleeping, working, playing, solitude, socializing, celebrating, eating, exercising, relating, learning, walking, breathing, moving, living, thinking, caring, loving, forgiving, and communion. Our very lives become an expression of contemplation in everything we are. We actually become our contemplation, a moving, living, working, loving experiment in contemplative living. This is our identity as the body of Christ in everyday life in the parish. We cannot allow it to be anything less. If we do, we will lose a sense of our humanity. New Monastic writer Jonathan Wilson-Hartgrove notes, "But this way of contemplation is not a technique. Contemplation is not a skill that we can perfect so as to ensure the right result. Perfection in contemplation is the realization that we do not know what we are doing."[12]

---

[12] Wilson-Hartgrove, "Commitment to a Disciplined Contemplative Life," 167-168.

"Now to him who is able to do immeasurably more than all we ask or imagine, according to his power that is at work within us, to him be the glory in the church and in Christ Jesus throughout all generations" (Ephesians 3:20-21). Christ will never assent to our expectations. The mystical imagination will have nothing to do with expectations and control in the place where we live. If we attempt this way of life, we will destroy ourselves. This must be deeply rooted in us in order to be the body of Christ in everyday life. Our contemplation allows Christ to work within us beyond our understanding. The mystical imagination embraces Christ's life within us at all times.

Contemplation is never instant. It takes a lot of patience, awareness, and mindfulness to understand how God works within us. There are numerous ways God communicates to us in the ordinary moments of our days through our imaginations. Sometimes it is in a conversation with friends, sometimes on a walk in the neighborhood, sometimes when we are cooking a meal, sometimes in solitude, sometimes at work, sometimes in silence, sometimes in listening, sometimes in learning, sometimes in exercising, sometimes in watching a movie, sometimes in reflecting, sometimes in buying something locally, sometimes in gardening, and sometimes in the making of art. God can communicate in any number of ways that we would not expect. So we need to take a contemplative attitude in all of life if we are to grow in wisdom as the body of Christ in our local community. Michael Casey states, "There is certainly nothing flashy about contemplation: there is nothing in it that can be translated into marketable commodities and subsequently traded for some temporal advantage. Contemplation is entirely gratuitous, pure grace. On God's part total gift, on ours total receptivity."[13]

Contemplation is so ordinary. A lot of people think it is too ordinary to be spiritual. Most of the time our contemplation does not accompany deep feelings of closeness to God. But it is a spiritual practice that is vital to our survival as the body of Christ in the parish. We need to

---

[13] Casey, *Toward God*, 170-171.

have the receptivity to become listening contemplatives in everyday life. Contemplation exists through the gift of grace. Our practice of contemplation ought to be pursued through grace, cultivated in grace, sustained in grace, and embodied through grace. It is worked out through the place we inhabit.

We need to see the danger in holding God hostage to any of our expectations. Expectations are premeditated resentments, as one of my friends always says. A lot of our expectations will never come to fruition. When that happens we can become resentful and angry. When we live contrary to our contemplative spirituality we tend to hurt a lot of people in our relational context. Jesuit Anthony De Mello says, "Do not approach contemplation with any preconceived notions at all. Approach it with a readiness to discover new experiences (that initially may not even seem like 'experience' at all) and to acquire brand-new tastes."[14]

We need to do away with expectations and embrace instead an attitude of receptive discovery. We also need to embrace new hungers, longings, or tastes in our lives together rather than try to control everything. When the posture of our lives becomes much more about "a readiness to discover new experiences" and "acquiring brand-new tastes," we become more holistic in our practice and become less caught up in our expectations.

This paradigm will liberate our communion with God to a level where there are not expectations or a desire to control, something we desperately need as the body of Christ in the parish. Ruth Burrows writes, "Instinctively we want to live life on our own terms, in our world, not God's. Even when we think we want God, it is as often as not with our own conditions, our own expectations."[15]

---

[14] De Mello, *Sadhana*, 61.

[15] Burrows, *Essence of Prayer*, 100.

Over the years of living in Downtown Tacoma, our Downtown Neighborhood Fellowship has learned how to be open, receptive, and patient in our practice of contemplation. We thought that God would work in a certain way, but we have oftentimes been led into something different than what we had anticipated.

At first we started a large gathering in a renovated longshoremen's hall, hoping to build a 24-hour drive-through coffee shop onto it. We had a music venue and living spaces in the building. I lived there when I first moved to the neighborhood.

Then we started partnering with a nonprofit organization in the neighborhood called the Northwest Leadership Foundation. We started an initiative called the Urban Leadership Collaborative. It was a community development initiative bringing together civic leaders throughout Tacoma. Then we wanted to integrate the church into civic life in a local context. So we created a more grassroots form of faith expression based solely on community development in the neighborhood and being the church together in everyday life. The emphasis became living in the neighborhood as an expression of the body of Christ.

Our contemplation has led us in many directions. We have always tried to focus on having a listening posture toward life in all that we are and in everything do. We wanted to cultivate a listening church. Listening has always put us on the path of receptive discovery and acquiring new tastes for new wine in new wineskins.

Part 3

Exploring the Depths: Cultivating Silence and Solitude

Chapter 7

Grounding Ourselves: The Mystery of Our Being

Listening to Mystery: Receiving the Beauty In Life

For many of us, listening is hard. Listening to others, listening to God, listening to our lives, listening to the true self, listening to our environment, listening to our local community, listening to mystery; these become problematic if we are not attuned to being silent together. There is always so much noise all around us. It's like we are addicted to noise and hurried activity. And yet God is calling us into the mystical imagination of silence and solitude as the body of Christ in the parish. We will not be able to embrace these without listening to life's mystery and beauty. They liberate us from our noise-addicted world. Paula Huston writes, "... we can take some practical steps to increase our capacity for listening."[1]

I believe there is an abundance of mystery and beauty throughout our lives in the place we inhabit together. They are all around us and live within us. Our problem is we have not trained ourselves to experience them. We have not practiced a faithful presence to the mystery and

---

[1] Huston, *A Season of Mystery*, 9.

beauty in life. But they remain there still, and Christ is leading us to seek them out.

We need to become a church that listens. Listening is the beginning of love. Without listening, we lose our true self. We lose our souls. We lose connection with the practice of humility and grace. The mystical imagination seeks a posture of listening to the mystery and beauty in life. Parker J. Palmer notes in his book *Let Your Life Speak:*

> ... learn to embrace mystery, something our culture resists. Mystery surrounds every deep experience of the human heart ... But our culture wants to turn mysteries into puzzles to be explained or problems to be solved, because maintaining the illusion that we can "straighten things out" makes us feel powerful. Yet mysteries never yield to solutions or fixes—and when we pretend that they do, life becomes not only more banal but also more hopeless, because the fixes never work.[2]

Silence and solitude cultivate a posture of listening to mystery. They are not to be feared but are in fact essential if we are to be sustainable as a local community. Our stability will break down if this posture is not present within us. John McKnight and Peter Block say:

> ... silence is associated with listening. In listening, we also open ourselves to the nature of our neighborhood. With silence, we can learn about the place where we live because we can hear and see the messages of the trees, the plants, animals, and the buildings around us. They are a part of our community with much to teach, once we listen.[3]

God uses the world around us to speak to us and teach us of its mystery and beauty. Our environment has a history and a specific context. If we do not listen to it, we will instead exploit it and become its enemies.

---

[2] Palmer, *Let Your Life Speak*, 60.

[3] McKnight and Block, *The Abundant Community*, 95.

There is abundant mystery and beauty in our particular place if we have eyes to see it. The Spirit is working out our salvation through our practice of silence and solitude in the parish. We are being led as we listen to the mystery and beauty in life together in the place we inhabit. The body of Christ is called to nothing less than this in everyday life. Keri Wyatt Kent states:

> In the Christian tradition, solitude and silence were foundational practices. Jesus himself modeled these practices, and his followers have been using them as tools for creating space to listen to God ever since. In post-modern America, where silence is "weird," it's a bit harder to engage in this practice. But we need it more than ever because our world is so noisy and hurried.[4]

Silence and solitude are oftentimes considered "weird" today, but they have a rich history behind them. Christ practiced silence and solitude as a means to listen deeply. Through this, he learned to embrace the mystery and beauty in life contextually. This was crucial for the life Jesus lived. Most of the followers of Christ throughout history have found a way to practice silence and solitude. This is so important to understand! Silence and solitude help us to cultivate a listening spirit in everyday life.

The mystery and beauty in life whisper to us in the place we inhabit. We can only listen to them if have cultivated the ground of silence and solitude within ourselves. This doesn't just mean being alone in a noiseless room. It is much more holistic than that. It means we live with an awareness and a mindfulness that roots our very being in silence and solitude in all that we are and do. We become an embodied expression of silence and solitude. In fact, there can be noise in the midst of silence, people in the midst of solitude. It doesn't matter if we're introverts or extroverts; silence and solitude can be cultivated within us as the body of Christ in the parish.

---

[4] Kent, *Listen*, 119.

"Then Jesus was led by the Spirit into the desert" (Mathew 4:1). Why was Jesus led by the Spirt to go into the desert? One reason might be to be tempted with the various compulsions to be successful, to be arrogant, and to be powerful. All of which Jesus had little interest in. Another reason might be so that he could listen more deeply to the mystery and beauty in life. Through the silence and solitude of the desert, he came to find the strength he needed to endure the temptations of success, arrogance, and power. Jesus understood that his life was to be about love, humility, and compassion; not something less than that. So the way Jesus listened to the mystery and beauty in life for 40 days, and all throughout his life up to this point, helped him through his temptations in the desert. The desert was surely not easy for Jesus, but it was essential to his longing to really listen deeply to what was within him.

What did Jesus do in the desert for 40 days? He probably found different ways to listen as he spent lots of time alone. It was something like just under 6 weeks that Jesus spent in the desert. That's a long time for most of us! Maybe the desert was a combination of many things for him such as longing, dreaming, reflecting, crying, walking, resting, and sleeping. He probably was bored, lonely, tired, and hungry at times. But he kept going because this was the process of disciplining himself to listen deeply and face his temptations. This was essential to his whole life.

Can we imagine what an extended time of silence and solitude would do for our capacity to listen as the body of Christ in the parish? We would be a much more authentic church if we experimented with finding our own silence and solitude. Letty M. Russell writes, "Each of us needs to search out our own ways of listening."[5]

We need to become seasoned practitioners of listening to all of life. We need a healthy approach in listening to mystery and to receiving beauty in life. We need to take this listening seriously through our practice of

---

[5] Russell, *Just Hospitality*, 96.

silence and solitude. We need eyes that long for this mysterious beauty to be seen, understood, and experienced in our local community. It is there, but we just have trouble seeing it because we do not always live a life of listening. Tony Jones says, "Ultimately, we keep silence and solitude so we can listen better—so we can hear what God is saying to us and to our world."[6]

Without silence and solitude, we cannot listen to what God is revealing to the world through our neighborhood. God is always manifesting seeds of revelation practically where people live. It is in the neighborhood where mystery and beauty are experienced. Without the neighborhood, we would have a hard time finding mystery and beauty in everyday life.

Mystery and beauty are oftentimes found through relationships in the place we inhabit together. It is always contextual and changing. Just when we think we have figured it out, we are surprised by a new expression of it. This happens all the time. We can't understand such things unless we are listening for them. Listening will make us better at being the body of Christ in everyday life. We need to embrace listening in our local community in order to create a holistic counterculture. Without listening, we are just insensitive talking heads with very little understanding and practice of loving our neighbors. The mystical imagination connects us to the mystery and beauty in life we will need if we are to love our neighbors day in and day out.

Our Downtown Neighborhood Fellowship has become better over the years at listening to the mystery and beauty in life. After practicing a lot of silence and solitude both alone and together, we have become more aware of our relational connection to this place we inhabit. We have begun to listen more. We are slowly discovering that there is so much beauty and mystery within the world as we become an expression of love in our context. We have begun to see the mystery and beauty around us in our neighborhood environment.

---

[6] Jones, *The Sacred Way*, 40.

I remember one time running and walking in the neighborhood in order to discover the freedom of the sky, the freedom of the sun, the freedom of the wind, and the freedom of the sidewalks. I sensed God using all of this to speak to me about the livability of this place. God was reminding me of the many days the sun has shone on this land. For countless years, God has been faithful to provide this place with sun and wind and sky. So many people decade after decade have walked these sidewalks. People of different races, socio-economic status, genders, lifestyles, and opinions have lived here. The rich and the poor alike have lived here.

God was reminding me to listen to the stories of the many beautiful Japanese people in the neighborhood who were forced into prison camps in the 1940s. God was reminding me of the pictures I had seen on the walls of a local coffee shop of what Downtown Tacoma looked like in 1910. I think to myself, "What a beautiful place this is." It was a very integrated community before the mall was built in the 1970s. Now Downtown Tacoma has a struggling local economy. It has been exploited and abused at times, but it still contains a lot of mystery and beauty.

As I was running another mile through the streets of Downtown Tacoma on a Saturday morning, God was teaching my soul to listen to everything around me and everything within me. I am reminded of the beauty and mystery in my struggles to embody love in this place with others. Our listening improves and becomes more seasoned with each day we practice silence and solitude in some form. Whether it's being alone in a room, or running or walking through the neighborhood, doing an artistic expression, or just some kind of thinking or learning, our listening reveals to us a lot of beauty and mystery that is otherwise hard to see. Henri J. M. Nouwen says:

> It seems more important than ever to stress that solitude is one of the human capacities that can exist, be maintained and developed in the center of a big city, in the middle of a large crowd and in the context of a very active and productive life. A man or woman who

has developed this solitude of heart is no longer pulled apart by the most divergent stimuli of the surrounding world but is able to perceive and understand this world from a quiet inner center.[7]

Silence and solitude can exist anywhere. This posture can be practiced within our relational context as the body of Christ in the parish. Everyday life is filled with moments where listening is required of us to see the mystery and beauty all around us. We need to live into this through the mystical imagination. No context should separate us from silence and solitude. It is a way of life in all things. All our relational encounters are to be practiced in silence and solitude with a deep listening intentionality. We should not be slow to have some receptivity to listening to mystery and receiving beauty in the place we inhabit together. Jesus is our example of this way of life. I love this expression by Karen Wilk of her longing for God to move her to embody a compassionate listening where she lives:

> Give me your eyes to see this community and its people as you do. Give me your ears to listen to their hearts as you hear them. Give me an open and attentive spirit to recognize where you are already at work. Fill me with courage that I might ask the right questions, accept the true answers, and follow your leading. Equip and empower me to engage in this place, to live among people just as you did.[8]

Reconnecting With Others: Mysterious Solidarity

Many people think that silence and solitude separate us from others, but I believe that they actually reconnect us with others. How is this possible? I really don't understand it fully, but I would say that it is a part of the paradox of our spirituality to be both alone and together at the same time in our local community. This is an embodied expression of the mystical imagination. It doesn't make sense to our overly rational minds that we could be alone and together at the same time. This is one

---

[7] Nouwen, *Reaching Out*, 38.

[8] Wilk, *Don't Invite Them To Church*, 104.

of the deep mysteries of our faith, but it is nonetheless authentically true. Murray Bodo says:

> In silence and solitude I relearn that I am in others and they are in me, whether or not we are physically present to one another. My own uniqueness discovered in the One who made me and dwells in me, is my simultaneous discovery of everything that is in the same One who inhabits silence and solitude—a silence and solitude I carry with me in the tabernacle of my deepest self. A silence and solitude I forget is there when I abandon retreating into that center and allow myself to be distracted by the proliferation of things and people, by noise and sound that obscure the way back into the center of myself where I realize how deeply connected I am to others. If I continue to immerse myself in other things and people, I paradoxically become alienated from them and myself. I lose myself in them and resent their demands on my time and attention. If I take the time to withdraw periodically into silence and solitude, I reconnect to myself and others from whom I've grown alienated.[9]

Silence and solitude always draw us into a mysterious solidarity with others in our neighborhood. There do not need to be a lot of words and speech for this to happen. We just need to have a practice of silence and solitude in the midst of everyday life in the place we inhabit. This will cultivate miraculous relational revelations as we find ourselves more connected with each passing day. Through this practice, we will become constantly reconnected to those we are called to love in our local community. Our presence to this practice makes all the difference.

Silence and solitude take us on a path of presence to ourselves and to one another. This practice helps us to never lose sight of our true self. In this, everyday life mediates the reality of relationship. Our local context constantly reconnects us to ourselves and others through the mystical imagination. Silence and solitude help us to feel our humanity in the depths of our being. Quaker writer Parker J. Palmer states:

---

[9] Bodo, *The Landscape of Prayer*, 146.

If we are to hold solitude and community together as a true paradox, we need to deepen our understanding of both poles. Solitude does not necessarily mean living apart from others; rather, it means never living apart from one's self. It is not about the absence of other people—it is about being fully present to ourselves, whether or not we are with others. Community does not necessarily mean living face-to-face with others; rather, it means never losing the awareness that we are connected to each other. It is not about the presence of other people—it is about being fully open to the reality of relationship, whether or not we are alone.[10]

There is an awareness that happens as we live with a posture of silence and solitude in everyday life. We become aware that we are connected to one another even though we might at times feel alone. But we are not alone. We are the body of Christ together even when we are not physically present to one another. We can still be present to one another through our spirits in silence and solitude. Even though we are alone, we are together through the mystical imagination. Margaret J. Wheatley notes, "None of us exists independent of our relationships with others."[11]

The mystical imagination brings us to a place of solidarity with others through the practice of silence and solitude. The times we spend alone may actually be the most profound times of reconnecting with others in our neighborhood. The mystic in us cries out for this connection in everyday life. This longing draws us into silence and solitude. Without it silence and solitude have no purpose. We are wasting our time. Benedictine Sister Jeremy Hall writes:

> … solitude is not antisocial. The person who embraces true solitude, either at certain times or as a way of life, is not running away from, not rejecting anyone. Rather, such a person is making room within, is preparing to welcome someone—God, others, self.

[10] Palmer, *A Hidden Wholeness*, 55.

[11] Wheatley, *Leadership and the New Science*, 35.

It is a positive choice, appropriate to a social being, and it is for a positive goal.[12]

The mystical imagination leads us to a profound connection of solidarity with others even when we are alone. We experience a deep level of our humanity being linked with the humanity of others. The ordinary mystic within us needs to be alone at times yet connected to others in everyday life in the parish. Silence and solitude cultivate a unity with others in our local community. We mysteriously become more connected to the place we inhabit together as the body of Christ in everyday life.

Physical solitude can be the source of the strength that brings us together. This practice can reconnect us again and again. God uses our silence and solitude to speak to our imaginations, to our passions, to our creativity, and to our love for others. But this isn't in the form of spoken words, but through an awareness of a deeper intuition that goes beyond words. Silence and solitude facilitate this mysterious listening and intuitive way of knowing one another as we live in community.

Our shared life together is touched and strengthened through silence and solitude. There can be no authentic shared life together without silence and solitude. Contemplative activist Dorothy Day has some wise words on the subject, "You must know when to find your own, quiet moments of solitude. But you must know when to open the door to go be with others, and you must know how to open the door. There's no point in opening the door with bitterness and resentment."[13]

Our shared life together is the making of the mystical imagination within us. Our common life cultivates togetherness through silence and solitude. The very core of who we are is moved, inspired, and encouraged in solidarity with others through our silence and solitude. We begin to embody this paradox of solitude and solidarity through the

---

[12] Hall, *Silence, Solitude, Simplicity*, 86.

[13] Day, *A Radical Devotion*, 130.

mystical imagination. Our common life together becomes an expression of the body of Christ in everyday life in the parish.

Silence and solitude bring us many relational gifts in everyday life. These gifts include: love, grace, humility, simplicity, compassion, awareness, mindfulness, listening, empathy, and creativity. All of them are experienced through our local context when we are present to the practice of silence and solitude. They involve everything we are, everything we do, and everything we long for. There is not one aspect of life that our practice of silence and solitude do not touch.

I remember several years back when some friends and I put together a silent retreat for those in our neighborhood. This was kind of new to all of us, but as I had been studying silence and solitude for years, I became convinced that our community needed more opportunities where they could be practiced together. We went to a monastery in the Seattle area and had a great time. We spent two days (about twelve hours in total) in silence and solitude together. I had planned out a schedule and facilitated most of it.

We ate our meals in silence. We had free time where we could go for a walk, journal, read, take a nap, or do some artistic expressions. We had a learning packet from Martin Laird's book *Into The Silent Land* that we had time to reflect on in silence. We did some *Lectio Divina* from the Psalms. We wrote down our longings for God. I sensed a powerful connection with my friends over those two days.

It was strange in a sense because we didn't talk to each other, but we could see each other. I believe our lives were experiencing a solidarity beyond words that logic cannot explain. Our mystical imaginations were being drawn closer together. Our connection to one another was being practiced beyond words. It was beautiful. It was freeing. It was one of the most precious memories I have of experiencing life with my friends.

This experience has helped us in our everyday lives together in Downtown Tacoma. Our practice of silence and solitude has helped us to embrace struggle and pain more honestly. It brought us a mysterious solidarity and unity with one another.

As I asked everyone what they thought about our time together over those two days, one of my friends said that she thought it was a revolutionary experience that needs to be practiced more often. Some felt that nothing spectacular happened, but I reassured everyone that their presence to God in silence and solitude had not been wasted. God always works through our silence and solitude without our proper understanding of what is happening. We all came away from this experience with a reconnection to one another and to ourselves.

Words have their limits. Language has its imperfections. Words and language can be used outside the context of relational care in a neighborhood. Silence and solitude free us from the potential abuse of words and language. They take away our addiction to noise. Silence and solitude destroy any controlling technique we might use. Silence and solitude cultivate our powerlessness in the parish which in turn reveals to us our interdependence. Richard J. Foster says:

> Silence frees us from the need to control others. One reason we can hardly bear to remain silent is that it makes us feel so helpless. We are accustomed to relying upon words to manage and control others. A frantic stream of words flows from us in an attempt to straighten others out. We want so desperately for them to agree with us, to see things our way. We evaluate people, judge people, condemn people. We devour people with our words.[14]

By contrast, silence and solitude help us to embrace people in love. We give up trying to control or manipulate others in our neighborhood. We live in a freedom to be in relationship with others without condemnation. Words become secondary to love. Others do not threaten us if they hold diverse perspectives on life. In silence and

---

[14] Foster, *The Freedom Of Simplicity*, 68.

solitude we give up our own perceptions of others by finding what we have in common. This reconnects us constantly as we practice silence and solitude within the mystical imagination.

"We live by faith, not by sight" (2 Corinthians 5:7). The mystical imagination is embodied by faith. We embody our spirituality trusting that our silence and solitude will lead us to a constant reconnection with others in everyday life. We have to believe that our silence and solitude will not lead us to isolation, but instead draw us closer to one another in solidarity. This is the ecology of silence and solitude.

Our silence and solitude are interconnected to our relational context. There is no more running from this. We must face one another through silence and solitude if we are to become a holistic and sustainable counterculture through all that life brings to us. The mystical imagination cultivates this among us in the parish. Ruth Haley Barton says in her book *Invitation to Solitude and Silence:*

> Without pressing or pushing or trying to do a great altruistic deed, we discover that much that happens in solitude and silence ends up being "for others"—as paradoxical as that may seem. Our speech patterns are refined by the discipline of silence, because growing self-awareness enables us to choose more truly the words we say. Rather than speech that issues from subconscious need to impress, to put others in their place, to compete, to control and manipulate, to repay hurt with hurt, we now notice our inner dynamics and choose to speak from a different place, a place of love, trust, true wisdom that God is cultivating within us. Over time we become safer. We are comfortable with our humanity, because we have experienced God's love and compassion in that place, and so it becomes very natural for us to extend love and compassion to others in their humanity.[15]

---

[15] Barton, *Invitation to Solitude and Silence*, 131-132.

"But Jesus often withdrew to lonely places" (Luke 5:16). Christ often went to lonely places to commune with the Father. Christ's silence and solitude are a mystery to us. We do not know a lot about how he practiced this. We just know that he did it.

Our process of being and becoming is wrapped up in following Christ's example. This needs to be a practice we take seriously in our lives together as the body of Christ in the parish. Our very identity comes from this practice of silence and solitude. It is our very being. As we practice silence and solitude, we start on the journey of becoming our true self, our true humanity, becoming the body of Christ together in everyday life.

This being and becoming is rooted in the place we inhabit. Christ was rooted in his local context through his practice of silence and solitude. They helped him to have the courage and strength to love, forgive, listen, inspire, and befriend others.

Silence and solitude are much less concerned with doing than they are with being. If the being is cultivated, we will not conform to the status quo, and we will not express a form of colonialism that is so often seen in our world. Instead, we will be listening to the mystery and beauty in life. We will become an expression of love as the body of Christ in the parish. Franciscan Richard Rohr, who founded the Center for Action and Contemplation, writes:

> I would almost describe spirituality as a concern for one's being, one's inner motivation and attitude, one's real inner Source, as opposed to any primary concern for one's "doing." Doing will always take care of itself when your being is right. It is our preoccupation with external forms and successes that make us superficial, judgmental, split off and often just downright wrong—without knowing it.[16]

---

[16] Rohr, *Things Hidden*, 89.

Our spirituality is often so external that we risk losing our true self and the mystical depth of our communion with God. We box everything up into judgments, categories, and tangible successes. But silence and solitude are about being and becoming. They are about our own spiritual formation as the body of Christ. They are less about what we do and more about how we are shaped in the process of life. Our being is not a project to complete, but an attentive cultivation of who we are within ourselves. All our doing is rooted in our being and becoming through the mystical imagination within. A lot of our doing will become self-destructive if our priority is not on being shaped within and becoming an expression of love as the body of Christ in everyday life together.

In our practice of silence and solitude we respond to the status quo not with hatred but with grace. We gracefully embody a holistic counterculture as the body of Christ in the parish. We have the strength to present an alternative to the status quo in our being. The mystical imagination helps us to see beyond the status quo and express something more abundant. The mystical imagination facilitates a discovered life of silence and solitude. We find a freedom from superficial living. We become more authentic and honest. Gunilla Norris says in her book *Inviting Silence*, "By making room for silence, we resist the forces of the world which tell us to live an advertised life of surface appearances, instead of a discovered life—a life lived in contact with our senses, our feelings, our deepest thoughts and values."[17]

The deepest parts of our humanity will be touched by our silence and solitude. Our humanity will start to long for what is beautiful. We will lose interest in the "advertised life of surface appearances" and discover more of ourselves and our neighbors as we listen to all of life in the place we inhabit. We are becoming loving nonconformists to the status quo as the body of Christ in everyday life together. Our silence and solitude will lead us to nothing less.

---

[17] Norris, *Inviting Silence*, 49.

Our silence and solitude connect us to our deepest values, thoughts, feelings, and senses. We become more aware of the things we are seeing, hearing, smelling, tasting, and touching in the place we inhabit. We discover so many things through our experience of living in our bodies. Our neighborhood becomes alive to us. The mystical imagination brings life to our senses.

Just as Christ practiced silence and solitude, we too need this practice. Without it, we will get carried away with the systems of the status quo. If we're not careful, the status quo will destroy the mystical imagination within us. It will destroy our being and our becoming, both of which can only be found through silence and solitude.

Without silence and solitude, we will destroy one another. Our love will break down. Our humility will be swallowed by arrogance. Our grace will turn to judgment. Our simplicity will turn to greed. We will speak more than listen. We will become less human. Beauty will start to die within us. The false self will emerge.

The practice of silence and solitude protects our souls from all of this. That is why we need it so much in our time. It is crucial for our survival as the body of Christ in the parish. Our sustainability and our connection to one another depend on it. The mystical imagination needs silence and solitude if it's to live. Tom and Christine Sine in their book *Living on Purpose* write, "We need to learn to richly cultivate our inner life."[18]

Our Downtown Neighborhood Fellowship has worked to make being and becoming an important value as we live out the gospel of love in our context. We have withdrawn from doing isolated projects and have become more attuned to living our everyday lives within the proximity of the neighborhood while being shaped from within. You might say, "What about the work of the gospel?" And we would say, "The integration of everyday life in the neighborhood brings about many

---

[18] Sine, *Living on Purpose*, 97.

holistic collaborations and partnerships which are based on valuing others while listening to our context. This is the work of the gospel."

We believe that isolated projects quickly become colonial because they typically are not integrated relationally to a listening spirit. We want to be rooted and living locally. We do the work of the gospel of love through being faithfully present and listening. This takes much longer and there are oftentimes no tangible successes that we can identify. But none of this is about numbers, effects or church growth. We have to be indifferent with being misunderstood. The institutional status quo might say we are irrelevant, foolish, or wasting our time. But we think otherwise.

Our silence and solitude are teaching us the importance of being and becoming. Our being and becoming makes us irrelevant a lot of the time to the values of society. But that is fine because we want out of the global prison of corporate propaganda that fills our culture telling us who we are and what to become. Instead, we want to embrace a way of becoming a holistic counterculture. Our lives are about being and becoming shaped from within us through silence and solitude in the place we inhabit. The work of the gospel is not to change the world, but to change ourselves by learning to embody love. It is our relational context that contributes to our salvation in everyday life. Christine D. Pohl notes, "A community that loves the truth will understand the wisdom of silence."[19]

Our everyday lives become a process of conversion within and through the mystical imagination. Our practice of silence and solitude shapes us from within as the body of Christ in everyday life. It connects us to ourselves, our experiences, and our histories in the place we inhabit. Henri J. M. Nouwen says:

> In our solitude, our history no longer can remain a random collection of disconnected incidents and accidents but has to become a constant call for the change of heart and mind. There we can break through the fatalistic chain of cause and effect and listen

---

[19] Pohl, *Living into Community*, 150.

with our inner senses to the deeper meaning of the actualities of everyday life.[20]

We are being and becoming our own change within. Our everyday lives call us to listen. Our everyday lives call us to a process of evolution on our journey of life. Our neighborhood demands our attention to the common good. Our neighborhood calls us into responsibility and stewardship. Our neighborhood teases out the beauty within us in our everyday lives of relational connections.

Our very strength is in our silence and solitude. Without them, we will not be shaped in healthy ways and will instead try to shape others to conform. Our emphasis on the conversion of others will hinder the mystical imagination as well as our being and becoming. We step into a realm that we cannot understand or control, even though we presume that we can. We do not see our limitations. Twentieth century mystic Thomas Merton says, "Silence is the strength of our interior life."[21]

Silence and solitude keep us on the path of being and becoming. They show us that we are the ones who need to change, that we are the ones who do damage to others and the place we inhabit sometimes. We cannot escape the need to change ourselves from within. This is the pressing call of the gospel of love, humility, and compassion. Silence and solitude is our source of interior strength that God uses to shape us within. This is what the mystical imagination is made of. Our strength is found in being and becoming the change we hope for in others. We need to look within to change. This will keep us from looking at others in judgment and condemnation. Maybe we don't have all the answers. Maybe others have something to teach us about ourselves and about God. Monica A. Coleman writes, "So are you willing to venture into the unknown? Are you ready to learn new ways of being in the world?"[22]

---

[20] Nouwen, *Reaching Out*, 52.

[21] Merton, *No Man is an Island*, 259.

[22] Coleman, *Not Alone*, 126.

Chapter 8

The Present Depth of Our Experience: Moving Beyond Fear

Living In the Present Moment: Opening to the Gift of Life

Our silence and solitude will lead us to embrace living in the present moment. The one needs the other. Our silence and solitude will cultivate a healthy, functional relationship with the present moment in the place we inhabit together. Without silence and solitude, we will abuse the present moment with our own agendas. We cannot directly see this relationship; we can only feel it in our relationships. We feel the energy it brings into our local community. David G. Benner says in his book *Soulful Spirituality:*

> Our relationship with the now will always shape every other relationship we have. A dysfunctional relationship with the present moment will be reflected in a dysfunctional relationship with our self, with others, with the world, and with life. But on the other hand, an embrace of the present moment opens us up to life and all we encounter.[1]

---

[1] Benner, *Soulful Spirituality*, 102.

Our self, our neighbors, and our locality will be the recipients of a colonial expression of faith if we do not cultivate a healthy relationship with the present moment through silence and solitude. It opens up the mystical imagination among us, and it causes the mystical imagination to come alive within us. And this in turn will shape the ecology of relationship in the place where we live and all that we are.

"Very early in the morning, while it was still dark, Jesus got up, left the house and went off to a solitary place" (Mark 1:35). I believe Christ practiced silence and solitude because he was cultivating a healthy relationship with the present moment in his life. It affected all his relationships as he embraced compassion as a way of life. It gave him solidarity with others. It made him into an expression of love in the world. Isn't this what the purpose of prayer is? Authentic forms of prayer will always lead us to this in everyday life: compassion, solidarity, and love in the present moment. Jesus understood the ecology of his relationship with others in the present moment. That is why he practiced silence and solitude. It was extremely important in his life. Thich Nhat Hanh states:

> Our true home is in the present moment. To live in the present moment is a miracle. The miracle is not to walk on water. The miracle is to walk on the green Earth in the present moment, to appreciate the peace and beauty that are available now. Peace is all around us—in the world and in nature—and within us—in our bodies and our spirits. Once we learn to touch this peace we will be healed and transformed. It is not a matter of faith; it is a matter of practice. We need only to find ways to bring our body and mind back to the present moment so we can touch what is refreshing, healing, and wondrous.[2]

We need to become connected to the present moment in our local community as the body of Christ in everyday life. This is our home. This is our identity. This is where the true self is discovered. It is an on-the-ground miracle to embody living in the present moment in the

---

[2] Nhat Hanh, *Touching Peace*, 1-2.

place where we live. This is where all beauty is found within and around us. When our bodies become rooted in the present moment we experience an ongoing sense of freedom, liberation, and gratitude. Mary Jo Leddy writes, "… there is a more ordinary mysticism to be found in discovering the liberating attitude of gratitude. This is not given rarely or only to a few but exists as a present possibility for all of us."[3]

There is peace, life, healing, rest, and epiphany within the present moment. Gratitude can only be practiced in the present moment, in the here and now of our lives. Our locality cries out for us to live constantly in the present moment in everyday life together. This is the way of the body of Christ in the parish. Sarah Cunningham notes:

> What if what God is doing right now is as important as anything I'll ever do? What if the way our life is playing out in this specific moment—this rhythm, this people, this work—is as much what we were born to do as any other activity we'll ever take on? If it is exactly what, through any series of unpredictable circumstances, would make our life count the most?[4]

We are only as alive to the extent we are present in the present moment. The present moment is speaking to us all of the time in our local community. It cultivates the mystical imagination within us. We can no longer let ourselves get caught up in either the past or the future. When we become united to the present moment we become connected to life, wisdom, and liberation. We become alive right where we are as the body of Christ in everyday life in the parish. Wendell Berry so eloquently writes, "We are alive only in the present moment, not in the previous moment or the following one."[5]

---

[3] Leddy, *Radical Gratitude*, 134.

[4] Cunningham, *The Well Balanced World Changer*, 220.

[5] Berry, *Citizenship Papers*, 186.

This is the only moment we have to share our lives together. Our solitude and silence help us to live in the present moment. Our everyday lives become the means of experiencing our silence and solitude in the present moment. It touches every aspect of our lives together as the body of Christ in the parish.

To become the body of Christ together we need this healthy relationship with the present moment in our local community. We cannot let ourselves become trapped in either the future or the past. When we do not live in the present moment, our false self leads us to places we do not want to go. There is nothing to be gained from either living for ideal notions of the future, or looking for identity in the past.

Our communion with God is always rooted in the present moment. It is not from two weeks ago, three days ago, ten years ago, four years ago, or six months ago that we draw our strength from God. It is always in the now that we listen authentically. God is not the God of the past or the God of the future, but is the God of the present moment in our lives. Our present God is alive within us as the body of Christ in the parish in everyday life. Suzanne Zuercher notes:

> God is no longer in our past experience, helpful as it may have been along the way to remember life there. Nor is God in our plans and visions for the future, because there is nothing of future life we can predict, let alone experience. We are only creatures in time who meet reality moment by moment.[6]

I remember hearing one of my friends talk about how he ate an apple in the present moment. He didn't just eat the apple, he ate it with an awareness to what was happening in the present moment. The way he described how his senses became alive was amazing to hear. The flavor he tasted was delicious and sweet. He could feel his body chewing and digesting the apple. He felt its texture with his hands. He pondered its color and shape and marveled at how God had created such a beautiful piece of fruit. He could hear the sound of the apple as he bit into it. He

---

[6] Zuercher, *Enneagram Spirituality*, 120.

smelled its freshness. As he savored the apple with all his senses, he became more alive. He described it as a very deeply human experience. The apple taught him about God, himself, and the beauty of creation.

The present moment came alive to him as he ate the apple in silence and solitude. He valued that moment. This experience opened him up to so many other ways of experiencing the present moment in our neighborhood through the mystical imagination. His silence and solitude helped him to cultivate more of living in the present moment in many unlikely ways, such as eating an apple on a cool spring day. This cultivated an ecology of living in relationship to the present moment and to all of life in the place where he lives. He has become my teacher in living in the present moment in the place we inhabit together as the body of Christ in everyday life.

Confining ourselves to the present moment may seem limiting, but it is actually the source of our liberation. The present moment opens us to the ecology of relationship in our neighborhood. Jean-Pierre De Caussade in his book *The Sacrament of the Present Moment* says, "We must confine ourselves to the present moment without taking thought for the one before or the one to come."[7] The present moment is the context where love and compassion are lived out in the place we inhabit. It is where God lives. Confining ourselves to the present moment cultivates the mystical imagination within us.

The mystical imagination does not live in the past or the future, but only in the present. Our silence and solitude are motivated by, and need to be connected to, the present moment. We must be mindful of the present moment and value it. The present moment is a sacrament of the body of Christ in everyday life that should not be taken for granted. We need to confine ourselves to it and be open to what it does within us. This sacrament will shape us from within, cultivating love, compassion, grace, humility, gentleness, and kindness. The mystical imagination is embodied through this sacrament.

---

[7] De Caussade, *The Sacrament of the Present Moment*, 15.

We need to have our body firmly planted in the present moment in the place we inhabit. If we are to be Christ's hands and feet in our world, they need to be in the present moment. This is where we find life and nowhere else. William Shannon, who has been profoundly shaped by the works of Thomas Merton, says:

> I think we all have the tendency to live with one foot in the present and the other in the past or the future. When this happens, we miss the richness of the present, because we are not fully aware of it. We aren't fully aware, because we are not fully in the present. So often we do something in order to be able to do something else: our thoughts are so concentrated on that something else that we don't really experience what we are doing. When we are continually jockeying back and forth between past and future, we often are not really there to the present. We are not truly aware of what is NOW. We don't enjoy what we are doing now, because our thoughts are on what we are going to be doing next. And because our thoughts are diverted from the present, we are never fully aware of what we are doing here and now.[8]

The present moment shows us relational revelations within and around us. If we hide from the present moment we will lose out on wisdom. We are relational only in the present moment. The present moment is calling out to be reconciled with the body of Christ in the place we live.

God sustains, strengthens, and inspires us through the present moment. God is always living in the present moment, even if we can't see it. Our silence and solitude help us to understand this. Donald Spoto notes, "God is at work every moment, sustaining everything in being."[9]

The present moment will not be controlled or explained! All of life is lived in the present moment. It is a living sacrament that can shape us

---

[8] Shannon, *Silence on Fire*, 75.

[9] Spoto, *In Silence*, 66.

from within. We need to integrate our lives with the present moment. This is where purpose and intentionality are found.

Living in the now will sustain our lives together. God sustains each present moment that we embody together, and so should we. God cherishes the present moment. God dreams of days when the church will not live in the past or the future, but embrace the present moment in the parish. The present moment should not be an enemy, but a friend. Sharon Daloz Parks writes, "The practice of presence is integral to the capacity to be a creative agent in the moment—poised on the edge between the known reality and the emergent possibility. Presence is the meeting place between the inner life of a person and the outer life of action in the world."[10]

Being present in the present moment is where we commune with God. This is where we experience God, faithfully present through our silence and solitude. It is only in the present moment that we find wisdom, beauty, and authenticity. Carl Arico says, "The only way we can really live is in the present. It is by being present to the present moment that we encounter God and God encounters us."[11]

We can only be authentically alive in the present moment. It is divine and full of possibility if we are present to it. Nadia Bolz-Weber states, "The greatest spiritual practice is just showing up. Showing up, to me, means being present to what is actually happening."[12]

The mystical imagination is always present to the present moment. It is where God is discovered in everyday life. We are being called to live in the present moment in the parish. This is the call of the gospel in our local community.

---

[10] Parks, *Leadership Can Be Taught*, 100.

[11] Arico, *A Taste Of Silence*, 187.

[12] Bolz-Weber, *Pastrix*, 198.

Creating Depth to Our Humanity: Developing Experiential Maturity

Silence and solitude can appear to our rational minds as nonsense. We might think that nothing important is happening within us. But God's greatest movements often will catch us unaware. We cannot force God to do anything, but we can cultivate a soul that listens deeply.

God is both hidden to us and revealed in our silence and solitude. This process can oftentimes seem like the winter seasons of life where it is cold or dark, where nothing appears to be happening. But these seasons cultivate a depth to our humanity that is necessary for our survival and sanity. They develop in us an experiential maturity that we can receive no other way. Wise spiritual director Jan Johnson writes:

> Silence and solitude both work in hidden ways, resembling the work that goes on during winter. In the cold months, it appears nothing is going on. Animals hibernate. Nothing grows. Everything is still and at rest. But in the important sleep of winter, life renews itself. In silence and solitude, God works in ways that are hidden, but nevertheless vital to life.[13]

A lot of life happens in the winter season. We cannot always understand this process. Our silence and solitude cause us to lose control of our life. Everything in this season of life is led by God, revealed by God, and shaped by God even though we cannot always see this completely. We do not control our communion with God. We can only allow the depth of our humanity to be shaped through silence and solitude in the place we inhabit. The mystical imagination always deepens our humanity.

There is so much wisdom to be learned from Christ in silence and solitude. There is so much depth to experience. We need not fear this in any way, because it is in the depths of our humanity that we discover the kingdom of God. Life cannot stop at believing. Our communion

---

[13] Johnson, *When the Soul Listens*, 80.

with God cannot remain a static belief system disconnected from the depths of our humanity. We must go deeper. This is the call of the body of Christ in the place we inhabit together. Sandra Maitri writes, "We suffer because we are living at a distance from our depths—it's as simple as that."[14]

There is so much more to our humanity than propositional belief. What we believe should not block us from entering into the depths of our humanity, but should instead intentionally cause us to keep growing our entire lives. Belief is always connected to depth or it is dead. It should never be used as a cliché to keep us from taking responsibility for our lives or something to justify our hiding.

Jenna Smith states, "Depth can be a scary thing."[15] We need to have the courage to face the depth of our humanity and all its potential—the opportunities, the unknown, the fear, the struggle against being marginalized by a world that usually lives on a superficial level. Going deeper opens up the mystical imagination in fascinating ways.

We practice silence and solitude to seek God in everyday life together. As we seek God in this way, we are adding depth to our humanity. Our silence and solitude prepare us to embrace a listening spirit. There is so much God is wanting to communicate to us, but many times our lives are too fragmented to really listen. We must never stop seeking God in silence and solitude in the place we inhabit. If we did, we would die within. The mystical imagination always seeks God. Twentieth century contemplative writer Thomas Merton says, "For inner silence depends on a continual seeking, a continual crying in the night, a repeated bending over the abyss. If we cling to a silence we think we have found forever, we stop seeking God and the silence goes dead within us."[16]

---

[14] Maitri, *The Spiritual Dimension of the Enneagram*, 46.

[15] Smith, *A Way*, 130.

[16] Merton, *Thoughts in Solitude*, 89.

The noise within us needs to stop or we'll never be able to listen long enough to embrace the depth of our humanity and develop an experiential maturity within. Our sanity depends on it. Our silence and solitude put us in touch with the depths of our humanity. There is no other way we can commune with God or experience life in creative ways.

Over the years I have seen my friend Danny cross from belief to depth in his humanity. When I first met Danny he didn't say a lot. He wasn't really sure exactly what he believed in. He just believed in Jesus. He was having trouble finding a deep connection to his humanity. Danny didn't seem to understand that Christ lives within his humanity and wanted to empower him to become fully alive and fully human. Isolation became pretty common for Danny and he did not have a lot of practice in silence and solitude.

Danny moved into Downtown Tacoma several years ago. Since then he has experienced a supportive community where he can find ways to practice silence and solitude. Today Danny lives a relational life with courage and compassion within our local community. This man has become a passionate community advocate for neighborhood collaboration and social capital. He is connected to the depth of his humanity through the love he shows his neighbors.

Our neighborhood would mourn if Danny were ever to leave. Danny is excited to live embodied in his humanity as an expression of love in the place we inhabit together. Danny is a model to us all. His love is very present to us in all kinds of ways. I thank God that Danny has moved from belief to depth over the course of the time I have known him. His journey opens us all to the possibility of the mystical imagination in our neighborhood.

Silence and solitude develop a receptivity in the depths of our humanity. We begin to listen deeply as the body of Christ in the parish. This receptive listening in turn cultivates relational revelations among us in the depth of our humanity. The mystical imagination is open to God in all of life in our local community. Jean Yves-Leloup says, "To become silent is to become receptive to God."[17]

When we are receptive to God, we are alive and human in the place we inhabit together. Expectations and control of others are done away with. We no longer try to conquer God with our techniques. God becomes a mystery to us and we follow the Spirit in silence and solitude.

We cannot dictate to the ways we would like Christ to support us in our ambitions. When we do this, we reduce the mystery within us to a proposition and deny the depth of our humanity; we forsake our silence and solitude for something less. Our silence and solitude will not play these games.

"Jesus went out to a mountainside ... and spent the night" (Luke 6:12). Christ spent the night on a mountainside. A night probably consisted of six to eight hours. This was not unusual for Christ. He saw it as part of his rhythm of life. It was essential to who he was and what he did on the earth. He found the depth of his humanity more as he practiced this kind of silence and solitude. Have we ever given God our complete attention in silence and solitude as Christ did? Maybe we should have the courage to experiment with this a little. Marcia Ford says, "Silence inspires awe when it diverts my attention away from the chatter in my head and toward the wonder that the rest of life—the authentic life—contains."[18]

This is the call of the mystical imagination in the place where we live. We need to develop a practice of seeking God in silence and solitude. We will never experience the depth of our humanity if we do not give this kind of attention to our communion with God. Mother Teresa

---

[17] Leloup, *Being Still*, 19.

[18] Ford, *Traditions of the Ancients*, 30.

writes, "We all must take the time to be silent."[19] We might think this is asking too much of ourselves, but I would say that this is the radical nature of following Christ in our local community. Our practice of silence and solitude will save us from dysfunction, fragmentation, and narcissism.

What would actually happen if we turned off our televisions and computers and gave some thought to seeking God in silence and solitude? Social activist Dorothy Day, who co-founded the Catholic Worker Movement, states, "… we must deepen our own interior life."[20] If we took several weeks or days out of the year and gave absolute attention to silence and solitude, this would shape our lives together tremendously as the body of Christ in everyday life.

Our silence and solitude could manifest lots of ordinary, everyday miracles in our ongoing relational connection to the place we inhabit over time. This call to silence and solitude has not been cultivated enough in North America. We are oftentimes too loud to take the time to listen. Let's practice a more silent way of life in the parish. Let us be done with a noisy life. Let's start to follow an authentic path in silence and solitude together in our local context. This will be for our own healing, restoration, and growth.

We live in a culture that oppresses us with words. Our faith traditions oftentimes oppress us with words. We oppress our relationships with words if they are not balanced with silence and solitude. We need to be free from this oppression. Silence and solitude could be our liberation as the body of Christ in the place we live. Kenneth Leech states:

> Our age is one which is marked and disfigured by the corruption and dehumanizing of language. We live under the constant onslaught of words from advertisements and from propaganda, and the clichés and slogans of the consumer technocracies. Words by

---

[19] Mother Teresa, "The Fruit of Silence is Prayer," 7.

[20] Day, "The Impact of Monasticism," 85.

the million wash over us in a wave of meaninglessness. But the recovery of meaning and of resistance to the oppression derives from the practice of inner silence.[21]

This loud, noisy life does an injustice to our very humanity. We will never discover the depth of our humanity as the body of Christ if we do not resist this oppression of words through silence and solitude. They are the bearers of so much undiscovered wisdom. We need to become expressions of our silence and solitude in the place we inhabit together. There is no other way to be free.

The mystical imagination will not be oppressed by words. It lives in a subversive kind of freedom from all this. The widely read mystic Thomas Merton, who spent over 25 years practicing silence and solitude, writes, "If I were the same person I was ten years ago, I certainly would be astonished. But I am not really the same person, except in appearance."[22]

The Fear of Silence and Solitude: Integrating Courageous Action

Our culture has taught us to fear silence and solitude. We have learned that it is not safe because it is uncomfortable, unpredictable, unknown, and mysterious most of the time. Did Jesus face his fear, the cost of practicing silence and solitude? I think he did. Silence and solitude gave Christ the courage in his humanity to be an expression of love all throughout his life. Without silence and solitude, Christ would not have been able to live as he did in the world. Christ embraced this practice with courage and authenticity. Tilden Edwards, who is the director of the Shalom Institute for Spiritual Formation, says this about silence:

> Something about it draws us deeper into reality: its stillness, its openness, its gentleness. As we feel its pull on us, though, we also

---

[21] Leech, *True Prayer*, 178.

[22] Merton, *The Sign of Jonas*, 31.

find that we are afraid of silence. We fear its lack of boundaries and its seeming emptiness. We don't know if we can trust what will happen if we let go into it; we wonder if there will be anything left of us if we fully join the silence.[23]

Will we have the courage to find our identity apart from cultural propaganda or colonial religion? Will we completely lose our ego-driven agendas? Will we find a false god we have tried to believe in all these years in the name of Christianity and inside of the unhealthy systems of what we have known as "church" in North America? Will our whole structure of "reality" become shattered through our practice of silence and solitude? We have to have the courage to face this.

Silence and solitude cultivate stillness, openness, and gentleness within us in the parish. If we hold onto clichés, agendas, and techniques, we will fear silence and solitude. They cannot coexist. If our clichés, agendas and techniques were disrupted, we would have to create our identity in authenticity. Silence and solitude have no boundaries. They cut through everything to the core of who we are or who we think we are. We will sometimes be left to our own emptiness in the process.

It's hard facing our emptiness. But our spirituality is birthed in the core of our emptiness. Our emptiness shows us how to live, trust, and listen out of desperation. It opens up our relational context. It shows us how to desperately dream with a mystical imagination. Our communion with God becomes our very survival. We have to "join fully the silence" and remain open to how God is shaping us as the body of Christ in the place where we share life together. When we participate in our silence and solitude, we embrace the mystical imagination.

"Jesus went as usual to the Mount of Olives. And being in anguish, his sweat was like drops of blood falling to the ground" (Luke 22: 39, 44). Christ experienced great anguish and pain in the last days before his life would end in crucifixion. His silence and solitude expressed tears, cries, questions, fears, and helplessness. This was Christ's longing: "Father, if

---

[23] Edwards, *Living in the Presence*, 35.

you are willing, take this cup from me; yet not my will, but yours be done" (Luke 22: 42). How could Christ experience this on the Mount of Olives? He was about to become tortured and covered with his own blood left to die in disgrace at a young age in his thirties.

Christ needed courage to practice silence and solitude. He needed courage to face his pain. Silence and solitude was hard for him and that is why he was sweating something like drops of blood as he sensed that he was going to die soon. This was probably one of the most intense experiences of Christ's life. He did not want to face it. He knew the pain would be unbearable. The breaking of his body would bring about what seemed like a betrayal by his Father. How could he face this in his silence and solitude? Alone and betrayed by his friends, his silence and solitude strengthened him in the midst of his fear of it. As the sweat from his body dropped to the ground, he cried in deep anguish in his silence and solitude on the Mount of Olives. C. W. McPherson states:

> … silence now seems abnormal. Remove the envelope of noise and we become anxious and nervous. Just as a long-term prisoner, released from jail finds freedom confining and longs for the regularity and predictability of life on the cell block, we long for what we know: noise. Our noisy world acts as a kind of insulation, a distraction from the serious concerns that silence often invites.[24]

We sometimes fear our own silence and solitude because we know God will "ruin our false selves." If we participate with our silence and solitude; our clichés, agendas, and techniques will be destroyed by God. We will have "Mount of Olives" experiences of sorts where we become the crucified in our context as we share life together. Our local community will crucify us through silence and solitude. Our relationships will crucify us in the place we inhabit. We will become helpless and powerless as we become an expression of love in the world. This is our paradox to embrace. Only in powerlessness will we discover compassion within ourselves. And this will lead us to vulnerability, lamentation, and pain at times. We will have fear because all our own

---

[24] McPherson, *Keeping Silence*, 4.

control is gone. As this happens, an authentic reality will slowly reveal itself within us as we practice silence and solitude in everyday life.

Living in constant noise is easy, comfortable, and culturally acceptable. We fear silence and solitude because they force us to honestly face ourselves, our relational context, and our communion with God. Gunilla Norris says, "In our present culture silence is something like an endangered species."[25] Our silence and solitude do not want to become an endangered species. The body of Christ cannot live without them in the parish. They are essential to our survival, sustainability, and sanity. Yet we're afraid because we don't understand that the way we change the world is by changing ourselves within through the mystical imagination. The mystical imagination doesn't fear silence and solitude. It embraces silence and solitude.

There is so much abundance of life to be discovered in silence and solitude if we would just adopt a lifestyle of experimenting with it. What if we lived into our questions? What if we practiced silence and solitude while living in our local community? What if we listened more than we spoke? What if we embodied silence and solitude? How would we be shaped? What would we become? What if we were able to face ourselves in silence and solitude? The mystical imagination wants us to explore, practice, and experiment with silence and solitude. The mystical imagination dreams of such things. Henri J. M. Nouwen notes, "One of our main problems is that in this chatty society, silence has become a very fearful thing. For most people, silence creates itchiness and nervousness. Many experience silence not as full and rich, but as empty and hollow. For them silence is like a gaping abyss which can swallow them up."[26]

I remember when I first started to practice silence and solitude. It wasn't like I planned on it or that I knew what I was doing. I just got tired of using lots of words in my communion with God. It felt

---

[25] Norris, *Inviting Silence*, 31.

[26] Nouwen, *The Way of the Heart*, 59.

unnatural and draining to me. If I was going to live in communion with God without dualistic postures in my life, I knew I had to find a way beyond words.

So in 1995, after I finished two years of community college, I moved out of my parents' house and rented my first apartment with a friend from school. I started to work for an after school program for elementary school-age kids. Then I worked for a construction company doing a lot of clean-up work at job sites.

I didn't have much to do after work. I knew that I wanted to grow in my faith. There wasn't much support from people that I knew. Churches didn't help. There was no community. There was no practice of presence in a place. So I just started to read more. I started to learn more. I started to practice silence and solitude more. I stopped watching TV and movies. I even stopped listening to a lot of music for a while so I could find this posture within myself.

The silence really was terrifying at first. I lived in a world of noise. A world of music, TV, movies, sports, and social events consumed my life. There was no room for silence and solitude within myself. I didn't know how to survive and live in a silence and solitude that saw beyond these things into something more intentional within.

My life became very solitary and silent for a period of about two years. I was afraid, but I felt I didn't have a lot of options. I wanted to seek God, but wasn't quite sure how. So all I knew at the time was to develop a focus on my interior life. I would spend hours reading, thinking, reflecting, writing out books of the Bible. I wrote out most of the New Testament in those two years. This helped me to learn more of what it was talking about. I spent hours in silence and solitude reading Scripture, reading books, and cultivating my longing for God.

I remember so many days and nights where the silence terrified me. Facing myself was difficult. Thinking was hard. I had to face God within myself. Feeling my pain was almost impossible. I had to be present to who I was and was not. Becoming more honest with myself scared me. I had to be truthful in my solitude. Even though I tried to run, I couldn't. Tears of pain soon became familiar to me. I felt abandoned by God. There was no one to share my experience with. Life felt dark, cold, and hopeless at times. Weakness, questions, and ambiguity were very present to me. I had to trust that God was holding me even though all my feelings shouted abandonment and confusion.

Was I going crazy in the name of communion with God? Could I hold the tension of silence? Would the silence become my friend or my enemy? I had to live into these questions before me. It was not easy and looking back I often wonder how I actually did it. I now believe that God was strengthening me in a way I could not understand at the time. Although it didn't feel like it at all, I now know that God had not abandoned me. My practice of silence and solitude was crucial for developing my identity as an authentic human being in the world.

My salvation was revealed to me more clearly in those formative years through silence and solitude. I experienced redemption. Wisdom grew in me as I began to better understand my spirituality. I began to listen. Silence and solitude became my journey to seeking God.

I have seen the importance of embodying the gospel of compassion and loving my neighbors in community together with others. What a gift my silence and solitude have been to me. I have needed courage to practice silence and solitude all these years because sometimes they lead me to frightening places. But God constantly calls us not to fear the silence and the solitude. Such is my path to authenticity.

We fear facing ourselves. Most of us have no idea who we truly are. We construct our identity almost entirely from the noise around us. We say, "What good is silence in the midst of all the noise? The noise is fun, exciting, controlling, and a product of progress." We have been extreme consumers of noise. Maybe we think we will cease to exist if there is an end to all the noise. Lillian Daniel states:

> There's no shame in being afraid. You just don't want to stay that way, to allow yourself to ... become like the dead. Because the heart of the resurrection is that new life is always possible. Nobody

should live in fear and be like the dead. God wants us to live like the living, not the dead. We're not meant to live like the dead.[27]

The noise keeps us from facing ourselves. It blinds us to our inner worlds. It destroys everything that gets in its way. But silence is stronger than noise. Silence destroys all the noise within us and around us. Noise is not a part of the mystical imagination. We need to have the courage to face ourselves in silence and solitude as the body of Christ in the place we inhabit together.

We typically are not too friendly toward silence. We do not advocate for silence. We do not like to practice it. Our silence and solitude threaten our existence by destroying our abstract clichés. Our addiction to preaching has left us fearful of silence and solitude. Silence and solitude are too controversial and too unpredictable. They recognize no boundaries. Our silence and solitude cultivate the mystical imagination within us. We would be wise if we stopped fearing silence and start practicing it more.

Our neighborhood will thrive through its citizens practicing silence and solitude. The place we inhabit will become sustainable through our silence and solitude. We cannot be the body of Christ in everyday life without them. Wayne Muller says, "We greet silence with fear, afraid it will show us the broken center at the core of the world and of ourselves. Afraid of what we will find there, we avoid the stillness at all costs, keeping ourselves busy not so much to accomplish but to avoid the terrors and dangers of emptiness."[28]

Silence and solitude reveal our brokenness. Silence and solitude reveal the shallowness of our relationships with one another. Silence and solitude reveal our apathy. We prefer busyness to the terrors of facing ourselves. We are not ready to be honest with the emptiness that is killing us on the inside. The mystical imagination helps us hold the tension between our emptiness and our peace, a tension we will experience our entire lives as the body of Christ in the place we inhabit in the world.

---

[27] Daniel, *When "Spiritual But Not Religious" is Not Enough*, 68.

[28] Muller, *Sabbath*, 42.

The Present Depth of Our Experience

Chapter 9

Understanding at a Deeper Level: Taking Our Growth Seriously

The Desert Experience: A Dark Night of the Soul

Silence and solitude will guide us to be more vulnerable, leading us at times to desert experiences, to dark nights of the soul. In this darkness all of our preconceived paradigms will be questioned. We will think that God has abandoned us. But this is the natural process of spiritual growth.

There is untapped wisdom to be found within us if we do not let these experiences frighten us to the point of giving up our pursuit of God. We need to seek God constantly through the desert experiences of our lives in the parish. They will teach us in ways we cannot understand. Our deserts break through all of our illusions of being in control of life.

Our practice of silence and solitude will help us to walk through our desert experiences with courage. The desert will expose our inner pain. But it's there that we will learn to trust in God through our pain and brokenness. We need to embrace our pain and not pretend that "Christ has completed us" by taking all our pain away. Our pain and brokenness makes us more human and gives us solidarity with others.

The mystical imagination is not afraid to hold our pain through the desert experiences of life. It is honest about the existence of pain and brokenness within our lives. Kathy Escobar states so eloquently:

> A theology of brokenness is a way of seeing the world that is contrary to much of what we've been taught. Instead of a "rise above mentality," a theology of brokenness ascribes to a "go lower and deeper one." It doesn't mean that we wallow in our brokenness or the brokenness of others, but instead, we acknowledge that success is not defined by everything looking neat and tidy ... Rejecting brokenness usually leads to a false faith where we are pretending instead of living authentically.[1]

Our souls will eventually heal, but not without some struggle through our desert seasons. As we work out our salvation through silence and solitude, we will feel our pain through all of the things we would prefer would stay hidden. We will become more honest with God, with ourselves, and with one another. We will be open to our brokenness in the place we inhabit. The mystical imagination is always connected to the condition of our souls. We may think that measuring up is all about morality, ethics, and doing all the preconceived right things; but maybe it is more about our authenticity. Howard Baker says:

> What is hard for many of us to accept is this: The journey of faith will take us through the many conditions of the soul. We may not have expected things to get tougher before they get better. Certainly, we did not expect to have our innermost selves exposed—our misgivings about God, our doubt, apathy, disillusionment, depression. Because many of us think like people who are supposed to have arrived, we do not think of these as interior conditions God may lead us through.[2]

A desert experience may cause us to experience ourselves differently. At times we will feel anger, pain, depression, loneliness, confusion, brokenness, powerlessness and limitation. We will deconstruct

---

[1] Escobar, *Down We Go*, 42.

[2] Baker, *Soul Keeping*, 59.

everything. A lot of what our life has become will bother us. We will not be content with the status quo. We will discover that there is so much more to the condition of our souls than an institutional morality that has little connection to local community. Our silence and solitude give us the ability to embody courage in the place we inhabit both internally and externally. We will experience God in one another through the desert experiences of life. My friend Christine Sine writes in her book *Return to Our Senses*, "Often the moves of God that are transforming our world grow as hidden mustard seeds planted in dark places. Sometimes the darkness seems to last a long time. Often the seeds sprout and grow before we even realize anything has changed."[3]

We are constantly moving to deeper levels of faith throughout our lives. If we are growing spiritually; we will learn to experience our life in holistic ways that are constantly new, alive and inspired by the mystical imagination. Our mystical imaginations will shape us in the moment, in the present places of our awakened life.

The desert experiences are normal processes of growth. They are not because we have necessarily done anything wrong or turned away from God. On the contrary, they are actually signs of a mature and serious follower of Christ. Thomas Keating notes:

> Every time we move to a new level of faith, there is an initial experience of disintegration, distress, confusion, and darkness. If we are not forewarned about the spiritual journey, it feels like something has gone wrong. This is the normal way that the present level of our understanding—our attitude toward ourselves, other people, and God—experiences that our life just does not work any more at that level. We are challenged or forced to move to a deeper level.[4]

The deserts push us to a liminal space where life can be experienced in ways that can feel like disintegration, darkness, confusion and distress.

---

[3] Sine, *Return to Our Senses*, 125.

[4] Keating, *Intimacy With God*, 52.

We do not have to fear the depths of our humanity in these times. What feels like defeat and loss is in fact moving us to a deeper level of faith. Barbara Brown Taylor writes, "This faith will not offer me much to hold on to. It will not give me a safe place to settle. Practicing it will require me to celebrate the sacrament of defeat and loss."[5]

Becoming honest through the desert experiences is never easy. They may be one of the most difficult things that the body of Christ must face together. It takes deeper levels of experiencing life if we are to practice silence and solitude and embody the mystical imagination within us. The desert is essential to our ongoing sustainability, growth, and maturity. Desert experiences are the way God shapes us.

We have to trust God that the darkness, desert, and distress will not destroy us. We must hold onto God through our pain and brokenness. We must learn to live through it with grace, courage, and gentleness. God's grace will sustain us through the desert experiences in the parish. Our silence and solitude will cultivate the mystical imagination as we process our pain. After caring for the dying in India for many years, Mother Teresa said when facing her own darkness:

> The darkness is so dark—and I am alone.—Unwanted, forsaken.— The loneliness of the heart that wants love is unbearable.—Where is my faith?—Even deep down, right in, there is nothing but emptiness & darkness.—My God—how painful is this unknown pain. It pains without ceasing.—I have no faith.—I dare not utter the words & thoughts that crowd in my heart—& make me suffer untold agony. So many unanswered questions live with me – I am afraid to uncover them—because of the blasphemy.—If there be God, please forgive me ... Love—the word—it brings nothing.—I am told God loves me—and the reality of darkness & coldness & emptiness is so great that nothing touches my soul.[6]

---

[5] Taylor, *Learning to Walk in the Dark*, 148.

[6] Mother Teresa, "My God, How Painful is This Unknown Pain," 187.

"I tell you the truth, unless a kernel of wheat falls to the ground and dies, it remains only a single seed. But if it dies, it produces many seeds" (John 12:24). The desert seasons of darkness are like seeds that are dying within ourselves to produce something else that we cannot understand at the time. Our silence and solitude facilitate the process of these seeds dying within us to bring about something unfamiliar, painful, and ambiguous. This is beyond what we can understand. It is a mystery that we don't have to understand. We will survive if we just listen deeply the best we can to our life's context.

The kingdom of God lives in little seeds within us in these seasons of life. It is these seeds that are cultivated in the desert. As one dies, another comes to life. This is the process of silence and solitude through these difficult seasons of life. Ann Voskamp says in her book *One Thousand Gifts*, "… all new life comes out of the dark places, and hasn't it always been?"[7] The desert experiences of darkness have always been the process of new expressions of life taking place within us. It is the path of the mystical imagination. It is the path of authentic wisdom. It is the path of my own experience.

I remember vividly the year 2000. It was a difficult year of darkness, death, and desert experiences. It was one of the worst years of my life. After graduating from Central Washington University with a teaching degree in education, I moved from the college town of Ellensburg to the city of Kent. This left me uprooted. I was alone in this new place working as a teacher in a public school. A sense of discouragement set in as I quickly found out that teaching was more about following a standardized curriculum and less about creativity. It became extremely difficult to like what I was doing as a teacher.

I lost interest in teaching altogether, but I had to keep working to pay off my student loans as well as other bills. After my first job as a teacher, I did some subbing and had a hard time finding work. Soon depression kicked in as I was living alone and struggling to make sense

---

[7] Voskamp, *One Thousand Gifts*, 96.

of life. I didn't know very many people in Kent at the time. My college degree was depressing me. Teaching didn't interest me anymore. Having all this debt, I thought I had made a mistake going to college in the first place.

When I was in community college, I met a young woman who I had become very fond of. After several years, she went off to Bosnia to work with a missionary organization for a couple of years. As she was at the end of her time there, she was coming back to Washington. I was excited to see her, and hoped we would become partners for life and possibly get married down the road. But when she got back, she told me that God was leading her in a different direction and it wasn't going to happen. I was even more crushed, numb, and depressed.

Not knowing what had happened, I walked away from a hard conversation with her in sadness, grief, and pain. All I could do was try to accept what had happened. I wasn't very good at it. My world was coming undone. I had a difficult time seeking God through all of this. Deep emotional pain consumed me. I was overwhelmed with sadness and grief not knowing what to do.

Sometime later that year, I noticed that I was starting to lose my hair. I was 26 years old, and I never expected this could happen at such a young age. Being very self-conscious about it, I worried about my appearance. I had a hard time understanding how this could happen. I cried, screamed, and was angry in my spirit. Losing my hair depressed me even more. With all these events happening in a matter of months, I lost the motivation to live. I started to sleep a lot to escape my pain.

I went to sleep every night not knowing if it was worth it to wake up the next day. The pain was deep. I was all alone and was struggling to seek God. It felt I had given up on my spirituality. I was paralyzed by fear, anxiety, and depression. There was no hope or future for me in this lonely place.

After the school year was over, I stopped working altogether. Having saved a bunch of money while I was working, I lived off that for a while. My family recommended that I seek counseling and go to social services for help. I followed their advice. I remember one day standing in line at a crowded social service office around Christmas just crying tears of pain.

I thought to myself, "I had not done anything wrong. I had not chosen these circumstances. I was not on drugs and alcohol. I had not been violent. I had never gone to prison. I have just graduated from college with a supposed bright future." I wondered where I would be in a year. "Would I be functional? Would I be institutionalized? Would I ever feel different about life?"

Someone recommended that I start to read about depression so I could understand its processes a little better. This led me to a book on cognitive therapy. I learned that I must not lose interest in my normal everyday activities, and that I must keep being social and work on my irrational thinking patterns that can occur in circumstances such as mine. As a result, I became so concerned about my health that I stopped sleeping so much. Showering, shaving and getting dressed everyday became my priority. Working again became important. Eating regularly began to be a part of my life again. I started going out of my apartment and socializing. I started to meet people in the place I lived. It was so hard. I had to work through a lot of residual pain as well as any spirituality that was left within me.

Then I met some people in Auburn (very close to Kent) who told me about this thing that many young people went to. It was based on cultivating a postmodern spirituality in our cultural context. They met in a coffee shop close by. I went to a meeting and met a lot of the people. And as the next couple of years went by, I integrated more into relationships there. That was very healing for me. I slowly found myself feeling good about life again. It took a long time, but I believe that I was experiencing God in my disintegration, distress, confusion, and pain although I could not see that at the time.

My desert experience had led me to a relational integration that has impacted my growth, clarity, awareness, passion, and imagination. My silence and solitude helped facilitate this process within me. I am thankful to God everyday for the dark night of the soul that creates in us who we will become and who we truly are. One of my favorite writers Kelly Bean says:

> Getting in touch with our own pain and becoming aware of our own brokenness is not an easy path, but it's one that leads to our own transformation as well as the possibility of forming authentic relationships. No matter how many good intentions we have, if we are not becoming more self-aware and taking active measures to continue toward growth and healing, our work and our relationships can only go so far and may end up causing more harm than good over time.[8]

Revealing Reality: Inviting the Nakedness of Life

Silence and solitude reveal reality. Our lives are based on too many illusions and idolatries. Our eyes are opened when reality is revealed and we listen. We need to be honest in our relationship with reality. We cannot make up or distort reality. Reality has its own naked existence.

We need to let reality shape us in our local community as the body of Christ in everyday life. We need to become one with reality. We need to become an expression of reality through our silence and solitude. Ronald Rolheiser says in his book *The Shattered Lantern*, "In standing naked before reality and letting reality be for us all that it is in itself, we allow reality into our lives in such a way that it becomes part of us and we become part of it."[9]

Reality lives within the mystical imagination. Our silence and solitude are constantly revealing reality to us. Christ is the teacher of the reality

---

[8] Bean, *How to Be a Christian Without Going to Church*, 194.

[9] Rolheiser, *The Shattered Lantern*, 66.

of our relational context. He is the teacher of the wisdom of silence and solitude.

Our embodied existence hinges on our practice of silence and solitude. Without silence and solitude, we will not be able to understand reality fully. We will not be able to experience reality in our local context as the body of Christ in everyday life. Dallas Willard states, "Solitude and silence are primary means for correcting the distortions of our embodied social existence."[10]

We are only alive when we experience our relational context free from our own distortions. We are only authentic when we experience reality through the mystical imagination within us in the place we share life together. Reality must become the dominant paradigm in which we live out an "embodied social existence" as the body of Christ in the parish.

Our communion with God is leading us to relational revelations. Our communion with God shows us how to treat others with truthfulness. Our silence and solitude help us to see the reality of our relational connection in everyday life. We need silence and solitude to sort through our distorted relational ways in our local community.

Christ practiced silence and solitude because he needed to embody a relational reality to those in his local context in the world. Scripture says, "… he went up on a mountainside by himself" (Matthew 14:23). He often practiced silence and solitude to embrace reality within the human context he inhabited. Christ lived within the real, authentic experience of his humanity. On mountainsides, in gardens, in the desert, on long walks, in lonely places, and in homes; Christ practiced silence and solitude to find an integration with the real. Reality was constantly being revealed through his embodiment of truthfulness in the way he treated others with love, respect, and dignity.

---

[10] Willard, *The Great Omission*, 153.

Christ embodied the kingdom of God in the world through his love for his neighbors. This was how he lived. This is how he died. This is how he grew up. His humanity was not separate from embodying love in the place where he lived. All he had was his local context on the earth to experience reality. All he had were the people around him to express his love and compassion.

Christ's silence and solitude opened him up to this reality. He was one with the real in his humanity, and we are called to this kind of union as we follow him in our local context. We are called to be his hands and feet in everyday life in the parish. The mystical imagination is constantly revealing reality to us in the place we inhabit together. Mary Jo Meadow writes, "God is always more than our present concept of God. We must always remain open to receive God's further self."[11]

God is always revealing reality to us in all of life. Our silence and solitude make us more aware of these revelations within us and all around us. But do we have the posture to listen and learn from them? These revelations happen moment by moment in the place where we live. But if we are not faithfully present we will never be able to really understand them. We are moving too fast and being too loud to be receptive to the ordinary moments of divine revelation. Mary Margaret Funk states, "Furthermore, although such fearful intimacy continues to overload my emotions on occasions, I nevertheless consider it a privilege to be so wholly known by God ... and to abide in a place of truth that, while raw and naked and deeply revelatory of my own abiding weakness, is entirely real."[12]

If God's nature is always revelation, our posture should be to live in receptivity as the body of Christ in the parish. Revelations are best understood in the local, everyday life of a place. They are best understood in the relational context that we share life with others in. It is as if these revelations are blowing in the wind. We can't grab them

---

[11] Meadow, *Christian Insight Meditation*, 109.

[12] Funk, *Into the Depths*, 153.

with our hands; we can only experience them in our lives. The condition of our souls will determine our receptivity to these revelations in everyday life.

God will never stop revealing dreams of beloved community. God will never stop inspiring the church to listen in the context of everyday life together. God will never stop living in the place we inhabit. God will never stop teaching us through the ordinary experiences of our lives. God's revelations are always integrated with the ecology of relational connection. Our silence and solitude are so important in this process. God is calling us to a life of constant inner revelation through the mystical imagination in the place we inhabit.

We have a hard time facing the reality of ourselves, others, and God. We have a hard time with the reality of authentic engagement as the body of Christ in everyday life in the parish. We don't like listening and we don't like allowing ourselves to be shaped by the place where we live. It is easy for us to live above place and not care. We think we have all the answers and want to create our own monopoly on reality. But reality is constantly revealing itself to be beyond our own agendas.

When reality reveals itself throughout everyday life together, all our preconceived clichés become meaningless. We look foolish before reality when we hold onto our clichés. They are nothing more than a disembodied spirituality that only exist in our minds and language. Our practice of silence and solitude facilitates the disappearance of our clichés, setting a new pace that allows us to become receptive to reality in everyday life. Barbara Erakko Taylor states, "There is also a pace within our lifestyle that allows silence to remain present and conscious within us."[13]

When our Downtown Neighborhood Fellowship was transitioning out of a large regional gathering and into a more local embodied expression, we practiced a lot of silence and solitude together. We

---

[13] Taylor, *Silent Dwellers*, 24.

would just listen in the silence. We would reflect on others and on God's dreams for our lives. We would hold our relational context in the silence. Sometimes we would write out expressions of what was going on within us. Sometimes we would just be still in our silence together.

We had many forms of this, but the focus was always on listening to our inner selves, listening to God, and listening to one another. As we slowly developed a theology of place, our silence and solitude were essential for these realities to be revealed to us. The more we listened in our silence, the more convinced we became of the importance of the parish for an embodied spirituality together.

We saw that we could not love our neighbors if we did not practice our faith in a local context. We abandoned focusing on buildings and meetings as a way to worship; instead we embraced proximity, a shared life in a particular place in everyday life together as a way to worship. Worship became the very fabric of relational care in our lives together in the parish. Worship shaped our ongoing identity through our lives together embodied in community.

The built environment, the local economy, the integration of diversity with the poor, the rich, and the middle class all became important to us. Caring for a place and rooting ourselves in a particular locality became the medium that began shaping us in our everyday lives together. Our silence and solitude together helped us, I believe, to have these revelations of reality as we have been working to become a holistic counterculture.

Our silence and solitude will always be revealing reality to us as the body of Christ in everyday life. We cannot get stuck in our past preconceived notions of God. We cannot put God in a box anymore. We cannot trap God into a distortion of our own reality. God needs to be free within us to be the revealing God.

The call of the gospel is to be constantly embracing God's revelations in the present moment of our experience. This is always evolving, growing, changing, and shaping us to become a holistic counterculture in the place we inhabit. It is a very fluid experience of adaptability and experimentation. Joan Chittister states, "God cannot be defined by yesterday. God is constantly revealing the fullness of God, more today than yesterday, more tomorrow than today."[14] The fullness of God's revelations will keep being made manifest if we will have the courage to listen in our souls.

God will be revealing reality to us all throughout our journey of life. This will never stop. It cannot stop if God is alive and present to creation. God lives to be the revealing God of the place we inhabit together. Yesterday does not define God anymore. The mystical imagination does not experience the God of yesterday. The mystical imagination experiences the God of the present moment who constantly is revealing reality within and around us.

Our practice of silence and solitude grounds us in a revealing reality that we can never turn away from. When reality breaks through to our fragmented lives it tastes so good. Our lives will long for this groundedness in reality because out of it comes all that is beautiful within the mystical imagination. Gus Gordon writes:

> Silence is the ground, the core of reality, and all else relates to it and emanates from it. Silence suffuses the core of our being. Silence is the primal and necessary human atmosphere that gives birth to all that is precious in becoming human.[15]

Silence and solitude touches "the core of our being." They create the environment to experience our humanity without distortions. Silence and solitude bring out all that is beautiful within us as the body of Christ in the parish. The world needs more practitioners of silence and solitude. The world needs more expressions of human beauty and

---

[14] Chittister, *Wisdom Distilled from the Daily*, 141.

[15] Gordon, *Solitude and Compassion*, 164.

listening postures within everyday lives. The world needs more of the mystical imagination to flourish in authentic human beings.

Understanding Ourselves: The Wonder of Self-Awareness

Our silence and solitude put us in a place of presence to ourselves. This in turn cultivates a presence to God and our relational context with others. When we are present to ourselves we start to understand ourselves, to know ourselves more. We start on the process of self-awareness. This self-understanding is important if we are to have an openness to knowing authentically who we are if we are going to seek God as the body of Christ in the parish. Stephan Chase says, "... if one is completely present to oneself, one is completely present to God, and if one is completely present to God, one is completely present to others."[16]

The mystical imagination facilitates a presence to ourselves and our relational context. It helps us in the process of understanding and knowing ourselves in the place we inhabit together. We cannot be closed off to being present to ourselves and remaining disembodied anymore. If we do not know ourselves, we will live with multiple identities. We will live with all kinds of inner sacred/secular dualities. This is not healthy and will catch up to us at some point. We are called to a deep understanding of our true self in everyday life.

Our true self cannot become co-opted by the narratives of media, consumerism, or entertainment. If we do not cultivate silence and solitude, we will never come to understand who we truly are without masks, techniques, or agendas. If we turn away from seeking self-understanding, we will never know the mystical imagination. And we will never cultivate the life-giving practice of listening to ourselves, to our local context, and to God. We could start an inner revolution of self-awareness in the practice of everyday life together. Changing the world starts within ourselves and nowhere else.

---

[16] Chase, *The Tree of Life*, 226.

If we are honest with ourselves, we will come to a place of not really knowing who we are. We will find that we are the lost ones. We have a hard time exploring the interior movements of our soul because the lives we lead have become overly busy and loud. We make too much noise in the way we live and are disconnected from within. We have no room to explore our silence and solitude. Jane Rubietta says in her book *Resting Place:*

> But our relationship with God and others has no honest context if we do not know ourselves. In solitude ... we can afford total honesty about failures ... In solitude I face my ugliness, unforgiveness, anger, laziness with others—including God. In solitude I also find, miraculously, hope—the capacity to love, forgive, grow, rest. There I notice gifts and dreams and hopes, in spite of broken places.[17]

There needs to be an inner revolution that changes how we embody ourselves, how we understand ourselves, and how we express ourselves in the world. We need to engage the mystical imagination and start to embrace some self-understanding. If we do not seek to understand ourselves, we will never seek God in everyday life. We must constantly question ourselves as we seek God together. Our identity is constantly being shaped as we listen intensely to our lives, the lives of others, and the life of God within.

"Not long after that, the younger son got together all he had, set off for a distant country and there squandered his wealth in wild living. After he had spent everything, there was a severe famine in that whole country, and he began to be in need. So he went and hired himself out to a citizen of that country who sent him to his fields to feed pigs. He longed to fill his stomach with the pods that the pigs were eating, but no one gave him anything.

When he came to his senses, he said, 'How many of my father's hired men have food to spare, and here I am starving to death! I will set out

---

[17] Rubietta, *Resting Place*, 63.

and go back to my father and say to him: Father, I have sinned against heaven and against you. I am no longer worthy to be called your son; make me like one of your hired men.' So he got up and went to his father.

But while he was still a long way off, his father saw him and was filled with compassion for him; he ran to his son, threw his arms around him and kissed him.

The son said to him, 'Father, I have sinned against heaven and against you. I am no longer worthy to be called your son.'

But the father said to his servants, 'Quick! Bring the best robe and put it on him. Put a ring on his finger and sandals on his feet. Bring the fattened calf and kill it. Let's have a feast and celebrate. For this son of mine was dead and is alive again; he was lost and is found.' So they began to celebrate" (Luke 15:13-24).

We are the lost ones when we do not seek to understand ourselves. It is not the other who is lost, it is ourselves. When we do not know ourselves, we become lost within ourselves not knowing who we are. Sixteenth century mystic Teresa of Avila says, "As I see it, we shall never succeed in knowing ourselves unless we seek to know God."[18]

We have a hard time understanding our identity as beloved children of God. We seek our identity elsewhere in a narrative of illusion. We think that our illusion of the "good life" will make us so "happy," but it is oftentimes arrogant and individualistic. Our silence and solitude help us to remember who we are as we seek to understand ourselves in the parish. We do not have to end up like a lost son or daughter. We can seek an understanding of ourselves that will prevent this from happening.

---

[18] Teresa of Avila, *Interior Castle*, 38.

When we seek to understand ourselves, we become authentically human. We sort out our identity in silence and solitude. Our whole lives should be a process of seeking God through this understanding of ourselves. We become our silence and solitude when we seek to understand ourselves as a way of life. We become walking expressions of silence and solitude through beauty, goodness, love, and compassion in our local community. Robert Faricy and Lucy Rooney note, "I can only relate to Jesus as myself. I do not have to try to be someone else, or different from myself."[19]

Silence and solitude bring clarity and healing to distorted ways of experiencing ourselves. They help us to have empathy for ourselves and open up the mystical imagination within us. Paula Huston writes, "The natural result of solitude and silence is a far clearer picture of ourselves, whether or not we really want to see it … The longer we look into the mirror of silence and solitude, the more we see."[20]

Silence and solitude are like a mirror where we come to see and understand ourselves more. They touch the core of our pain and native passion. They create an inner revolution of the mystical imagination as the body of Christ in the parish.

Understanding ourselves is important to our presence in life. It helps us work through trust issues, fear, loneliness, self protection, and defensiveness. We come to a place of honesty and authenticity in all of life. When we live on the path to understanding ourselves; we do not need to hide from ourselves, from others, or from God. We can be ourselves right where we are in the place where we live.

I have been on a path to understanding myself for the past two decades. It all started back in the early 90s. It has felt confusing, difficult, and impossible at times. I have recognized that my own humanity is very complex and has very deep levels that I do not always fully understand.

---

[19] Faricy and Rooney, *The Contemplative Way of Prayer*, 34.

[20] Huston, *The Holy Way*, 61.

I crave food, sleep, sex, comfort, rest, companionship, rhythms, integration, purpose, learning, thinking, contemplating, silence, meaningful work, healing from pain, freedom from anger, the disappearance of sadness, looking good, cleanliness, exercise, leisure, celebration, touch, affirmation, happiness, money, possessions, and fun experiences.

In the midst of sorting out what is a healthy expression of my humanity, I have had to cultivate a practice of listening in silence and solitude. There are boundaries, liberties and limitations to all the things I experience within myself. My silence and solitude have helped me to discern what is going on inside of me. I ask the hard questions of myself constantly to try to understand myself. I have gotten much better at this over the years, but working out my identity in the parish is a lifelong process. Thomas Merton writes in his book *Contemplation in a World of Action:*

> He who attempts to act and do things for others or for the world without deepening his own self-understanding, freedom, integrity and capacity to love will not have anything to give others. He will communicate to them nothing but the contagion of his own obsessions, his aggressiveness, his ego-centered ambitions, his delusions about ends and means, his doctrinaire prejudices and ideas.[21]

The more we understand ourselves, the more ability we will have to live relationally in our local community. When we are on the path of self-understanding, we will start to experience our spirituality more holistically. Our self-awareness becomes alive and free within the mystical imagination. It leads us deeper into ourselves and the place we inhabit together. Phileena Heuertz says in her wonderful book *Pilgrimage of a Soul*, "Self-Awareness is central to becoming whole and connected."[22] If we are not connected to one another in our local

---

[21] Merton, *Contemplation in a World of Action*, 160-161.

[22] Heuertz, *Pilgrimage of a Soul*, 47.

context, it is because we are not seeking to look inside and understand ourselves.

Silence and solitude ensure our identity will not become fragmented. If we are to embody compassion in our local community, we cannot have multiple identities at the core of who we are. Our identity needs to be holistically one with our true self. Henri J. M. Nouwen writes, "Solitude is the place where we find our identity."[23] In the practice of silence and solitude, we will experience our identity.

Our identity will become integrated with our humanity, and our humanity will become integrated with the place we inhabit as the body of Christ together. We will have a hard time finding our identity outside of our practice of silence and solitude. Our identity needs the mystical imagination that comes from our silence and solitude. The mystical imagination leads us to an identity that is one with our humanity in the parish. Silence and solitude need to be practiced with intentionality, seriousness, and intensity. We will never discover our true self that makes up our identity any other way.

---

[23] Nouwen, *Clowning in Rome*, 19.

Part 4

Re-imagining Our Interior World: Welcoming Reflection and Rest

Chapter 10

A New Paradigm: Dreaming, Awakening, and Remembering

Unlearning Old Ways: Dreaming Beyond the Status Quo

We have forgotten how to dream in ways that are not individualistic and all about us. We have forgotten the beautiful dreams that God has for our lives together as the body of Christ in the parish. The mystical imagination is teaching us to dream together, not alone. Wendy R. McCaig, Executive Director of Embrace Richmond, says, "I have come to realize that dreamers are not born but made, often through pain and suffering. What sets dreamers apart is their willingness to allow their pain to bring healing to others."[1]

The mystical imagination is teaching us to be an expression of these dreams as the body of Christ in everyday life. Our everyday lives will become expressions of these dreams when we learn to re-imagine the paradigms of our lives together through reflection and rest. God is calling us to an inner revolution of reflection and rest that breaks through status quo living.

---

[1] McCaig, *From the Sanctuary to the Streets*, 158.

We need to allow God's dreams to live within us through the place we inhabit. We need to learn how to dream in holistic ways that are for the common good. Our dreams need to be an expression of love in our local community. We should model our lives after Christ's ways of love and compassion for all people. Alexia Salvatierra and Peter Heltzel state:

> That's what dreams do: they ignite our prophetic imagination. They give us language that can unite and inspire us across racial, ethnic and religious differences, even across differences in societal power. Dreams bring people together, and when we organize our efforts based on our dreams and visions for our communities, the game often changes, and a different kind of agreement becomes possible.[2]

God wants to express and embody these dreams through us. Our reflection and rest are so important to this process of spiritual formation in us as the body of Christ in everyday life. The mystical imagination needs them in order to embody these dreams within us.

The mystical imagination is a powerful strength within us that dreams on behalf of the common good of the world around us. Michael Frost and Alan Hirsch say, "We need to dream again, and to do this we must cultivate a love for imagination."[3] We must love the imagination. We must cultivate the dreams of the mystical imagination within us. This is how Christ lives within us.

When we are engaged in the practice of reflection and rest, we are present to the dreams within us in the parish. Learning to dream through a love of the mystical imagination is not always the easiest thing to do in a cultural context that promotes individualism. We need to fight for the freedom to practice reflection and rest so we can dream in ways that honor our neighbors in the place we inhabit.

---

[2] Salvatierra and Heltzel, *Faith-Rooted Organizing*, 41.

[3] Frost and Hirsch, *The Shaping of Things to Come*, 188.

The empire of the Untied States promotes a narrative that we all need to fall into without resistance. We all need to be happy, mobile, wealthy, consumers who work for this system and promote it by the way we live. Our values need to align or there might be a disruption. We might just find what is authentic in our midst if a disruption in the system occurs. God forbid that this ever happens. We like things just the way they are.

We can enclose ourselves in our wealth and forget about everyone else. But these are not the dreams of the mystical imagination. The narrative of the empire kills the mystical imagination by killing our expression of the body of Christ in everyday live in the parish. We need to practice reflection and rest if we are to dream beyond the narrative of the empire. Brian J. Walsh and Sylvia C. Keesmaat note, "An alternative to the empire requires different dreams, animated by a different narrative."[4]

We need to become unique expressions of dreams that subvert the empire in the place we live. Our reflection and rest will facilitate the mystical imagination to begin to dream again. We will be able to find a narrative of relational care together in our context and forsake the spoon-fed, selfish lifestyle that the empire gorges us with.

God is the creator of the subversive dreams within us. Our gift to the world is the expression and embodiment of our dreams in the parish. "It seems like we never give ourselves enough open space and permission to dream and hope boldly and aloud with one another. It's like somehow we don't think that's an okay thing to do," states Enuma Okoro.[5]

Following our subversive dreams is how the Spirit leads us in everyday life as the body of Christ in the parish. The following of our dreams is a gift to our neighborhood and our neighbors in every local, particular

---

[4] Walsh and Keesmaat, *Colossians Remixed*, 171.

[5] Okoro, *Reluctant Pilgrim*, 175.

aspect of life. Our reflection and rest always connects us more to our dreams within.

What do we hope for? What do we long for? How can we become an expression of our hopes and longings together? The process of wrestling with these questions throughout life could be our greatest gift to the world. Jan Johnson writes, "When we're seeking God's dreams for us, it changes what we do."[6]

Our Downtown Neighborhood Fellowship has dreamed of becoming an expression of the body of Christ in everyday life in the parish we live in. Our reflection and rest have helped us in this. Our theology of place was a dream we have had for a long time and which has taken us through many lessons. It has not been easy. But after ten years of experimenting with embodied forms of this in Downtown Tacoma, I feel we are now on our way to creating a holistic counterculture. Our dream has been to allow others to see and experience in and through us the body of Christ in everyday life.

We are still working out our salvation together. We have not arrived and probably never will, but we have been listening to our local context for awhile now. We have been shaped by our local community. The mystical imagination is growing within us. The inner revolution has begun and will continue. Our reflection and rest have helped us to dream of what others have said is impossible. It is truly a gift to have an embodied, local expression of the body of Christ in all dimensions of everyday life.

> Consequently, you are no longer foreigners and aliens, but fellow citizens with God's people and members of God's household, built on the foundation of the apostles and prophets, with Christ Jesus himself as the chief cornerstone. In him the whole building is joined together and rises to become a holy temple in the Lord. And in him you too are being built together to become a dwelling in which God lives by his Spirit (Ephesians 2:19-22).

---

[6] Johnson, *Enjoying the Presence of God*, 82.

We need to dream of becoming citizens of our place together as our call and identity. The Spirit within us is leading us to love our neighbors in this way, to dream subversive dreams of becoming the body of Christ in the parish. We must follow our dreams to embody love, humility, vulnerability, and compassion in everyday life together.

If Christ is our chief cornerstone, we must allow his life to embody itself through our everyday experiences in our local community. We must follow Christ's example of love, grace, reflection, and rest.

In the neighborhood among neighbors is where God is continually working in the world. Our reflection and rest will help us to re-imagine our neighborhood as the parish. Our dreams must be advocates for this. The mystical imagination longs for this.

We need to see the practice of learning to dream as essential and nonnegotiable. We cannot re-imagine anything beautiful in our local context without it. We cannot find life without a vibrant mystical imagination for the parish. Frederika Carney says, "That is our task today: to dream and hope for a better world."[7]

We should be advocates for the place where we live. This is our task, our duty, our way of life, and our subversive practice. Affecting the world with goodness, beauty, and love always starts in small ways through what is happening locally among us. It starts within us in the place we inhabit through our reflection and rest. Our locality needs to be embraced as sacred in everyday life. The world will not become anything different and history will repeat itself, if we do not take this call seriously. The mystical imagination is calling out to us to come alive and embrace an expression of love that starts through the local community we live in.

---

[7] Carney, "To Dream and Hope for a Better World," 98.

Reflection and rest will bring us to a place of profound awakening in everyday life together. They will awaken our sensuousness deep within us. We will start to experience the gospel sensuously as we get in touch with the authentic reality of our experience. We will become alive to all that we authentically taste, see, hear, touch, and smell in our relational context in the place we inhabit. Our sensuousness will undergo an awakening of its sacredness. Our reflection and rest bring us to this kind of awakening within ourselves. The mystical imagination embraces a sacred sensuousness in all of life. David Steindl-Rast says in his book *A Listening Heart:*

> Discovering sacred sensuousness is like waking up from a stupor into which Christian spirituality fell in spite of itself, long ago. This awakening is the beginning of a genuine incarnational spirituality. Sacred sensuousness takes it seriously that God is not only beyond all that we can imagine, but is also the very source of the sensuous reality that feeds our imagination. What a privilege for us to be alive in this period of history when more and more people are waking up to the realization that sensuousness is sacred.[8]

This sacred sensuousness cultivates the mystical imagination within us. An incarnational spirituality touches our sensuousness as we share life together. We need to become more connected to the gift of sensuousness in our bodies. This will bring life to the mystical imagination within us. No longer can we live a life that is disconnected from our sensuousness. This is a distortion of reality. God is calling us to an awakening of our sensuousness as the body of Christ in the parish.

We can't make awakening happen within us. We have to listen and let it live through our bodies in the natural rhythms of our experience. We need to trust this process of awakening to become a part of us in the depths of our being. Reflection and rest are essential to our awakening.

---

[8] Steindl-Rast, *A Listening Heart*, 43.

We need this. We long for this. Stephan Bodian notes, "In the end, the only conclusion we can make about the awakened life is that it assumes the form and personality of the person who lives it. You can't imitate it or will it to happen; you can only wake up, live the truth of your awakening and notice how life lives through you."[9]

All of our lives need to embody an evolving awakening in everyday life. It must become part of our shared life together in community. Awakening does not hold back life within us. It is mysterious and uncontrollable. It shatters all the perceptions we might hold onto tightly to out of fear. It can be frightful and unkind to our illusions. But awakening will cultivate the mystical imagination in all of life as we practice reflection and rest. Leonard Sweet writes, "Western Christianity went to sleep in the modern world by the gods of reason and observation. It is awakening to a postmodern world open to revelation and hungry for experience."[10]

When will we awaken to love one another? When will we awaken to humility? When will we awaken to compassion? Catherine Whitmire says, "The opportunity before us in every moment is to choose to live awakened lives."[11]

We cannot make awakening happen within us, but we can create a posture of openness to awakening. We can practice reflection and rest as a way to be hospitable to awakening. Awakening is bound to happen within all of us if we listen deeply. We are created for ongoing awakening as the body of Christ in the parish. We can choose to seek God in our context and live awakened lives. Our reflection and rest hold this before us in the place we inhabit

---

[9] Bodian, *Wake Up Now*, 213-214.

[10] Sweet, *Post-Modern Pilgrims*, 29.

[11] Whitmire, *Plain Living*, 52.

Awakening can bring us great fear because it exposes what we want to hide within. But awakening can also help us to experience connection, contentment, and mystery. Paula D'Arcy writes, "I resist my own awakening. I push hard against that for which I most deeply long. I sense, deep within, that there is more: more to know, more to experience, more reality than my careful definitions of God."[12] Awakening brings unity to the mystical imagination in everyday life. We come to a point of facing ourselves honestly.

God's love, goodness, beauty, grace, and kindness are for our awakening. This movement starts within us as we listen deeply through reflection and rest in everyday life. God is always leading us to awakening in the parish. Everything we go through in life calls out for our awakening. It is important for us to remain open to this all throughout our journey of life. God is constantly showing us more wisdom through the mystical imagination as our everyday lives are opportunities for awakening. Diana Butler Bass states, "... awakening is marked by insistence on connection, networks, relationship, imagination, and story instead of dualism, individualism, autonomy, techniques, and rules."[13]

"Come with me by yourselves to a quiet place and get some rest" (Mark 6:31). We must learn to rest in the midst of life. In our rest comes a deep sense of self-reflection. We come to experience our lives in all their sensuousness as the body of Christ in the parish. And our sensuousness leads us to practice an ongoing, authentic reflection and rest.

Christ is calling us to follow him into interior reflection and rest. If we do not rest, we will not have the strength to live into a way of love for ourselves and others. Nor will we slow down enough to experience our sensuousness as the body of Christ in the parish. If we do not live a reflective life, we will never live authentically in our relational context.

---

[12] D'Arcy, *A New Set of Eyes*, 10.

[13] Bass, *Christianity After Religion*, 237.

The need for reflection and rest is so crucial in our time. We need to find some solitude where both can be practiced, cultivated, and nurtured. Our reflection and rest will bring life to our weary bodies. We will be grounded by the mystical imagination within us. Christ is calling us to follow a way of life into reflection and rest. Through reflection and rest, we begin to hunger and long for awakening. We will live into a posture of seeking awakening in all of life together. Cynthia Bourgeault in her book *Mystical Hope* says:

> From the first century onward there has been a subterranean but distinct vein of Christianity known as the "inner tradition." In contrast to the mainstream, which came to emphasize doctrinal correctness and institutional loyalty, the inner tradition kept its focus squarely on the path of inner awakening taught and modeled by Christ.[14]

We need an awakening to the presence of God. We cannot come into and go out from the presence of God in our world. God is present within us and all around us in the place where we live in our everyday lives. We need this kind of awakening as the body of Christ in our everyday lives together. This awakening could change everything about our lives and the place we inhabit. Reflection and rest will help us to live awakened to the presence of what is real, mysterious, and authentic. Brian D. McLaren says in his book *Naked Spirituality*, "How much higher and wider and deeper and richer our lives become when we awaken to the presence of the real, wild, mysterious, living God, who is bigger than our tame concepts of God."[15]

God cannot be confined by our boundaries or techniques. Our "tame concepts of God" are deconstructed when they are put to the test of embodiment in the parish.

---

[14] Bourgeault, *Mystical Hope*, 91.

[15] McLaren, *Naked Spirituality*, 37.

In my own life, I have been experiencing awakening for quite some time now. It has been a process of change, growth, shaping, and listening. Growing up as a Catholic, I went to a church building almost every Sunday with my parents and siblings. I became an altar boy and rang the bells during the Eucharist at Mass. My first Communion, CCD, and confirmation were all things I completed throughout elementary school, middle school, and high school.

After going to hundreds of Masses growing up, I believed in God from a very young age, although thinking a lot about God was not something I liked to do. I didn't think God was relevant to this life. I thought God was only present to the afterlife.

Toward the end of my high school days, I had a profound awakening. I loved playing basketball. It was what I lived for and took part in for years throughout middle school and high school.

When I was in high school, I played under a tough coach who made me feel like quitting the basketball team. He yelled a lot, and I experienced a lot of fear of making mistakes. I got to the point of hating practices so much that I quit the team for good. This brought me to a place of depression.

It got so bad that I was having a difficult time wanting to finish my senior year of high school. Dropping out crossed my mind more than once. I didn't want others calling me a quitter. Facing this was extremely hard. It seemed I was alone and afraid in a state of withdrawal and depression. It was one of the most difficult experiences of my life up to this point.

Soon I met a youth worker within the Christian Missionary Alliance who was hanging out at my high school. He would tell me that God cares for my life. I would think to myself, "Whatever." We started to spend time together. He seemed to listen to me. The guy was kind of strange to me, but he became a friend. I would listen to him talk about

God's love for me, the kind of stuff that I now can see is very common among church culture.

My excruciating loneliness and pain kept me listening carefully. Becoming even more depressed was something that I didn't want to experience. I didn't want to turn to drugs and alcohol to relieve my pain, so I slowly became open to God. I thought to myself, "I am so messed up I might as well try being open to God. I don't have a lot of options at this point. Where will I be in a year?" I said this out of a deep fear. At the age of 18, I was extremely scared and depressed. Not a place you want to be right before graduating high school. I didn't know what to do.

So I started to trust God in my own way. I started to cry out to God. Knowing pretty much nothing of theology at the time, all I knew was my pain and my need, but that was enough. I had virtually no knowledge of the Protestant church.

As I trusted in God and slowly began to practice reflection and rest, I experienced an awakening within myself. I started to show signs of hope as the depression began receding over the course of the year. Finding some kind of identity in God really helped me to ground myself in a sense of peace in life. My identity as a basketball player had died when I quit the team. This dream was crushed and gone forever which was hard to take. But I wanted to live again, to believe that life was worth living. I had a hope for the future of my life that I hadn't thought was possible before.

I didn't really understand what was happening, but I just wanted to keep seeking God more. I had a conscious awakening over time to becoming more mindful of God in everyday life. This was troubling in a way because what I experienced of church always seemed to have a sense of disconnection and disillusionment for me. I never seemed to fit in. I tried getting involved in Campus Crusade for Christ in college along with the Christian Missionary Alliance and Calvary Chapel denominations. But still things didn't seem to work for me that well.

After college, I went through another stage of depression in 2000. I began exploring the Emergent Church movement when I realized there were all these other North Americans who were disillusioned with their experience of church. Learning about postmodern culture through much reading, conversation, as well as many new relationships in my life, I had an awakening to the context I was living in and being shaped by. I soon had more awakenings to the Missional Church movement, New Monasticism, and the Catholic Worker movement.

And now I am having more awakenings toward what community means as embodied in a particular place in a local context together in everyday life. The words or phrases "parish," "neighborhood," "theology of place," "rebuilding," "authenticity," "practices," "embodiment," "faithful presence," and the concept of being "rooted and linked" have all been a part of my journey to understand the mystical body of Christ in the world today. I am sure more awakenings will happen the longer I live and the more I experience life. I am sure more awakenings will happen as I practice reflection and rest in the parish where I live in community with my neighbors.

Remembering: Recovering Our Individual and Collective Memory

Our reflection and rest help us to remember. We remember one another. We remember our place. We remember the divine mysteries within us and all around us. We remember who we are as the body of Christ in everyday life together. We remember all that we have is not of our own making and is gift. We remember all the wisdom that God has imparted to us. We remember the Scriptures and all that they speak to our lives together. We remember the crucifixion and resurrection of Christ. We remember where we have come from. We remember how we have changed and been shaped over the years. Anthony Bloom says, "We must remember that all we possess is a gift."[16]

---

[16] Bloom, *Beginning to Pray*, 40.

Everything that we embody, think, feel, experience, and embrace is a gift in the place we live. Nothing can escape this gift paradigm. When we forget about the gift of the body of Christ, we will start to become fragmented. We will not remember the importance of our connection to one another, our connection to the ground we walk on, and our connection to the mystical imagination within us.

"Therefore, since the promise of entering his rest still stands, let us be careful that none of you be found to have fallen short of it" (Hebrews 4:1). We need to embody the rest of God. There is a promised rest for the body of Christ. We do not have to give up. We can find strength through reflection and rest. We can find strength through the mystical imagination.

There is perseverance and wisdom in reflection and rest. We fall short of our promised rest when we do not remember who we are together and forget to care for ourselves or one another. Our memory is stifled and lost when we do not practice reflection and rest. Cynthia Bourgeault notes, "One of the greatest losses in our Christian West has been the loss of memory (in fact, almost a collective amnesia) about our own Wisdom heritage."[17]

Our mystical imagination suffers without the practice of reflection and rest, and we forget all that is valuable and beautiful in one another in community. We need space for the mystical imagination to develop through reflection and rest. Kester Brewin writes:

> Our problem today: the space for imagination to expand and take shape is inversely proportional to the speed at which we live. Driven hard and fast, we lack the time to allow alternate worlds and possibilities to form, careening past small turnings and exits, bound to follow the obvious straight paths of the present arrangement. Yet if we stop and wait, and close our eyes to the "buy now, take me now" images, and rest our weary retinas, we will

---

[17] Bourgeault, *The Wisdom Way of Knowing*, 4.

begin to remember, new worlds will form, new exits will become apparent. Only the exercise of memory will allow this possibility.[18]

When we practice reflection and rest, we exercise our memory. We remember who we are as the body of Christ together in the parish. We slow down to reflect on the beauty that is sometimes hard to see if we are not intentionally looking for it. We remember the experiences of beauty, authenticity, and goodness that happen within us. "Alternative worlds" will begin to form in our imaginations. Our possibilities will come alive. We will understand that we are not bound to the status quo. There is another way to follow Christ in the place we inhabit together in everyday life. Our reflection and rest will cultivate an inner revolution of relational care within our locality. We will experience the freedom of being centered and kind to ourselves and our neighbors.

When we lose our sense of remembering who we are in the place we inhabit, we lose our strength. John B. Hayes states, "When we lose our memory, we lose our way."[19] We must practice what will help us to remember the paradoxes and mysteries of our lives, what will lead us to care for ourselves and one another. Our refection and rest will keep us from apathy. Our reflection and rest will show us our salvation together.

We cannot lose our way to sanity and courage in the parish. We cannot lose our way of love and grace, patience and kindness toward ourselves and our neighbors. The mystical imagination refuses to forget what is valuable in our lives together and what will bring us together in everyday life. James K.A. Smith says, "We are called to be a people of memory."[20]

---

[18] Brewin, *Signs of Emergence*, 57.

[19] Hayes, *Sub-Merge*, 236.

[20] Smith, *Desiring the Kingdom*, 159.

Memory is subversive to the status quo. Memory is life-giving to us both individually and collectively as the body of Christ. What is the body without memory? If we do not remember what is important in life, we will be dysfunctional. Memory infuses the mystical imagination. To have a memory of the beautiful is a powerful practice in the parish. Our reflection and rest hold this memory within our souls. We need to remember the divine mysteries all around us and within us.

All of us are called to memory in the place we inhabit together. The memory cultivates the mystical imagination within us. It calls us to be ourselves and to re-imagine. It calls us to love, grace, and humility. The memory is calling for an inner revolution that is decentralized, organic, and subversive by connecting us to authenticity and honesty.

God's rest is our abundance, our strength, and our identity as the body of Christ in everyday life together. Our reflection and rest put us in a posture of vulnerability, honesty, and listening to our local community. Lynne M. Baab writes, "… our rest indicates that we depend completely on the God who created and sustains us."[21] God is the one we remember through each other and the parish.

We are all created in the image of God. How can we not remember God through one another? God lives in the very fabric of our being. We depend completely on our Creator who sustains us when we practice reflection and rest. We can learn to practice something that may be new to us. Ashley Bunting Seeber states, "Remember that life doesn't have to be the way we're used to."[22]

Our Downtown Neighborhood Fellowship has had to practice remembering where we came from. We have practiced remembering the struggles and the hardships we have experienced together over the years. We have practiced remembering our joy and our pain together.

---

[21] Baab, *Sabbath Keeping*, 42.

[22] Seeber, "Just Perspectives," 149.

We have practiced remembering one another in our neighborhood. Our reflection and rest have sustained us and taken us a long way together.

I remember times of practicing a listening to the Scriptures through *lectio divina* (a form of hearing a passage with no commentary) and writing out the ways that Christ was teaching us. I remember recently reading parts of the Sermon on the Mount. We listened to Jesus teach on oaths, turning the other cheek, love for enemies, and giving to the needy among us. This was a time of reflecting and resting on Christ. We remembered his presence within us and around us in our local community.

Someone shared that the Scriptures we were resting in were all for the purpose of our relational connection to one another. We were reminded of the manifestation of love through the body of Christ that we are all called into. We were encouraged to manifest this love in our neighborhood, to our neighbors, and to one another. As we reflected and rested in the teaching of Christ, we were all encouraged to remember and embody the life of Christ within us.

Chapter 11

Pursuing Meaning: Responding to the Questions of Life

Responding to Life: Posturing Ourselves to Attentiveness

The mystical imagination responds to life in our context. The reflective and restful life puts us into a posture of listening and cultivates a responsiveness to life. The body of Christ is called to respond to its locality in loving ways. Ken Gire says, "The reflective life is a life that is attentive, receptive, and responsive to what God is doing in us and around us."[1] We become aware of what God is doing in us and around us through our refection and rest.

We are called to a responsiveness, not a reaction, to life in the parish. To respond is to become attentive and receptive to all the mysteries within us. The mystical imagination always responds to life while avoiding reaction, which is always rooted in anger, bitterness, and hostility. Our reactions break down our spirituality into dysfunctional, unhealthy ways of life. They blind us to love and kill our sense of togetherness in our neighborhood. We become more like separate parts working independently rather than a holistic body. The Scriptures say,

---

[1] Gire, *Seeing What is Sacred*, 4.

"… for anyone who enters God's rest also rests from his own work, just as God did from his. Let us, therefore, make every effort to enter that rest" (Hebrews 4:10-11). This is what Jesus means when he talks about abiding in him. When we abide in Christ we will find rest for our souls. Our practice of reflection and rest will help us to respond to God's rest within us.

We can never react to God's rest. It doesn't work. It buries the mystical imagination within us. We will find great rest from our own work in the parish if we practice a reflective life. A reflective life is healing, peaceful, and attentive. How can we live in our unreflective reactions when there is so much to embrace and respond to, when there is so much rest to be experienced through the mystical imagination? Joyce Rupp writes:

> Our willingness to go within rests on courage to move beyond trepidation, faith to believe in our inner bountifulness, and hope that what we find will be a source of further growth … The best encouragement of all is the actual experience of gaining insight into who we truly are, of discovering a gem of authenticity that liberates and brings peace.[2]

Our reflection and rest shape our identity. We become restful and reflective people in our local community. We need to listen to the ordinary, everyday lives we lead together.

Ordinary life is what we embrace in reflection and rest. This is enough for us. The ordinariness of true restfulness becomes for us a source of divine strength. We respond with great trust that God is shaping us within. The ordinariness of life opens us up to respond in life with wonder, attentiveness, surprise, and gratitude. Ronald Rolheiser notes, "True restfulness, though, is a form of awareness, a way of being in life.

---

[2] Rupp, *Open the Door,* 67-68.

It is living ordinary life with a sense of ease, gratitude, appreciation, peace … We are restful when ordinary life is enough."[3]

To rest in God and embody a peaceful way of life in the ordinariness of it all is a miraculous gift. Our work is to live into our refection and rest and to experience this miraculous gift within us. We will be content with how God is shaping us to be an expression of love in the parish, in the place we live.

Growing up as a Catholic, I always thought that Christianity was about being a good moral person. I had a hard time embracing an attentiveness to God as a lifestyle as part of the body of Christ in a particular place. If I could be good on my own, why did I need the church?

Most of the time I was the model moral kid if ever there was one. Drinking, smoking, and swearing were things I didn't do. Treating others with kindness and respect were things I valued highly. I was very quiet and shy, a nice boy.

One time someone at a movie theatre that I worked at asked me if I was a Christian. I told them that I was, even though I thought being a Christian meant being a moral person. Now this is important in life for sure, but I was not really responding to life out of an attentiveness to or longing for God. It was only because it made sense to me in a kind of self-righteous way.

I was disinterested and apathetic toward things like church or reflection and rest. I was an individualist, but a good moral individualist. Calling the moral shots felt good to me. I took pride in being a good kid.

Sometimes I would try to read the Bible out of a sense of moral obligation to God, not out of any desire for a deeper attentiveness to or longing for God. After experiencing some depression and a loss of

---

[3] Rolheiser, *The Shattered Lantern*, 41.

identity involving the things I was building my life on, I came to realize that Christianity is not about a self-made morality. It is about cultivating and responding to an attentiveness and longing for my Creator. Morality can become a trap if the priority is on being a good, self-righteous person over longing for God through reflection and rest.

Our lack of reflection and rest will effect not just us personally, but will ultimately effect the world around us. Wayne Muller states, "Our lack of rest and reflection is not just a personal affliction. It colors the way we build and sustain community, it dictates the way we respond to suffering, and it shapes the ways in which we seek peace and healing in the world."[4]

We cannot respond to life properly without reflection and rest. They sustain and give meaning to our shared life together in our neighborhood. They help us to seek a peaceful way of life with others who might be "different" from us. Reflection and rest bring healing to the world through us as the body of Christ in the parish as we pursue unity with one another. The mystical imagination is interconnected to our practices of sustainability in the place where we live.

Resting can be a challenge in our noisy, hyper-busy world. Reflecting on Christ, the Scriptures, good literature, and life will challenge the status quo within us. We need to learn how to live a reflective life as the body of Christ in the parish. Marva J. Dawn writes, "Therefore we … need to help each other learn to rest. Ideally, we could covenant together to celebrate our … restful ways—taking gentle walks together, encouraging each other to sleep, helping each other know that the grace of God has set us free from the need to accomplish things."[5]

Resting and reflecting take a lot of work. We have to be open to working out our salvation together in this fashion. Resting and reflecting put us in postures of attentiveness and responsiveness to life in our local community together. Resting is so important in order for

---

[4] Muller, *Sabbath*, 3.

[5] Dawn, *Keeping the Sabbath Wholly*, 71.

our souls to stay centered and focused. Reflection is a discipline that will help us respond to life out of love and grace instead of reflexive reactions.

We need the love and grace that are born out of a reflective way of life to become a part of our everyday lives. They will help us become a gift to ourselves and to our neighbors as we learn from them in our local community. The grasping, grabbing, controlling, and manipulative ways of reacting to life are fragmenting us as the body of Christ in everyday life. This leaves us restless and unreflective, crowding out the mystical imagination within us. There is an essential need for reflection and rest today in our local context. We cannot inhabit the parish together without practicing them. Our manipulative ways need to be reevaluated. Our controlling habits need to be abandoned.

Our bodies, minds, and spirits need seasons of reflection and rest if they are to respond to life holistically. They need to become one with both the mystical imagination and our souls if they are to become one with our true selves. French mystic Jeanne Guyon states, "Now in this state of rest, is your soul active or passive? It is active! You are not in a passive state, even if you are resting."[6]

We need to live the reflective life of wisdom as the body of Christ in everyday life. We need to follow the reflective way of Christ in our local community. The restful and reflective path is the way of attentiveness and a way of life in the parish.

Living Into Questions: Unraveling Everything

Certainty leaves no room for reflection or rest. We need to lose our certainty about everything we think we know, and live into our questions. Certainty says it is okay to stop seeking God because we already have all the answers. Certainty will not experiment or learn anything new. It stops at propositional theology. It will not explore a

---

[6] Guyon, *Experiencing the Depths of Jesus Christ*, 111.

theology or spirituality of place. Certainty pushes away the local community and embraces our intellect only at the expense of our bodies. Peter Rollins says in his book *Insurrection*, "... in Christianity when one is crushed by a deep, existential loss of certainty, one finds oneself in Christ."[7]

Let us stop pretending that we understand everything about one another, life, and God. There are too many mysteries to live in certainty. Through uncertainty, questions, and a process of discovery, we come to know in more holistic ways. We come to understand that it is in our questions that we most effectively seek God. This is where we find an integration of the divine life within us.

Christ is the opener of a world of possibilities as we embody living into questions in our local community. Christ poses contextual questions to us as we are called to follow him into a posture of listening and learning. Our parish is too complex for us to pretend that we know everything about its context. Living into our questions will over time give us greater clarity and wisdom. It takes a decade just to start to understand how to become an expression of love together in a place.

"Come to me, all you who are weary and burdened, and I will give you rest" (Matthew 11:28). Christ wants us to come to a conscious awareness of his presence. We need to come into a Christ-consciousness in the place we inhabit. Our union with Christ becomes alive through reflection and rest. It is embodied in our questions. Our questions will speak of this union with Christ in our context. Our reflection and rest will cause us to unravel as we live into our questions. Spiritual director Kathy Escobar notes in her wonderful book *Faith Shift:*

> During Unraveling, all we once held dear is stripped away and the things that have held us together come undone. Here we deconstruct deeply held beliefs, practices, and ways of intersecting

---

[7] Rollins, *Insurrection*, 24.

with God, others, and even ourselves. For many, it can be painful, terrifying, and unpredictable. Others find it liberating and even exhilarating to be finally free of their former trappings. It is where our faith really comes undone—and from where it can eventually be rebuilt.[8]

Christ is calling us to listen and learn from our reflection and rest. Christ will give us rest deep within our souls if we are open to it. Christ will heal our restless and unreflective lives if we take on a posture of openness to our questions. It is revolutionary and innovative to live inside of questions that cause us to completely unravel, creating new life from within.

We must not fear our questions. Our questions could open up new possibilities for an authentic way of life in the place we inhabit and help shape us from within as the body of Christ in everyday life together. "There's an art to living your questions," writes Sue Monk Kidd. "You peel them. You listen to them spawn new questions. You hold the unknowing inside."[9]

Answers oftentimes keep us from sharing life together. It is our questions that bring us together as the body of Christ. Our reflection and rest cultivate our questions. We embody our questions together as a way of life in our local community. Answers destroy our trust in the divine mysteries within and around us. Answers ignore a listening posture in the parish. Answers tend to dismiss others in our relational context. We don't need questions when we have the answers. We don't need one another when we have answers. We don't need reflection and rest when we have answers. Answers are misleading. Answers are a lot of times an illusion. We think we know a lot with answers, but maybe we don't know as much as we think we do. Richard Rohr says:

[8] Escobar, *Faith Shift*, 65.

[9] Kidd, *When the Heart Waits*, 159.

> Answers make trust unnecessary, they make listening dispensable, they make relations with others superfluous. Having my answers, I don't need you in order to take my journey. I need only my head, my certainties, and my conclusions. It's all private. But Jesus said we have to live in this world so as to be dependent on one another.[10]

Our questions promote unity with one another. Our questions show us our need for a local community to inhabit together. Our questions help us to see more clearly. We have become so addicted to answers that we have almost completely stopped asking questions. But reflection and rest embrace our questions and call us to live into them in the place we share life together.

There is no mystery to answers. But questions abound with mystery. Christ's gospel is the mystery of the good news in our relational context. We can spend our entire lives on questions such as, "What is this good news?" Questions are the beginning of a process of discovery, a covenant epistemology in the parish. There is no paradox with easy answers. Questions embody paradox. Answers seek to control. Questions embrace listening. We need to embody our questions. Our questions should be never-ending. Rachel Held Evans writes in her book *Evolving in Monkey Town*, "And yet slowly I'm learning to love the questions ... My hope is that if I am patient, the questions themselves will dissolve into meaning, the answers won't matter so much anymore, and perhaps it will all make sense to me on some distant, ordinary day."[11]

Answers are the enemy of questions. They estrange us from God and disconnect us from our true self. They will eventually betray our confidence. The mystery of God will not be boxed up into all the "right" answers. The mystery of God will not fit into our neat boxes of control

---

[10] Rohr, *Simplicity*, 162.

[11] Evans, *Evolving in Monkey Town*, 225.

and propositional statements. Our questions do not need boxes for God to live in. Our questions do not need clichés to help us self-protect.

Without mystery, paradox, and questions, there is no authenticity. Everything becomes clichéd and meaningless even if we are supposedly using all the right words through our arrogant answers to life. The mystical imagination will have none of this. It is time we started to live into our questions.

Wisdom comes through us living into our questions, transforming our entire lives. Our reflection and rest reveal to us how uncertain we are about so many things. This uncertainty is not a bad thing, because it pushes us to listen. Our questions become essential to our embodied practice. Calenthia Dowdy states, "It is our calling ... to embrace an ongoing journey of transformation."[12] Our everyday lives need an authentic wisdom that comes through reflection and rest. The mystical imagination needs to embody our questions in everyday life.

Questions are much more important than the security of our answers. We do not need answers to be alive, but we do need our questions if we are to follow an authentic path in the place we inhabit together. Our questions are powerful and bring us inner sustainability. We tend to think that answers will bring us the sustainability and wisdom we need, but this is not true. Our answers cannot be contextualized, but our questions can in the place we share life together with others. Living into our questions is the beginning of all relational wisdom.

Our Downtown Neighborhood Fellowship has asked many questions over the years. We like the question: "What is the good news?" When we first started to live into this question through reflection and rest, we had to deconstruct a lot of propositional theology. We had no idea what this meant to us. We struggled with it for many years. If we couldn't get along with one another, then how could we embody good news in our neighborhood? Our reflection and rest led us to some

---

[12] Dowdy, "Race and Community," 212.

uncomfortable places within ourselves. And over time even more questions surfaced as a result of this one question.

Here are some of the other questions that emerged: What does the good news mean when we feel our pain? when we want to move away from close proximity? when we are frustrated and angry? when we see so many living in poverty? What does the good news mean in the midst of injustice and the way we treat each other? in our communion with God? in our local economy? in our artistic expression? in our local politics? in our life together in everyday life? in the way we celebrate together? in our use of resources? in the way we use our time? in what we value in life? What does the good news mean when it comes to our possessions?

Our Downtown Neighborhood Fellowship has not come to any conclusions on these multifaceted questions, but we are in a process of listening and discovery through them. We believe our questions are being prompted by the Holy Spirit in our local context of everyday life together. We believe there is a lot of mystery to our questions that will take decades to live into. We do not impose clichés and easy answers on anyone, but instead we seek to listen to God in our uncertainty. This is the posture that God has called us into. We want to live into our questions together and not pretend we have all the answers.

Can we survive losing all our answers in everyday life together? Can we survive losing control? Can we survive losing our institutional Christianity? Can we survive losing our power and our identity? Can our faith be made new? Can we remain lost and still be okay? Can we search for questions and not answers? Can we see doubt and questioning as divine leadings of the Spirit? Can we own our faith together in the midst of uncertainty? My Australian friend Michael Frost states:

> Lostness, questioning, doubting—this is the stuff of a search for real faith, a faith that we can own, rather than have dumped on us by others. And like the bone that breaks and heals stronger at the

broken place, it is a stronger faith than it was before because it has learned it can survive the loss of faith. Faith that can survive the loss of faith![13]

We need to be seeking God in the place we inhabit together through our questions and through our reflection and rest. This is the path to sanity. Our questions are a big part of seeking God and an authenticity within us. Our questions embrace the mystical imagination. We will risk everything to find the questions which we need to embody in the parish. The questions are our healing and our rest. They make the mysteries of God come alive to us in our local context.

Doing Nothing: The Paradox of Spirituality

We cultivate our spirituality when we do nothing through our reflection and rest. Doing nothing can help us to embrace the mystical imagination while detaching us from the cultural patterns of escapism. Doing nothing creates a revolution within us. It is dangerous and needs to be practiced with a lot of courage. Doing nothing is both powerful and subversive.

Our reflection and rest teach us to embrace a different narrative that values reflection and rest. We embrace a narrative of listening to the world we live in, the relational context in which we find ourselves. We embrace a narrative of love and grace. Doing nothing actually becomes our greatest source of strength. This is a paradox in our spirituality. Most of us can only handle doing nothing for so long. William Shannon says, "In the production-orientated culture we live in, we are not good at doing nothing. Just being seems difficult precisely because instinctively we feel that we ought to be usefully involved with something or other."[14] Doing nothing cultivates the mystical imagination within us in the parish.

[13] Frost, *Seeing God in the Ordinary*, 159-160.

[14] Shannon, *Seeking the Face of God*, 128-129.

We are not very good at just being, at just resting and reflecting. Our consumer society always pushes us to do something and refuses to just let us be content with doing nothing. Beatrice Bruteau states, "We can't bear simply to be still and do nothing."[15]

Doing nothing manifests itself in local acts of attentiveness and awareness. One of the best of these manifestations is being faithfully present. That may not seem like anything much, but it is a divine act of love and grace. It is useful to our spirituality. Richard Mahler states:

> In modern Western industrialized countries, we now enjoy such a general surfeit of money, comforts, and amusements that deliberately stopping to "do nothing" or "look inward" seems unthinkable, even ludicrous. If we "do nothing," we reject all the things we could be doing. The implication is that we are shunning what others have worked so hard to provide, insulting our fellow humans in the process. We are choosing bread and water over the delectable feast laid before us.[16]

Doing nothing takes practice and discipline. The mystical imagination embraces the embodiment of doing nothing. It is hard to lay down our colonial ways as the body of Christ in the parish. We need to stop doing things and learn to "look inward."

Our practice of reflection and rest will slow us down so we can be faithfully present to all of life in the place we inhabit. Doing nothing will shape us to love one another. Our reflection and rest will lead us to look within and discover a deeper life of mystery and paradox. We can be content with doing nothing. Our presence and our love are enough in our relational context.

"Be still and know that I am God" (Psalm 46:10). It is so hard in a world that values achievement to be still that most of us soon give up.

---

[15] Bruteau, *Radical Optimism*, 16.

[16] Mahler, *Stillness*, 61.

Most of us think being is not enough, but it is. Our being shapes us as the body of Christ in the parish.

Our reflection and rest move us to stillness within. We are doing something profound when we do nothing and rest in our inner stillness. Our stillness could shape the body of Christ to become a holistic counterculture in our local community. The mystical imagination needs this stillness within ourselves to help us to re-imagine life.

God is in the stillness and the silence and the rest. To be is to allow God to live within us freely and subversively, to allow God's wisdom to come alive in our embodiment of love. To do nothing is to do everything within us that cultivates life. To do nothing is to hold the mystical imagination within ourselves freely and openly. We allow ourselves to be shaped by God through our relational context in the parish.

Doing nothing leaves us with being. Being is uncomfortable in a noisy world of colonialism, domination, and activity. Being is the core of the mystical imagination. It is discovered through refection and rest. Being is where we listen to life together as the body of Christ in the place where we live. Jane E. Vennard says, "The spaciousness of pure being terrifies us."[17] And yet our souls need this reflection and rest, this stillness within in order for the mystical imagination to come alive.

Being will shake us out of our ego agendas. Being will transform us if we live by the Spirit of Christ. Doing nothing leaves us in a posture of vulnerability. Doing nothing puts us in touch with our souls and saves us from the meaningless of accomplishment. Doing nothing speaks to our purpose to be a faithful presence as the body of Christ in everyday life in the parish.

Doing nothing makes room for a listening spirit. It holds us in the practice of reflection and rest. "The more I'm able to enjoy rest, the

---

[17] Vennard, *Praying With Body and Soul*, 21.

more others will see God's life in me," states Bonnie Gray. "When my soul is at rest, I am free to please God right where I am."[18]

We need to rediscover doing nothing and resting in our being. It is essential to our sustainability and life together. If we value accomplishment above doing nothing, we will become colonial and our medium will communicate anything but love. Accomplishment has value only if it is grounded in refection and rest. We cannot do something without first doing nothing. Wayne Muller notes:

> We have lost this essential rhythm. Our culture invariably supposes that action and accomplishment are better than rest, that doing something—anything—is better than doing nothing. Because of our desire to succeed, to meet these ever-growing expectations, we do not rest. Because we do not rest, we lose our way. We miss the compass points that would show us where to go, we bypass the nourishment that would give us succor. We miss the quiet that would give us wisdom. We miss the joy and love born of effortless delight. Poisoned by this hypnotic belief that good things come only through unceasing determination and tireless effort, we can never truly rest. And for want of rest, our lives are in danger.[19]

When we do not live a reflective and restful life, we will live in the danger of neglecting our being. And it is this danger that is pulling us apart as the body of Christ in everyday life in the parish.

Our Downtown Neighborhood Fellowship has been criticized at times for our lack of interest in programs and projects. Although we do participate in them at times, we have instead tried to cultivate a culture of refection and rest in the everyday, ordinariness of life together. We do not want to accomplish anything. We simply want to live our everyday lives together rooted in the place where we live. All we want is to be more connected to and integrated into our neighborhood of Downtown Tacoma. We are good at doing nothing. It doesn't make

---

[18] Gray, *Finding Spiritual Whitespace*, 230.

[19] Muller, *Sabbath*, 1.

sense to some, but we just want to be faithfully present in our local community.

Others say to me, "What does your fellowship do?" I simply say, "Nothing." We listen. We love. We live relationally. These are the values that are important to us. We do not punch time cards and go in and out of our neighborhood. Our whole lives are centered in the neighborhood. We have stepped into the proximity of everyday life together. We live, play, and work within the relational context of our neighborhood. We live and sleep there. We are present to that more than we are to any program, service, or project.

When we do nothing, we allow life to speak to us through reflection and rest, we listen deeply in the parish, and we embrace the mystical imagination within us. We learn from others more than they learn from us. We are more interested in being engaged in life, taking ownership in life, and listening to life in the place we inhabit, than in controlling it. Kathryn J. Hermes writes, "Doing nothing is the art of letting life reveal itself to you rather than scheduling life's events."[20]

We need to practice "the art of letting life reveal itself" to us as we listen. It has everything to do with the mystical imagination within us. When we do nothing and allow life to reveal itself to us as the body of Christ in the parish, we will be satisfied with just being. That will be enough for us.

---

[20] Hermes, *Beginning Contemplative Prayer*, 21.

Chapter 12

The Core of Our Humanity: Nurturing a Christ-Consciousness

Examining the Shape of Our Lives: Truthfulness, Honesty, and Consciousness

Our practice of reflection and rest help us to examine the shape of our lives together. We are constantly tested by our local community to see if what we believe about the gospel is being embodied in our everyday lives together. Examining the shape of our lives together requires honesty and truthfulness. It's hard. It's like looking in the mirror, a reality check that will either affirm us or convict us of the need for greater authenticity. Reflection and rest cannot escape this examining of our lives together in the parish. There is a freedom in this kind of self-examination as we develop together an inner reflective spirit. Leighton Ford writes:

> The rest God offers is the freedom to be fully present in the moment, free to reflect and enjoy what has been; to let go of the deficits and regrets that wear us down; free to envision what will be, what we are being re-created for; free to unburden ourselves of

regretful thoughts about our yesterdays and anxious thoughts about our tomorrows.[1]

Our freedom is embodied in the ways we learn from our past as we re-imagine the present and unburden ourselves from the future. We constantly re-imagine the present, what God has for us now and the days to come. Through the mystical imagination in reflection and rest, we will free ourselves to work through our anxieties and regrets. Our yesterdays and our tomorrows can bring out the life of Christ within us in our local community.

Examining the shape of our lives together can be one of our greatest hopes as the body of Christ in the parish. We must look into the mirror and stare into our own eyes to find what is authentically there. Our regrets, deficits, and anxieties will not weigh us down as much as we practice examining the shape of our lives together. In the process, we will create a new sense of Christ-consciousness within us. We will find the enjoyment of sharing life together through our everyday experiences more powerful than any other emotional state. Becky Garrison asks the question, "Can I really not worry about my life and put all my trust in God?"[2]

"Do not be anxious about anything" (Philippians 4:6). In the examining of our lives together, we do not need to fear that anxiety could destroy our present experience together in the parish. God will lead us into the path of honesty if we will have some openness to one another through the process. Learning to trust God and one another is difficult in everyday life, but is an authentic possibility. Our reflection and rest will help us to create some boundaries that will protect us and over time heal us from the anxiety we wrestle with. Kathleen Finley notes,

---

[1] Ford, *The Attentive Life*, 178.

[2] Garrison, *Jesus Died for This?*, 21.

"Listening to, and reflecting on, our lives is a natural part of resting in God's love."[3]

Examining the shape of our lives together will uncover and cultivate the mystical imagination within each of us in our own unique way. It will bring us to a place of embracing with courage our tomorrows and yesterdays. Our anxiety will blind us if we allow it to control us because it cultivates division and fragmentation, not community and collaboration.

We are all called into the courage of following Christ where we live. Anxiety lacks this courage and cannot understand it. And isn't our spirituality about courage and love more than anything else? Any practice that does not lead us there is a fruitless waste of time. That is why we need to practice reflection and rest as the body of Christ in everyday life. This will take all the courage and love we possess within.

Examining the shape of our lives together guides us to question our attitudes and motives. We have to ask, "Is this action motivated by love for our neighbor?" Many times when we practice refection and rest, we will come to see that our attitudes, motives, and behavior are not founded on love but on something less. Our reflection and rest keep us from losing the power of our imagination. Mark Scandrette says, "We reimagine our lives by allowing the Creator to examine our thoughts, attitudes, motives, and behavior."[4]

When we allow God to examine our lives within, we become alive. We make it our priority to re-imagine everything about how we embody love for our neighbors. Reflection and rest will not let us leave this place of re-imagining life until it has redefined our love. Examining the shape of our lives together embraces and cultivates the mystical imagination within.

---

[3] Finley, *Savoring God,* 90.

[4] Scandrette, *Soul Graffiti,* 222.

Practicing reflection and rest is easiest and most natural for me when I lie down on the floor, on a couch, or on my bed. I like the act of laying down my body somewhere and resting my head on something soft like a pillow or a cushion. Lying on my back or side indicates vulnerability and receptivity. If I am laying on my back on the floor, I usually have my legs bent. I like lying down because it symbolizes the rest that God is calling me into as I examine the shape of my life. I look at the highs and lows, where I am tired and where I am energized, where I am joyful and where I am sad, where I am struggling and where I am thriving. Consenting to the action and presence of God's life within me is what I seek as I listen deeply.

Sometimes I imagine that Christ is the pillow or cushion beneath my head. I imagine Christ holding me as I rest my head upon him. Sometimes I imagine a powerful wind like a tornado that is trying to sweep me away from Christ. All I have keeping me from being blown away are my hands gripping Christ tightly. I imagine Christ holding me with all of his strength. We hold each other through the storm blowing all around us. This is what I imagine the practice of reflection and rest is like. It is how we keep from getting blown away from one another by remaining open to rest in the unexpected gifts of life that we discover through the storm.

We all sleep. We all lay our bodies down to rest. For me, this is a powerful practice because it is common to us all. We just have to put some imagination to our resting.

We are missing out on the opportunity to live fully if we do not practice examining our lives together through reflection and rest. God is calling us to a life that is free from the trap of anxiety. Esther De Waal in her book *Lost in Wonder* notes, "Whatever it may be, in any particular situation there is the danger that we are wasting the God-given possibility of living life to the full. I long for fullness of life and it is frightening to think that I might be wasting that most precious of God's gifts, the chance to live fully and freely."[5]

Our everyday lives need to be examined through reflection and rest as the body of Christ in the parish. The "God-given possibility" of reflection and rest is within us. It needs to be practiced and embodied in the place we inhabit together.

Reflection and rest enlighten us from within, and give us the ability to re-imagine our everyday lives. New Monastic activist Shane Claiborne writes, "I think that's a good sign—the ability to change and rethink things."[6] We need to be always evolving our human consciousness through the examining of our lives together.

"Let us examine our ways and test them" (Lamentations 3:40). We need to examine constantly our lives together as the body of Christ in the parish. If we practice examining our lives through reflection and rest, we could build some social capital and do away with the "weird, individualistic ways" of being the church that are so common. We must be tested by our local community to see if we are just talk with no love for our neighbors. Henri J. M. Nouwen says:

> It is remarkable how much of our life is lived without reflection on its meaning. It is not surprising that so many people are busy but bored! They have many things to do and are always running to get them done, but beneath the hectic activity they often wonder if anything is truly happening. A life that is not reflected upon eventually loses its meaning and becomes boring.[7]

Reflection and rest are not always easy within us. Some days they come easier than other days. Most of the time they are very intentional and difficult. We become more natural at them over time, but we must

[5] De Waal, *Lost in Wonder*, 3.

[6] Claiborne, *Follow Me to Freedom*, 209.

[7] Nouwen, *Here and Now*, 73.

always start as a beginner no matter how old we are or how many years of intentionality we have lived. Diane J. Chandler asks, "Can we establish healthy rhythms of rest ... to provide life balance?"[8] I think we can with much practice and experimentation. We are not used to the balance of examining the shape of our lives through a resting posture while remaining active and engaged in our world.

Reflection and rest prepare us to practice our spirituality together as life goes on over many years of pain, sorrow, sadness, celebration, and joy. We will not be worn out when we practice examining our lives through a resting posture. We will be inspired instead to live within the mystical imagination as the body of Christ in the parish. This is our expression of honesty and truthfulness toward God, one another, and the world we live in.

Becoming Human: Reconciling Ourselves to an Expression of Love

We have sometimes forgotten what it means to be human. We have had a loss of memory toward the ways of compassion, humility, grace, vulnerability, and gentleness that Jesus taught us. Our humanity has escaped us oftentimes. It has been disconnected from our everyday lives together. We need to reconcile our humanity within ourselves as an expression of love in the world. Our humanity has been buried under the illusion of the false self. The body of Christ needs to rediscover its humanity in the parish.

Our humanity is created in the image of God. Why do we focus so much on sin and not on the possibilities of God's life within us? We have made sin too strong of an emphasis at the neglect of our Christ-consciousness. Do we believe that Christ lives within us? Do we believe this in practice or is it just a propositional statement of theology? Our reflection and rest help us to become human again in our lives together.

---

[8] Chandler, *Christian Spiritual Formation*, 208.

Our humanity is beautiful, our greatest asset, and is extremely sacred. It is not to be taken for granted. Reflection and rest give us the chance to feel our humanity and live in it with all its multifaceted dimensions. We experience everything we know in life through our humanity. Nothing escapes our humanity if we are living authentically. It is the filter of discernment. It is intertwined with the place where we live our everyday lives.

We are our humanity. It is the basis for the true self, incarnational embodiment, and authenticity. The body of Christ is manifested through our humanity in the parish. It is the medium of our giving and receiving love. Love can only be experienced through our humanity in everyday life together. When we are disconnected from love, we are disconnected from our humanity. Reflection and rest help us to rediscover the dignity of our humanity within us.

Reflection and rest put us on the path of working out our salvation together as the body of Christ in everyday life. As we do so, we are in the process of becoming more deeply human. Becoming human is a practice of presence and embodiment. Becoming fully human puts us on a path of listening and allows us to live in peace with our neighbors. We become the kind of people who manifest the peaceful ways of the indwelling Christ. We become inseparably one with God and with one another.

Solidarity with others is a big part of manifesting love in our local community. This is what it means to become fully alive and deeply human. Ilia Delio writes, "To be human is to be on the way to salvation, that is to be brought into relationships of wholeness and healing in union with God."[9] When we become human through reflection and rest, we develop relationships of "wholeness and healing." Reconciliation with others becomes a huge theme in our purpose and existence as the body of Christ in everyday life together. We experience the mystery of our salvation through constantly being reconciled with

---

[9] Delio, *Franciscan Prayer*, 22.

others in the place where we live. We lay down our prejudices, our biases, our opinions, our perceptions, and our arrogance in order to really see someone else in our common humanity.

Jesus lived in his humanity in the place he inhabited. He had to learn how to become human. His incarnation manifested all that is good, beautiful, loving, compassionate, empathetic, kind, and authentic in humanity. We too are called to manifest this way of humanity. We are called to be deeply human as the body of Christ in everyday life in the parish. Christ is calling us to become human just as he was as we live in our context in the twenty-first century world.

To live compassionately is to become human. To live as an expression of love is to become human. To work out our salvation together is to become human. To live in the freedom of the Spirit of reconciliation and grace toward others is to become human. Our reflection and rest help us to become human. The mystical imagination is calling us to become human by showing us that our humanity is beautiful. We need to honor and cultivate this beauty within us at all times. It is a subversive practice to become an expression of love, grace, and humility as we live restful lives. Brene Brown states, "Making the choice to rest … is, at best, counterculture."[10]

"In rest is your salvation, in quietness and trust is your strength" (Isaiah 30:15). Our salvation is intertwined with our refection and rest in community. Our salvation is our strength, rooted and experienced in the place we inhabit. Our salvation cries out from the earth. The earth blossoms our salvation. Our lives experience our salvation in everyday life together as the body of Christ in the parish. Our salvation is intertwined with our humanity. When we are deeply human, we will become an expression of love and compassion together. We cannot become human without a love for the particular place on earth that God has placed us. We cannot become human if we abandon our

---

[10] Brown, *The Gifts of Imperfection*, 102.

neighbors. Salvation cannot be separated from the love of our neighbors and engagement in the world any longer.

The earth that we live on is the place where we become human through reflection and rest. The earth cannot be destroyed by us any longer. We must honor the beauty of the earth, our humanity, and our local community. We must honor the beauty of the world through acts of love, compassion, kindness, empathy, and deep listening in our humanity. We trust God and one another through our reflection and rest in the parish. Our strength will be discovered in our relational connection to one another and God in the place we inhabit.

Our spirituality cannot be holistic until it becomes fully human through our love. Our spirituality needs to be lived through reflection and rest. It needs to be embodied in our humanity. David G. Benner writes, "For only a lived, holistic spirituality can be transformational, integrative, and capable of helping us become fully alive and deeply human."[11] Without our humanity, we cannot be the body of Christ together in everyday life. There would be no possibility of life, no humility or compassion, and no relational connection in our local community. Without our humanity, there is no faithful presence.

Without our humanity, we have pretty much nothing but our greed, prejudices, biases, perceptions, violence, arrogance, hatred, and divisions. We are shells of individualistic illusions. We bring colonialism and destruction to the land. We need our humanity more than we realize. We are pretty much narcissistic without our humanity. We need to practice reflection and rest to become human as we cultivate the mystical imagination in the parish.

In reflection and rest, we experience the mystery of the gospel within ourselves. We experience an everyday conversion as we change the world through allowing this change to happen in us. The gospel is for us more than it is for others because we live it out without words to

---

[11] Benner, *Soulful Spirituality*, 21.

define it. We need to experience the good news in us, in our local community, to become human. We need to constantly convert ourselves to a relational way of life in the place we inhabit together. My friend Tony Kriz says, "… the gospel has something to say about every aspect of existence and particularly every part of the human experience."[12]

Our humanity is about all of human existence. All dualities become irrelevant when we live in our humanity. Dualities cannot exist when we become human. Our experience of life needs to be holistic as the body of Christ in the parish. The mystical imagination embraces a holistic spirituality in the place we inhabit. The mystery of the gospel is intertwined with our practice of reflection and rest. God is always speaking to us in mysterious ways in everyday life through our relational context.

Our Downtown Neighborhood Fellowship partakes in a practice of remembering Christ's death and resurrection through bread and wine that has helped us to become human together. The practice of remembering the suffering and love he embodied his entire life helps us to see the possibility of following Christ in our local context in the world. This is a formative practice that has helped us become human through our reflection and rest.

We take the bread and say, "This is the body of Christ broken for you," as we pass the bread around. This helps us to focus on the humanity of Christ's embodied life. We remember how human he was and how divine he was. We remember him calling us into our humanity. We reflect and rest on his life within us. We reflect and rest on his life within the place we inhabit together in everyday life.

We all fill up our glasses with wine and drink together as a remembrance of Christ's blood that was shed for the flourishing of our humanity throughout the world. We remember how this practice of

---

[12] Kriz, *Welcome to the Table*, 111.

reflection and rest has been practiced throughout the world. We embrace the contextualization of our experience to the historical reality of the experiences of others throughout time. We embrace an ancient-future faith as the body of Christ in the midst of our postmodern culture of Downtown Tacoma. Our neighborhood becomes a place of communion for us in our everyday lives together.

Our practice of reflection and rest has helped us to become human in Downtown Tacoma. Without it, I believe we would soon have lost our desire for the common good of our neighbors and become individualistic consumers who have abandoned our humanity in the process. I am always moved by the simple practice of partaking the bread and wine together with my friends as a symbol of our love for the place we inhabit, the struggles we endure, and the celebration we experience in everyday life.

As a result, I experience a greater solidarity with the body of Christ. Reflection and rest are leading me to becoming human again. I am content to live in the freedom of my humanity. I am free to be myself. Running, jumping, screaming within myself, and dancing in the place where I live are things I like to do without shame. Being free to love makes me happy. The pressures of conformity to the system are falling away. Reflection and rest are the subversive elements in all of this as I partake in the bread and wine with my friends.

It takes a lot of courage to embrace our humanity in twenty-first century America. But we need to practice an intentional courage if we are to survive. All the talk of "liberty and justice for all," when this is clearly not the case, leaves us yearning for an authentic way of life where freedom for all is found within. Peter Rollins states, "… we must be courageous enough to fully and unreservedly embrace our humanity."[13]

---

[13] Rollins, *Insurrection,* 112.

The mystical imagination lives into a liberty and justice for all. Our humanity needs to be embodied in the parish. Our practice of reflection and rest give us the courage to live in our local community with an intentional courage. Courage is intertwined within the mystical imagination. It will take all our humanity to follow Christ in America because the popular culture shuns reflection and rest as a waste of time. It does not make sense to rest when we should all be working to the point of exhaustion.

We all think we are human. But we have truly lost the meaning of our humanity and our sanity. We have become an individualistic, violent people who have little time for reflection and rest. This is how we interact with each other in life. We have become colonial. We have become exploiters of the land. We have become murderers thanks to our subtle hatred and divisions all in the name of God. We have taken the love out of Christianity. We have cultivated a Christianity with no interior life of reflection and rest.

Our courage could help us in the process of becoming human in the place we find ourselves in. We can follow and be like Christ in our humanity. To be like Christ is to become human. To be like Christ is to embody courage. To be like Christ is to practice reflection and rest in our humanity. To be like Christ is to be vulnerable and find our strength in our weakness. To be like Christ is to be present to our local community, to live in it, and to love it. Christ was alive in his local community, and we should be too. Marva J. Dawn says, "God has more need of our weakness than our strength ... By our union with Christ in the power of the Spirit in our weaknesses, we display God's glory."[14]

Loving our neighbors in the parish is why we practice refection and rest. This is how we become human and how we love God in the place we inhabit together. There is no way around this. We are called to be an expression of love. Our reflection and rest is only authentic if we love our neighbors in everyday life together. God is constantly working

---

[14] Dawn, *Powers, Weakness, and the Tabernacling of God*, 47.

within us and among the neighbors all around us. Our humanity becomes sensitive to this mystery. Our reflection and rest help us to re-imagine it. We embrace and experience God through the diverse faces of our neighbors. Ken Gire in his book *Seeing What is Sacred* writes,

> To better love God and other people is the goal of the reflective life. But before we can love them, we must see them. And we must see them not as we would like to see them or as they would like to be seen. We must see them as they are. Otherwise we don't love the person. We love the image we perceive the person to be. f we are to love people as they are, we must see them as they are. Which means seeing all that lies hidden within them.[15]

Seeing our neighbors rather than exploiting them isn't easy. We have to unlearn so much. To see our neighbors is to become human in the process. We must see them with the eyes of love. To see God through their faces is important to becoming human. This is crucial to being an expression of love in the place we inhabit. Seeing God in the beauty of our neighbors is a new paradigm we all need to explore. Through our practice of reflection and rest, we can learn to see our neighbors differently. We must become human and see our neighbors as the mystical imagination sees them. As we become human, may we never close our eyes to our neighbors.

---

[15] Gire, *Seeing What is Sacred*, 142.

The Core of Our Humanity

Study Guide Questions

The Mystical Imagination: Seeing the Sacredness of All of Life

Chapter 1 - Developing Rhythms of Discipline: Continually Seeking God as a Way of Life

1. How can we seek God more intentionally in our lives and not leave this up to chance?
2. Have you ever longed for God to lead you to embody an undistracted way of life? In what ways?
3. What can help us to develop a deep, sustained focus in everyday life together?
4. How do you respond to the word "discipline"? Is it frightening? Or do you embrace it with possibility?
5. What is one specific and concrete thing that you need to choose to do for you to live with more discipline in your life?
6. How can we create rhythms that cultivate an awareness of God's presence in the place where we live?
7. What do you think about listening? Have you explored listening in your context?
8. Have you ever explored a healthy discipline in your spirituality?
9. How can we live with a sense of balance given the pace of our lives?
10. How can we find some sense of freedom from the dominant narratives of the mainstream culture?

11. How can we re-imagine a personal practice of radical obedience as a lifestyle of worship?

12. Do we have the potential to reflect the image of God within ourselves in the world? How have you experienced this in your own life?

13. How have we divorced worship from everyday life?

14. Do you believe you are more than just a "sinner" and created in the image of God to become a beautiful expression of love in the world? What is stirring in your imagination around this?

15. How are you being invited into collaboration and partnership with God in the place where you live?

Chapter 2 – The Embodiment of Mystery: Embracing the Wisdom of Seeing

1. Do you agree that the primary phenomenon of human persons is the lived body? Why or why not?

2. How is the body sacred, unique, beautiful, mystical, powerful, intuitive, intelligent, and the holder of all imagination?

3. How have we become a displaced, disembodied, dislocated society that has rejected the potential and limitations of the body?

4. What are some of the things you have done to practice living in your body?

5. How is the body a great reservoir of wisdom?

6. How have you dismissed the mystical nature of Christianity and settled for abstract ideas about God? How have you become aware of the wonder and preciousness of the ordinary, everyday experiences of life?

7. Do you believe God can be figured out? How can we live into God as a mystery to participate in?

8. How is the life of the mystical imagination both inward and outward? How can we experiment with the mystery of this paradox?

9. How does mystery invite you into wonder in everyday life?

10. How do we move closer to becoming a community of persons committed to place, growth, understanding, wisdom, and discipline?

11. How have you experienced discipleship and discipline as interconnected in life?

12. How can we see more clearly through the cultural narrative that says when things get difficult, just move on? Do we realize that we take ourselves wherever we go?
13. Do you think discipline is the natural structure of the human soul? What have you ever accomplished without some sense of discipline in life?
14. How have you experienced discipline as liberation?
15. Have you ever longed for eyes to see yourself, others, and God more clearly? In what ways?

Chapter 3 – Creative Insecurity: Learning to Live Life

1. How can we seek God by becoming lifelong learners in everyday life?
2. How can we dedicate more time to the discipline of reading?
3. Can you come up with some traits that describe lifelong learners?
4. Have you ever thought of books as your friends that accompany you in life?
5. How can we remain open to discovery throughout our lives learning from different perspectives?
6. In what ways have you experienced creativity, risk, freedom, and courage in everyday life with others?
7. How is being insecure our greatest freedom as we live by faith? How is this possible? Is it a contradiction or a paradox to embrace?
8. How is security bought at the cost of freedom?
9. Does freedom represent to you a responsibility to place, or is this anything but freedom in your experience?
10. How is the denial of freedom a denial of responsibility?
11. Why is thinking about death so difficult for us?
12. Does thinking about death often affect our priorities? In what ways?
13. Do you associate honesty and authenticity with thinking often about death?
14. How does the fear of death keep us from coming fully alive?
15. How could the practice of embracing our mortality help to us pursue God as our very survival and sanity?

Chapter 4 – The Value of Awareness and Mindfulness: Recovering from Our Dualistic Thinking

1. In what ways have you practiced cultivating an awareness of God's presence in everyday life?
2. How are we absent to God? How can we live into a new sense of our own presence to God?
3. How are you cultivating seeds of contemplation within yourself?
4. Why aren't we more aware of God's presence within us and around us in the world?
5. What are some of your struggles with developing a contemplative spirituality?
6. How can we embrace all of life as sacred?
7. In what ways can we subvert the sacred/secular divide?
8. How is our divided life a wounded life? How do we heal from this?
9. How can we unlearn the embedded illusion of the secular?
10. What kind of wisdom and liberation would we embrace if we learned to experience all of life as sacred?
11. In what ways was Christ the most mindful person who ever lived?
12. What comes to mind when you think of practicing mindfulness?
13. How can we cultivate the little seeds of love, compassion, grace, and humility within us through mindfulness?
14. Do you realize that Christianity is from the Eastern part of the world and is not American? In what ways have we made Jesus an American?
15. How can we cultivate an "ecology of the mind" that sees everything as interconnected?

Chapter 5 – The Kingdom of God Within Us: Sustainability for Our Work in the World

1. How are longing and listening intertwined?
2. Why is it so difficult to live into a vulnerable nakedness that listens deeply?
3. How can we be hospitable to the longing within us?
4. How can we explore our interior life with more intentionality and intensity?

5. Do you think that your longing for God is the truest thing about you? How so?
6. How can we cultivate the kingdom of God within us, the life of Christ within us?
7. In what ways do we live in our bodies as Christ lives within us?
8. How can we honor the image of God in others as Christ lives within us?
9. In what ways have you reflected on the radical nature of the life of Christ living within you?
10. How can we allow the mystery of life within us to be manifested instead of trying to manipulate God?
11. Can you articulate how a contemplative spirituality is important when we think about sustainability in our work in the world?
12. How have you neglected your soul in difficult times in your life? How can you live into something more nurturing?
13. How can a contemplative spirituality help us to respond to the difficulties of life with serenity and grace?
14. How can we live out contemplation as a way of life?
15. How can you become a contemplative critic who is not afraid to be considered a fool or a danger to society because you do not embrace the status quo anymore and live by risk?

Chapter 6 – Seeds of Ordinary Revelation: Uncovering the True Self

1. In what ways have you discovered the true self within you?
2. Have you experienced how love always comes from the truest part of ourselves?
3. How does discovering our true self reveal our identity as an authentic human being over the course of our lives?
4. Does the true self support an authentic contemplative spirituality? How?
5. In what ways is your true self a gift to the world?
6. Have you explored your capacity to have grace, listen deeply, and demonstrate humility through the true self within you? Has this shaped you in different ways?
7. Do you realize that there is only one you and no one else can live out your true self but you? How does this make you want to live with intentionality?

8. Is listening to the true self a countercultural experience? How have you embodied this in everyday life?
9. What comes to mind in the phrase "a beginner of new revelations"?
10. In what ways is struggle a sign of growth and maturity?
11. How have we boxed up contemplation into a program, activity, or method instead of an attitude or outlook?
12. In what ways have you noticed God working in you in ordinary ways in everyday life?
13. How can we have an openness and receptivity to grace in our practice of contemplative spirituality?
14. In what ways can we approach our practice of contemplative spirituality without any preconceived notions and expectations?
15. How have we practiced being a listening church, rooted in the neighborhood and letting go of our expectations and control?

Chapter 7 - Grounding Ourselves: The Mystery of Our Being

1. What practical steps can we take to develop a listening posture in life?
2. How do we lose connection with our souls when we do not listen?
3. How did Jesus practice silence and solitude?
4. Why do we label silence and solitude as "weird" in our culture today?
5. How can we search out our own ways to listen?
6. Does the practice of silence and solitude connect us to others? How?
7. In what ways does community mean never losing the awareness that we are connected to one another?
8. In what ways is solitude not anti-social, but a making room within for God, others, and self?
9. Intuitive ways of listening go way beyond words. How has this been true in your experience?
10. How is our shared life together touched in silence and solitude?
11. How is our identity connected to the practice of silence and solitude?
12. In what ways can we move beyond an advertised life of surface appearances toward a discovered life?

13. Why do silence and solitude touch the deepest part of our humanity?
14. In what ways can we learn to richly cultivate our inner lives?
15. Is there a process of conversion going on within you? How have silence and solitude been integral to this process?

Chapter 8 - The Present Depth of Our Experience: Moving Beyond Fear

1. How do silence and solitude open up the possibility to live in the present moment?
2. When have you created a dysfunctional relationship with the present moment? When have you created a healthy relationship with the present moment?
3. How have you found the present moment to be your true home?
4. How can we be more present to what we are doing here and now?
5. Will we lose out on wisdom if we do not live in the present moment? In what ways is wisdom discovered in the present moment?
6. How do silence and solitude seem like the winter season when it is cold and dark? Do you think that life and growth are happening in this season? What has been your experience?
7. Have we suffered because we do not live from the depths of our humanity? How has this hindered us in everyday life?
8. How can our silence and solitude divert our attention away from the chatter in our lives and into an authentic life of wonder?
9. Why do you think we need to take time to be silent?
10. What do you think would happen if we turned off our televisions or computers and gave more attention to silence and solitude?
11. In what ways do you fear embracing silence and solitude?
12. What do you think would happen if you fully joined the silence in your life?
13. Are we afraid that our whole structure of "reality" will be shattered through silence and solitude? Have you believed in a God made in your own image? What cultural propaganda have you assented to?
14. Do you experience silence as full and rich or empty and hollow?
15. How does noise blind us to our inner worlds?

Chapter 9 - Understanding at a Deeper Level: Taking Our Growth Seriously

1. Have you ever experienced a desert season in your life where it felt like a dark night of the soul? What happened?
2. How can we be more honest about our pain and brokenness through the desert experiences of life?
3. Why do we always want a life that looks neat and tidy without pain and struggle?
4. How can doubt, apathy, disillusionment, and depression be necessary conditions of our own growth sometimes?
5. Have you ever noticed hidden mustard seeds growing in the dark over a long period of time in your life without realizing it?
6. In what ways can we embrace reality in nakedness and vulnerability?
7. Do silence and solitude correct the distortions of our embodied social existence? How have you experienced this?
8. Have you ever abided in a place of truth that is raw, naked, and deeply revelatory of your own weakness? What keeps you from being constantly rooted there in an ongoing way? Are you afraid of this abiding place?
9. In what ways do silence and solitude make us receptive to God?
10. How is silence the atmosphere that gives birth to all that is precious in becoming human?
11. Why is it so hard to explore the interior movements of your soul?
12. How have you grown to know yourself more through solitude?
13. In what ways have you listened intensely to your life, the lives of others, and the life of God within you through silence and solitude?
14. Have you asked the hard questions within yourself? What are these questions?
15. In what ways is deepening your own understanding of yourself important to an active life?

Chapter 10 - Unlearning Old Ways: Dreaming Beyond the Status Quo

1. How can we become dreamers who allow our pain and suffering to bring healing to others?

2. How have you allowed God's dreams of love and compassion to live inside you?
3. How can we see reflection and rest as resistance to the dominant narrative of the empire we live in? What do you think that dominant narrative is?
4. In what ways can we dream again? What small steps can we take?
5. Do we dream and hope for a better world? How have reflection and rest helped you in this longing?
6. How have we become disconnected from our sensuousness?
7. In what ways can you listen to awakening and let it live through your body?
8. Have you lived the truth of your own awakening? How so?
9. How can we embody an evolving awakening experience?
10. Do you feel that reflection and rest are crucial for our context in the twenty-first century world? Why?
11. In what ways can we learn to care for ourselves?
12. How can we allow the exercise of memory to create alterative worlds, narratives and possibilities to emerge?
13. Is slowing down something you have worked at? What rhythms help you in this?
14. How can the memory connect us to authenticity and honesty?
15. What are some of the ways you have experimented with resting in God?

Chapter 11 - Pursuing Meaning: Responding to the Questions of Life

1. How can we be responsive, attentive, and receptive to all of life?
2. Have you had the courage to rest and look within to find gems of authenticity? What have you found as you have practiced this way of life?
3. Is ordinariness divine to you? In what ways?
4. How is resting challenging to you in our hyper-busy world?
5. How can we help one another learn how to rest?
6. How is certainty a default mode of knowing?
7. In what ways do our questions open up a world of possibilities?
8. How do answers make trust and listening dispensable?
9. Have we become addicted to our preconceived answers to everything? Do you agree or disagree?

10. What are the questions you have spent your entire life living into?
11. Does doing nothing freak you out? Does the active life override your sense of reflection and rest?
12. In our production-oriented culture why do you think it is so hard to focus on our being?
13. How is God in the stillness, silence and rest?
14. In what ways does being embrace countercultural ways of life?
15. How can we learn to enjoy rest and allow the life of God to live in us right where we are?

Chapter 12 – The Core of Our Humanity: Nurturing a Christ-Consciousness

1. How can the examining of our lives together bring us greater rest within?
2. In what ways can we listen to, and reflect on our lives?
3. Can we possibly live a meaningful life of purpose without reflection and rest?
4. What are the desires within you that you would like to see flourish?
5. How can we become more about love and less about talk?
6. Why are we so busy and bored?
7. How can we develop healthy rhythms of rest and embody life balance?
8. In what ways can reflection and rest keep us from becoming worn out?
9. How can we rediscover our humanity as an expression of love in the world?
10. Do you believe your humanity is sacred and that Christ lives in you? How does this shape you?
11. In what ways do you see your humanity as a sacred gift of life?
12. Do you honor the beauty of the earth, the world through the local community you live in? How have you practiced this?
13. How do we become fully alive and deeply human?
14. In what ways can we live out the gospel without words and allow it to speak to every aspect of the human experience?
15. In what ways have you had the courage to fully and unreservedly embrace your humanity?

Resource List – Recommended Reading

Books by Thomas Merton on the contemplative life

1. *No Man Is An Island* by Thomas Merton
2. *Thoughts in Solitude* by Thomas Merton
3. *The Silent Life* by Thomas Merton
4. *Spiritual Direction and Meditation* by Thomas Merton
5. *Contemplative Prayer* by Thomas Merton
6. *The Inner Experience: Notes on Contemplation* by Thomas Merton edited by William H. Shannon
7. *New Seeds of Contemplation* by Thomas Merton
8. *The Springs of Contemplation: A Retreat at the Abby of Gethsemani* by Thomas Merton
9. *Contemplation in a World of Action* by Thomas Merton
10. *Mystics and Zen Masters* by Thomas Merton

Books on contemplative activism

1. *Waiting for God* by Simone Weil
2. *Simple Spirituality: Learning to See God in a Broken World* by Christopher L Heuertz
3. *An Altar in the World: A Geography of Faith* by Barbara Brown Taylor
4. *Pilgrimage of a Soul: Contemplative Spirituality for the Active Life* by Phileena Heuertz

5. *Friendship at the Margins: Discovering Mutuality in Service and Mission* by Christopher L. Heuertz and Christine D. Pohl
6. *The Irresistible Revolution: Living as an Ordinary Radical* by Shane Claiborne
7. *Loaves and Fishes: The Inspiring Story of the Catholic Worker Movement* by Dorothy Day
8. *Colossians Remixed: Subverting the Empire* by Brian J. Walsh and Sylvia C. Keesmaat
9. *Pedagogy of the Oppressed* by Paulo Freire
10. *Moving in the Spirit: Becoming a Contemplative in Action* by Richard J. Hauser

Books silence and solitude

1. *Sadhana A Way to God: Christian Exercises in Eastern Form* by Anthony De Mello
2. *A Sunlit Absence: Silence, Awareness, and Contemplation* by Martin Laird
3. *Silent Dwellers: Embracing the Solitary Life* by Barbara Erakko Taylor
4. *Inviting Silence: Universal Principles of Meditation* by Gunilla Norris
5. *Radical Optimism: Practical Spirituality in an Uncertain World* by Beatrice Bruteau
6. *The Power of Solitude: Discovering Your True Self in a World of Nonsense and Noise* by Annemarie S. Kidder
7. *Poustinia: Encountering God in Silence, Solitude and Prayer* by Catherine Doherty
8. *Solitude and Compassion: The Path to the Heart of the Gospel* by Gus Gordon
9. *Listening Below the Noise: A Meditation on the Practice of Silence* by Anne D. LeClaire
10. *Invitation to Solitude and Silence: Experiencing God's Transforming Presence* by Ruth Haley Barton

Books on the true self, consciousness, awareness

1. *The Sacred Gaze: Contemplation and the Healing of the Self* by Susan R. Pitchford
2. *Touching Peace: Practicing the Art of Mindful Living* by Thich Nhat Hanh

3. *Becoming Who You Are: Insights on the True Self from Thomas Merton and Other Saints* by James Martin

4. *The Spiritual Dimension of the Enneagram: Nine Faces of the Soul* by Sandra Maitri

5. *Merton's Palace of Nowhere: A Search for God Through Awareness of the True Self* by James Finley

6. *The Wisdom Way of Knowing: Reclaiming an Ancient Tradition to Awaken the Heart* by Cynthia Bourgeault

7. *Immortal Diamond: The Search for Our True Self* by Richard Rohr

8. *Awareness: The Perils and Opportunities of Reality* by Anthony De Mello

9. *Spirituality and the Awakening Self: The Sacred Journey of Transformation* by David G. Benner

10. *Open the Door: A Journey to the True Self* by Joyce Rupp

Books on distraction and rhythms

1. *Wisdom Distilled From the Daily: Living the Rule of St. Benedict Today* by Joan Chittister

2. *Godspace: Time for Peace in the Rhythms of Rest* by Christine Sine

3. *Distracted: The Erosion of Attention and the Coming Dark Age* by Maggie Jackson

4. *Seven Sacred Pauses: Living Mindfully Through the Hours of the Day* by Macrina Wiederkehr

5. *Enjoying the Presence of God: Discovering Intimacy With God in the Daily Rhythms of Life* by Jan Johnson

6. *Finding Spiritual Whitespace: Awakening Your Soul to Rest* by Bonnie Gray

7. *Mudhouse Sabbath* by Lauren F. Winner

8. *Sabbath Keeping: Finding Freedom in the Rhythms of Rest* by Lynne M. Baab

9. *Simplifying the Soul: Lenten Practices to Renew Your Spirit* by Paula Huston

10. *Let Your Life Speak: Listening to the Voice of Vocation* by Parker J. Palmer

Resource List

Books on intentionality and discipline

1. *A New Set of Eyes: Encountering the Hidden God* by Paula D' Arcy
2. *Seeking the Face of God* by William H. Shannon
3. *The Spirit of the Disciplines: Understanding How God Changes Lives* by Dallas Willard
4. *The Holy Way: Practices for a Simple Life* by Paula Huston
5. *A Hidden Wholeness: The Journey Toward an Undivided Life* by Parker J. Palmer
6. *Nature as Spiritual Practice* by Stephan Chase
7. *Here and Now: Living in the Spirit* by Henri J.M. Nouwen
8. *Practicing Our Faith: A Way of Life For A Searching People* edited by Dorothy C. Bass
9. *Return to Our Senses: Re-imagining How We Pray* by Christine Sine
10. *A Listening Heart: The Spirituality of Sacred Sensuousness* by David Stendl-Rast

Books on spiritual formation

1. *Faith Shift: Finding Your Way Forward When Everything You Believe is Coming Apart* by Kathy Escobar
2. *Practicing the Way of Jesus: Life Together in the Kingdom of Love* by Mark Scandrette
3. *Falling Upward: A Spirituality for the Two Hales of Life* by Richard Rohr
4. *Faith-Rooted Organizing: Mobilizing the Church in Service to the World* by Alexia Salvatierra and Peter Heltzel
5. *Dorothy Day: Selected Writings* edited by Robert Ellsberg
6. *Sacred Rhythms: Arranging Our Lives for Spiritual Transformation* by Ruth Haley Barton
7. *When the Heart Waits: Spiritual Direction for Life's Sacred Questions* by Sue Monk Kidd
8. *Compassion: Living in the Spirit of Saint Francis* by Ilia Delio
9. *Hope Against Darkness: The Transforming Vision of Saint Francis in an Age of Anxiety* by Richard Rohr and John Bookser Feister
10. *Invitation to a Journey: A Road Map for Spiritual Formation* by M. Robert Mulholland Jr.

Books on community

1. *Living into Community: Cultivating Practices that Sustain Us* by Christine D. Pohl
2. *How To Be A Christian Without Going To Church: The Unofficial Guide to Alternative Forms of Christian Community* by Kelly Bean
3. *Slow Church: Cultivating Community in the Patient Way of Jesus* by C. Christopher Smith and John Pattison
4. *Down We Go: Living into the Wild Ways of Jesus* by Kathy Escobar
5. *Incarnate: The Body of Christ in an Age of Disengagement* by Michael Frost
6. *The Cost of Community: Jesus, St. Francis and Life in the Kingdom* by Jamie Arpin-Ricci
7. *Unexpected Gifts: Discovering the Way of Community* by Christopher L. Heuertz
8. *The Wisdom of Stability: Rooting Faith in a Mobile Culture* by Jonathan Wilson-Hartgrove
9. *The New Parish: How Neighborhood Churches are Transforming Mission, Discipleship and Community* by Paul Sparks, Tim Soerens and Dwight J. Friesen
10. *Making Neighborhoods Whole: A Handbook for Christian Community Development* by Wayne Gordon and John M. Perkins

Books on developing a contemplative spirituality in everyday life

1. *Stand On Your Own Feet: Finding a Contemplative Spirit in everyday Life* by Natalie Smith
2. *Lost in Wonder: Rediscovering the Spiritual Art of Attentiveness* by Esther De Waal
3. *Beginning Contemplative Prayer: Out of Chaos Into Quiet* by Katheryn J. Hermes
4. *Open Heart, Open Mind: The Contemplative Dimension of the Gospel* by Thomas Keating
5. *When the Soul Listens: Finding Rest and Direction in Contemplative Prayer* by Jan Johnson
6. *The Naked Now: Learning to See as the Mystics See* by Richard Rohr

7. *Into the Silent Land: A Guide to the Christian Practice of Contemplation* by Martin Laird
8. *The Contemplative Heart* by James Finley
9. *Prayer of the Heart: The Contemplative Tradition of the Christian East* by George Maloney
10. *The Big Book of Christian Mysticism: The Essential Guide to Contemplative Spirituality* by Carl McColman

Bibliography

Arico, Carl. *A Taste of Silence: A Guide to the Fundamentals of Centering Prayer.* New York: The Continuum International Publishing Group Inc., 1999.

Arpin-Ricci, Jamie. *The Cost of Community: Jesus, St. Francis and Life in the Kingdom.* Downers Grove: InterVarsity Press, 2011.

Baab, Lynne M. *Sabbath Keeping: Finding Freedom in the Rhythms of Rest.* Downers Grove: InterVarsity Press, 2005.

Baker, Howard. *Soul Keeping: Ancient Paths of Spiritual Direction.* Colorado Springs: NavPress, 1998.

Bartholomew, Craig G. *Where Mortals Dwell: A Christian View of Place for Today.* Grand Rapids: Baker Academic, 2011.

Barton, Ruth Haley. *Invitation to Solitude and Silence: Experiencing God's Transforming Presence.* Downers Grove: InterVarsity Press, 2004.

Bass, Diana Butler. *Christianity After Religion: The End of the Church and the Birth of a New Spiritual Awakening.* New York: HarperOne, 2012.

Bean, Kelly. *How to Be a Christian Without Going to Church: The Unofficial Guide to Alternative Forms of Christian Community.* Grand Rapids: Baker Books, 2014.

Benner, David G. *Soulful Spirituality: Becoming Fully Alive and Deeply Human.* Grand Rapids: Brazos Press, 2011.

Benson, Robert. *In Constant Prayer.* Nashville: Thomas Nelson, Inc., 2008.

Berry, Wendell. *Citizenship Papers.* Washington, DC: Shoemaker & Hoard, 2003.

_____. *The Way of Ignorance: And Other Essays.* Berkeley: Counterpoint, 2005.

Bloom, Anthony. *Beginning to Pray.* Ramsey: Paulist Press, 1970.

Blue, Debbie. *Sensual Orthodoxy.* Saint Paul: Cathedral Hill Press, 2004.

Bodian, Stephan. *Wake Up Now: A Guide to the Journey of Spiritual Awakening.* New York: McGraw-Hill Books, 2008.

Bodo, Murray. *The Landscape of Prayer.* Cincinnati: St. Anthony Messenger Press, 2003.

Bolz-Weber, Nadia. *Pastrix: The Cranky, Beautiful Faith of a Sinner and Saint.* New York: Jericho Books, 2013.

Bourgeault, Cynthia. *Centering Prayer and Inner Awakening.* Lanham: Cowley Publications, 2004.

_____. *Mystical Hope: Trusting in the Mercy of God.* Boston: Cowley Publications, 2001.

_____. *The Wisdom Way of Knowing: Reclaiming an Ancient Tradition to Awaken the Heart.* San Francisco: Jossey-Bass, 2003.

Brewin, Kester. *Signs of Emergence: A Vision for Church that is Organic, Networked, Bottom-Up, Communal, Flexible {Always Evolving}.* Grand Rapids: Baker Books, 2007.

Brown, Brene. *The Gifts of Imperfection: Let Go of Who You Think You're Supposed to Be and Embrace Who You Are.* Center City: Hazelden, 2010.

Bruteau, Beatrice. *Radical Optimism: Practical Spirituality in an Uncertain World.* Boulder: Sentient Publications, 2002.

Burrows, Ruth. *Essence of Prayer.* Mahwah: HiddenSpring, 2006.

Cain, Susan. *Quiet: The Power of Introverts in a World that Can't Stop Talking.* New York: Crown Publishers, 2012.

Campolo, Tony and Mary Albert Darling. *The God of Intimacy and Action: Reconnecting Ancient Spiritual Practices, Evangelism, and Justice.* San Francisco: Jossey-Bass, 2007.

Campbell, Jonathan S. and Jennifer Campbell. *The Way of Jesus: A Journey of Freedom for Pilgrims and Wanderers.* San Francisco: Jossey-Bass, 2005.

Carney, Frederika. "To Dream and Hope for a Better World." In *Contemplation in Action*, edited by Richard Rohr and Friends et al., 98. New York: The Crossroad Publishing Company, 2006.

Casey, Michael. *Toward God: The Ancient Wisdom of Western Prayer.* Liguori: Liguori/Triumph, 1996.

Chandler, Diane J. *Christian Spiritual Formation: An Integrated Approach for Personal and Relational Wholeness.* Downers Grove: InterVarsity Press, 2014.

Chase, Steven. *The Tree of Life: Models of Christian Prayer.* Grand Rapids: Baker Academic, 2005.

Chittister, Joan. *Wisdom Distilled from the Daily: Living the Rule of St. Benedict Today.* New York: HarperOne, 1991.

Christensen, Michael J. and Rebecca Laird. *Henri Nouwen: Spiritual Formation: Following the Movements of the Spirit.* New York: HarperOne, 2010.

Claiborne, Shane. T*he Irresistible Revolution: Living as an Ordinary Radical.* Grand Rapids: Zondervan, 2006.

_____ and John M. Perkins. *Follow Me to Freedom: Leading and Following as an Ordinary Radical.* Ventura: Regal, 2009.

Cleveland, Christena. *Disunity in Christ: Uncovering the Hidden Forces That Keep Us Apart.* Downers Grove: InterVarsity Press, 2013.

Coleman, Monica A. *Not Alone: Reflections on Faith and Depression.* Culver City: Inner Prizes, Inc., 2012.

Cross, Simon. *Totally Devoted: The Challenge of New Monasticism.* London: Authentic Media Limited, 2010.

Cunningham, Sarah. *The Well Balanced World Changer: A Field Guide for Staying Sane While Doing Good.* Chicago: Moody Publishers, 2013.

Daniel, Lillian. *When "Spiritual But Not Religious" is Not Enough: Seeing God in Surprising Places, Even the Church.* New York: Jericho Books, 2013.

D' Arcy, Paula. *A New Set of Eyes: Encountering the Hidden God.* New York: The Crossroad Publishing Company, 2002.

Dawn, Marva J. *Keeping the Sabbath Wholly: Ceasing, Resting, Embracing, Feasting.* Grand Rapids: William B. Eerdmans Publishing Company, 1991.

_____. *Powers, Weakness, and the Tabernacling of God.* Grand Rapids, Michigan: William B. Eerdmans Publishing Company, 2001.

Day, Dorothy. *On Pilgrimage.* Grand Rapids: Wm. B. Eerdmans Publishing Co., 1999.

_____ and Robert Coles. *Dorothy Day: A Radical Devotion.* Georgetown: Da Capo Press, 1987.

_____. "Day After Day." In *Dorothy Day: Selected Writings*, edited by Robert Ellsberg, 52. Maryknoll: Orbis Books, 2007.

_____. "The Impact of Monasticism." In *Searching for Christ: The Spirituality of Dorothy Day*, by Brigid O' Shea Merriman, 85. Notre Dame: University of Notre Dame Press, 1994.

De Caussade, Jean-Pierre. *The Sacrament of the Present Moment.* New York: HarperSanFrancisco, 1989.

Delio, Ilia. *Compassion: Living in the Spirit of St. Francis.* Cincinnati: St. Anthony Messenger Press, 2011.

————. *Franciscan Prayer.* Cincinnati: St. Anthony Messenger Press, 2004.

De Mello, Anthony. *Sadhana, A Way to God: Christian Exercises in Eastern Form.* New York: Image Books, 1978.

De Waal, Esther. *Lost in Wonder: Rediscovering the Spiritual Art of Attentiveness.* Collegeville: Litrugical Press, 2003.

Dowdy, Calenthia. "Race and Community." In *Widening the Circle: Experiments in Christian Discipleship*, edited by Joanna Shenk et al., 212. Harrisonburg: Herald Press, 2011.

Edwards, Tilden. *Living in the Presence: Spiritual Exercises to Open Our Lives to the Awareness of God.* New York: HarperSanFransico, 1995.

Ellul, Jacques. "The Humiliation of the Word." Grand Rapids: Wm. B. Eerdmans Publishing Co., 1985.

————. *The Subversion of Christianity.* Grand Rapids: Wm. B. Eerdmans Publishing Co., 1986.

Escobar, Kathy. *Down We Go: Living into the Wild Ways of Jesus.* Folsom: Civitas Press, 2011.

————. *Faith Shift: Finding Your Way Forward When Everything You Believe is Coming Apart.* New York: Convergent Books, 2014.

Evans, Rachel Held. *Evolving in Monkey Town: How a Girl Who Knew All the Answers Learned to Ask the Questions.* Grand Rapids: Zondervan, 2010.

Faricy, Robert and Lucy Rooney. *The Contemplative Way of Prayer: Deepening Your Life with God.* Ann Arbor: Servant Books, 1986.

Farrington, Debra K. *Living Faith Day by Day: How the Sacred Rules of Monastic Traditions Can Help You Live Spirituality in the Modern World.* New York: Perigee, 2000.

Feinberg, Margaret. *Wonderstruck: Awaken to the Nearness of God.* Brentwood: Worthy Publishing, 2012.

Finley, James. *The Contemplative Heart.* Notre Dame: Sorin Books, 2000.

Finley, Kathleen. *Savoring God: Praying With All Our Senses.* Notre Dame: Ave Maria Press, 2003.

Ford, Leighton. *The Attentive Life: Discerning God's Presence in all Things.* Downers Grove: InterVarsity Press, 2008.

Ford, Marcia. *Traditions of the Ancients: Vintage Faith Practices for the 21st Century.* Nashville: Broadman & Holman Publishers, 2006.

Foster, Richard J. *The Freedom of Simplicity: Finding Harmony in a Complex World.* New York: HarperSanFrancisco, 2005.

Frost, Michael. *Seeing God in the Ordinary: A Theology of the Everyday.* Peabody: Hendrickson Publishers, 2000.

_____ and Alan Hirsch. *ReJesus: A Wild Messiah for a Missional Church.* Peabody: Hendrickson Publishers, 2009.

_____ and Alan Hirsch. *The Shaping of Things to Come: Innovation and Mission for the 21st–Century Church.* Peabody: Hendrickson Publishers, 2003.

Fryling, Alice. *Seeking God Together: An Introduction to Group Spiritual Direction.* Downers Grove: Intervarsity Press, 2009.

Funk, Mary Margaret. *Into the Depths: A Journey of Loss and Vocation.* Brooklyn: Lantern Books, 2011.

Garrison, Becky. *Jesus Died for this? A Satirist's Search for the Risen Christ.* Grand Rapids: Zondervan, 2010.

Gerth, Holly. *You're Already Amazing: Embracing Who You Are, Becoming All God Created You to Be.* Grand Rapids: Revell, 2012.

Gire, Ken. *Seeing What is Sacred: Becoming More Spiritually Sensitive to the Everyday Moments of Life.* Nashville: W Publishing Group, 2006.

Gordon, Gus. *Solitude and Compassion: The Path to the Heart of the Gospel.* Maryknoll: Orbis Books, 2009.

Gray, Bonnie. *Finding Spiritual Whitespace: Awakening Your Soul to Rest.* Grand Rapids: Revell, 2014.

Griffin, Emilie. *Doors into Prayer: An Invitation.* Brewster: Paraclete Press, 2001.

Guyon, Jeanne. *Experiencing the Depths of Jesus Christ.* Sargent: SeedSowers, 1981.

Hall, Jeremy. *Silence, Solitude, Simplicity: A Hermits Love Affair with a Noisy, Crowded, and Complicated World.* Collegeville: Liturgical Press, 2007.

Hall, Thelma. *Too Deep for Words: Rediscovering Lectio Divina.* Mahwah: Paulist Press, 1988.

Hoffman, Elizabeth Hanson, and Christopher D. Hoffman. *Staying Focused in an Age of Distraction: How Mindfulness, Prayer & Meditation Can Help You Pay Attention to What Really Matters.* Oakland: New Harbinger Publications, Inc., 2006.

Hayes, John B. *Sub-Merge: Living Deep in a Shallow World: Service, Justice and Contemplation Among the World's Poor.* Ventura: Regal, 2006.

Heath, Elaine A. *The Mystic Way of Evangelism: A Contemplative Vision for Christian Outreach.* Grand Rapids: Baker Academic, 2008.

Hermes, Kathryn J. *Beginning Contemplative Prayer: Out of Chaos into Quiet.* Cincinnati: Servant Books, 2001.

Heuertz, Phileena. *Pilgrimage of a Soul: Contemplative Spirituality for the Active Life.* Downers Grove: InterVarsity Press, 2010.

_____ and Darren Prince. "Devotional." In *Living Mission: The Vision and Voices of New Friars,* edited by Scott A. Bessenecker et al., 122. Downers Grove: InterVarsity Press, 2010.

Hope, Susan. *Mission-Shaped Spirituality: The Transforming Power of Mission.* New York: Seabury Books, 2010.

Huston, Paula. *A Season of Mystery: 10 Spiritual Practices for Embracing a Happier Second Half of Life.* Chicago: Loyola Press, 2012.

_____. *The Holy Way: Practices for a Simple Life.* Chicago: Loyola Press, 2003.

Illich, Ivan and David Cayley. *The Rivers North of the Future: The Testament of Ivan Illich.* Toronto: Anansi Press Inc., 2005.

Imbach, Jeff. *The River Within: Loving God, Living Passionately.* Colorado Springs: NavPress, 1998.

Jackson, Maggie. *Distracted: The Erosion of Attention and the Coming Dark Age.* Amherst: Prometheus Books, 2008.

Johnson, Jan. *Enjoying the Presence of God: Discovering Intimacy with God in the Daily Rhythms of Life.* Colorado Springs: NavPress, 1996.

_____. *When the Soul Listens: Finding Rest and Direction in Contemplative Prayer.* Colorado Spring: NavPress, 1999.

Jones, Tony. *The Sacred Way: Spiritual Practices for Everyday Life.* Grand Rapids: Zondervan, 2004.

Keating, Thomas. *Intimacy With God: An Introduction to Centering Prayer.* New York: The Crossroad Publishing Company, 2005.

_____. *Invitation to Love: The Way of Christian Contemplation.* New York: The Continuum International Publishing Group Inc, 2004.

_____. *Open Heart Open Mind: The Contemplative Dimension of the Gospel.* New York: The Continuum International Publishing Group Inc, 1992.

Keel, Tim. *Intuitive Leadership: Embracing a Paradigm of Narrative, Metaphor and Chaos.* Grand Rapids: Baker Books, 2007.

Kent, Keri Wyatt. *Listen: Finding God in the Story of Your Life.* San Francisco: Jossey-Bass, 2006.

Kidd, Sue Monk. *When the Heart Waits: Spiritual Direction for Life's Sacred Questions.* New York: HarperCollins Publishers, 1990.

Kidder, Annemarie S. *The Power of Solitude: Discovering Your True Self in a World of Nonsense and Noise.* New York: The Crossroad Publishing Company, 2007.

King, Ursula. *The Search for Spirituality: Our Global Quest for a Spiritual Life.* New York: BlueBridge, 2008.

Kriz, Tony. *Welcome to the Table: Post-Christian Culture Saves a Seat for Ancient Liturgy.* Eugene: Wipf & Stock Publishers, 2011.

Laird, Martin. *A Sunlit Absence: Silence, Awareness, and Contemplation.* New York: Oxford University Press, 2011.

_____. *Into the Silent Land: A Guide to the Christian Practice of Contemplation.* New York: Oxford University Press, 2006.

Lamott, Anne. *Stitches: A Handbook on Meaning, Hope and Repair.* New York: Riverhead Books, 2013.

LeClaire, Anne D. *Listen Below the Noise: A Meditation on the Practice of Silence.* New York, HarperCollins Publishers, 2009.

Leddy, Mary Jo. *Radical Gratitude.* Maryknoll: Orbis Books, 2002.

Leech, Kenneth. *True Prayer: An Invitation to Christian Spirituality.* Harrisburg: Morehouse Publishing, 1995.

Leloup, Jean-Yves. *Being Still: Reflections on an Ancient Mystical Tradition.* Mahwah: Paulist Press, 2003.

MacDonald, Gordon. *Ordering Your Private World.* Nashville: Thomas Nelson, Inc., 2003.

Mahler, Richard. *Stillness: Daily Gifts of Solitude.* Boston: Red Wheel, 2003.

Main, John. *The Way of Unknowing: Expanding Spiritual Horizons Through Meditation.* New York: The Crossroads Publishing Company, 1990.

Maitri, Sandra. *The Spiritual Dimension of the Enneagram: Nine Faces of the Soul.* New York: Penguin Putnam, Inc., 2000.

Martin, James. *Becoming Who You Are: Insights on the True Self from Thomas Merton and other Saints.* Mahwah: HiddenSpring, 2006.

McCaig, Wendy R. *From the Sanctuary to the Streets: How the Dreams of One City's Homeless Sparked a Faith Revolution that Transformed a Community.* Eugene: Cascade Books, 2010.

McColman, Carl. *The Big Book of Christian Mysticism: The Essential Guide to Contemplative Spirituality.* Charlottesville: Hampton Roads Publishing, Inc., 2010.

McKnight, John and Peter Block. *The Abundant Community: Awakening the Power of Families and Neighborhoods.* San Francisco: Berrett-Koehler Publishers, Inc., 2010.

McLaren, Brian D. *More Ready than You Realize: The Power of Everyday Conversations.* Grand Rapids: Zondervan, 2006.

_____. *Naked Spirituality: A Life With God In 12 Simple Words.* New York: HarperOne, 2011.

McLuhan, Marshall and Quentin Fiore. *War and Peace in the Global Village.* Corte Madera: Gingko Press, 2001.

McNeil, Brenda Salter. *A Credible Witness: Reflections on Power, Evangelism and Race.* Downers Grove: InterVarsity Press, 2008.

McPherson, C.W. *Keeping Silence: Christian Practices for Entering Silence.* Harrisburg: Morehouse Publishing, 2002.

Meadow, Mary Jo. *Christian Insight Meditation: Following in the Footsteps of John of the Cross.* Somerville: Wisdom Publications, 2007.

Meek, Esther Lightcap. *Loving To Know: Covenant Epistemology.* Eugene: Cascade Books, 2011.

Merton, Thomas. *Contemplation in a World of Action.* Notre Dame: University of Notre Dame Press, 1998.

_____. *Life and Holiness.* Garden City: Image Books, 1964.

_____. *Mystics and Zen Masters.* New York: The Noonday Press, 1967.

_____. *New Seeds of Contemplation.* New York: New Direction Books, 1961.

_____. *No Man is an Island.* Orlando: Harcourt Brace & Company, 1983.

_____. *The New Man.* New York: Farrar, Straus & Giroux, 1961.

_____. *The Sign of Jonas.* Orlando: Haircourt, Inc., 1981.

_____. *Thoughts in Solitude.* New York: Farrar, Straus & Giroux, 1986.

Miles, Sara. *City of God: Faith in the Streets.* New York: Jericho Books, 2014.

Morse, MaryKate. *Making Room for Leadership: Power, Space and Influence.* Downers Grove: Intervarsity Press, 2008.

Mother Teresa. "The Fruit of Silence is Prayer." In *A Simple Path*, compiled by Lucinda Vardey, 7. New York: Ballantine Books, 1995.

_____. "My God, How Painful is This Unknown Pain." In *Come Be My Light*, edited by Brian Kolodiejchuk, 187. New York: Doubleday, 2007.

Muller, Wayne. *Sabbath: Finding Rest, Renewal, and Delight in Our Busy Lives.* New York: Bantom Books, 1999.

Myers, Joseph R. *Organic Community: Creating a Place Where People Naturally Connect.* Grand Rapids: Bakers Books, 2007.

Nhat Hanh, Thich. *Touching Peace: Practicing the Art of Mindful Living.* Berkley: Parallax Press, 1992.

Norris, Gunilla. *Inviting Silence: Universal Principles Of Meditation.* New York: BlueBridge, 2004.

Norris, Kathleen. *Acadia and Me: A Marriage, Monks, and a Writer's Life.* New York: Riverhead Books, 2008.

_____. *The Cloister Walk*. New York: Riverhead Books, 1996.

Nouwen, Henri J.M. *Clowning in Rome: Reflections on Solitude, Celibacy, Prayer, and Contemplation*. New York: Image Books, 1979.

_____. *Here and Now: Living in the Spirit*. New York: The Crossroads Publishing Company, 1994.

_____. *Reaching Out: The Three Movements of the Spiritual Life*. New York: Image Books, 1975.

_____. *The Inner Voice of Love: A Journey Through Anguish to Freedom*. New York: Doubleday, 1996.

_____. *The Way of the Heart: Desert Spirituality and Contemporary Ministry*. New York: HarperSanFrancisco, 1981.

_____. *The Wounded Healer*. New York: Image Books, 1979.

Okoro, Enuma. *Reluctant Pilgrim: A Moody, Somewhat Self-Indulgent Introvert's Search for Spiritual Community*. Nashville: Fresh Air Books, 2010.

Palmer, Parker J. *A Hidden Wholeness: The Journey Toward an Undivided Life*. San Francisco: Jossey-Bass, 2004.

_____. *Let Your Life Speak: Listening to the Voice of Vocation*. San Francisco: Jossey-Bass, 2000.

Parks, Sharon Daloz. *Leadership Can Be Taught: A Bold Approach for a Complex World*. Boston: Harvard Business School Press, 2005.

Paulsell, Stephanie. "Honoring the Body." In *Practicing Our Faith: A Way of Life for a Searching People*, edited by Dorothy C. Bass et al., 15. San Francisco, Jossey-Bass, 1997.

Pennington, M. Basil. *Centered Living: The Way of Centering Prayer*. Liguori: Liguori/Triumph, 1999.

Percy, Walker. *Signposts in a Strange Land*. New York: Farrar, Straus and Giroux, 1991.

Pitchford, Susan R. *The Sacred Gaze: Contemplation and the Healing of the Self*. Collegeville: Liturgical Press, 2014.

Pohl, Christine D. *Living into Community: Cultivating Practices that Sustain Us*. Grand Rapids: William B. Eerdmans Publishing Company, 2012.

Rakoczy, Susan. *Great Mystics and Social Justice: Walking on the Two Feet of Love*. Mahwah: Paulist Press, 2006.

Rohr, Richard. *A Lever and a Place to Stand: The Contemplative Stance, The Active Prayer*. Mahwah: HiddenSpring, 2011.

_____. *Everything Belongs: The Gift of Contemplative Prayer*. New York: The Crossroad Publishing Company, 2003.

_____. *Falling Upward: A Spirituality for the Two Halves of Life*. San Francisco: Jossey-Bass, 2011.

_____. *Immortal Diamond: The Search for Our True Self.* San Francisco: Jossey-Bass, 2013.

_____. *Simplicity: The Freedom of Letting Go.* New York: The Crossroad Publishing Company, 2003.

_____. *Things Hidden: Scripture as Spirituality.* Cincinnati: St. Anthony Messenger Press, 2008.

Rolheiser, Ronald. *The Shattered Lantern: Rediscovering a Felt Presence of God.* New York: The Crossroad Publishing Company, 2004.

Rollins, Peter. *Insurrection: To Believe is Human to Doubt, Divine.* New York: Howard Books, 2011.

_____. *The Fidelity of Betrayal: Towards a Church Beyond Belief.* Brewster: Paraclete Press, 2008.

Rubietta, Jane. *Resting Place: A Personal Guide to Spiritual Retreats.* Downers Grove: InterVarsity Press, 2005.

Rupp, Joyce. *Open the Door: A Journey to the True Self.* Notre Dame: Sorin Books, 2008.

Russell, Letty M. *Just Hospitality: God's Welcome in a World of Difference.* Louisville: Westminster John Knox Press, 2009.

Salvatierra, Alexia and Peter Heltzel. *Faith-Rooted Organizing: Mobilizing the Church in Service to the World.* Downers Grove: InterVarsity Press, 2014.

Scandrette, Mark. *Soul Graffiti: Making a Life in the Way Of Jesus.* San Francisco: Jossey-Bass, 2007.

Schumacher, E.F. *Small is Beautiful: Economics as if People Mattered.* New York: Harper & Row Publishers, Inc., 1973.

Seeber, Ashley Bunting. "Just Perspectives." In *The Justice Project*, edited by Brian McLaren, Elisa Padilla, and Ashley Bunting Seeber et al., 149. Grand Rapids: Baker Books, 2009.

Shannon, William. *Seeking the Face of God.* New York: The Crossroad Publishing Company, 1988.

_____. *Silence on Fire: Prayer of Awareness.* New York: The Crossroad Publishing Company, 2000.

Silf, Margaret. *Companions of Christ: Ignatian Spirituality for Everyday Living.* Grand Rapids: William B. Eerdmans Publishing Company, 2004.

Sine, Christine. *GodSpace: Time for Peace in the Rhythms of Life.* Newberg: Barclay Press, 2006.

_____. *Return to Our Senses: Re-Imagining How We Pray.* Seattle: Mustard Seed Associates, 2012.

_____ and Tom Sine. *Living on Purpose: Finding God's Best for Your Life.* Mill Hill: Monarch Books, 2002.

Smith, James K.A. *Desiring the Kingdom: Worship, Worldview, and Cultural Formation.* Grand Rapids, MI: Baker Academic, 2009.

Smith, Jenna. *A Way: The Story of a Long Walk.* Portland: Urban Loft Publishers, 2014.

Smith, Natalie. *Stand On Your Own: Finding a Contemplative Spirit in Everyday Life.* Allen: Thomas More Publishing, 2001.

Spoto, Donald. *In Silence: Why We Pray.* New York: Penguin Compass, 2004.

Starr, Mirabai. *God of Love: A Guide to the Heart of Judaism, Christianity and Islam.* Rhinebeck: Monkfish Book Publishing Company, 2012.

Steindl-Rast, David. *A Listening Heart: The Spirituality of Sacred Sensuousness.* New York: The Crossroad Publishing Company, 1999.

_____. *Gratefulness, the Heart of Prayer: An Approach to Life in Fullness.* Mahwah: Paulist Press, 1984.

Suico, Eileen. "With." In *The Gospel After Christendom: New Voices, New Cultures, New Expressions,* edited by Ryan K. Bolger et al., 277. Grand Rapids: Baker Academic, 2012.

Sweet, Leonard. *Post-Modern Pilgrims: First Century Passion for the 21st Century.* Nashville: B & H Publishing, 2000.

Taylor, Barbara Brown. *An Altar in the World: A Geography of Faith.* New York: HarperOne, 2009.

_____. *Learning to Walk in the Dark.* New York: HarperCollins Publishers, 2014.

Taylor, Barbara Erakko. *Silent Dwellers: Embracing the Solitary Life.* New York: The Continuum Publishing Company, 1999.

Teresa of Avila. *Interior Castle.* Translated by E. Allison Peers. 1961. Reprint, New York: Doubleday, 1989.

Underhill, Evelyn. *Mysticism: A Study in the Nature and Development of Man's Spiritual Consciousness.* New York: E.P. Dutten, 1961.

Vanier, Jean. *Becoming Human.* Toronto: Anansi Press Inc., 2008.

Vennard, Jane E. *Praying With Body and Soul: A Way to Intimacy With God.* Minneapolis: Augsburg Fortress Publishers, 1998.

Vest, Norvene. *No Moment Too Small: Rhythms of Silence, Prayer, and Holy Reading.* Boston: Cowley Publications, 1994.

Von Speyr, Adrienne. *Light and Images: Elements of Contemplation.* San Francisco: Ignatious Press, 2004.

Voskamp, Ann. *One Thousand Gifts: A Dare to Live Fully Right Where You Are.* Grand Rapids: Zondervan, 2010.

Walsh, Brian J. and Sylvia C. Keesmaat. *Colossians Remixed: Subverting the Empire.* Downers Grove: InterVarsity Press, 2004.

Weber, Carolyn. *Holy is the Day: Living in the Gift of the Present.* Downers Grove: InterVarsity Press, 2013.

Weil, Simone. *Waiting for God.* New York: HarperCollins Publishers, 2001.

Wheatley, Margaret J. *Leadership and the New Science: Discovering Order in a Chaotic World.* San Francisco: Berrett-Koehler Publishers, Inc., 1999.

Whitmire, Catherine. *Plain Living: A Quaker Path to Simplicity.* Notre Dame: Sorin Books, 2001.

Whitney, Donald. *Spiritual Disciplines for the Christian Life.* Colorado Springs: NavPress, 1991.

Wiederkehr, Macrina. *Seven Sacred Pauses: Living Mindfully Through the Hours of the Day.* Notre Dame: Sorin Books, 2008.

Wilhoit, James C. *Spiritual Formation as if the Church Mattered: Growing in Christ Through Community.* Grand Rapids: Baker Academic, 2008.

Wilk, Karen. *Don't Invite Them To Church: Moving from a Come and See to a Go And Be Church.* Grand Rapids: Faith Alive Christian Resources, 2010.

Willard, Dallas. *Renovation of the Heart: Putting on the Character of Christ.* Colorado Springs: NavPress, 2002.

_____. *The Great Omission: Reclaiming Jesus's Essential Teachings on Discipleship.* New York: HarperSanFrancisco, 2006.

Wilson-Hartgrove, Jonathan. "Commitment to a Disciplined Contemplative Life." In *School(s) for Conversion: 12 Marks of New Monasticism,* edited by The Rutba House et al., 167-168. Eugene: Cascade Books, 2005.

Winner, Lauren F. *Mudhouse Sabbath.* Brewster: Paraclete Press, 2003.

Wirzba, Norman. *Living the Sabbath: Discovering the Rhythms of Rest and Delight.* Grand Rapids: Brazos Press, 2006.

Wolf-Devine, Celia. *The Heart Transformed: Prayer of Desire.* New York: St. Pauls, 2009.

Zuercher, Suzanne. *Enneagram Spirituality: From Compulsion to Contemplation.* Notre Dame: Ave Maria Press, 1992.

About the Author

Mark Votava lives in the Pacific Northwest in Tacoma, Washington where he has rooted himself in the neighborhood of Downtown Tacoma for the past decade. He is a core member of the Tacoma Catholic Worker, local practitioner, contemplative activist, and ordinary mystic. His life is dedicated to exploring and practicing a more subversive, creative, and contemplative way of life in the twenty-first century that is engaged relationally in the world. He is the author of *The Communal Imagination: Finding a Way to Share Life Together* and blogs regularly at markvotava.com.

Website // markvotava.com
Twitter // @MarkVotava

About Urban Loft Publishers

Urban Loft Publishers focuses on ideas, topics, themes, and conversations about all things urban. Renewing the city is the central theme and focus of what we publish. It is our intention to blend urban ministry, theology, urban planning, architecture, urbanism, stories, and the social sciences, as ways to drive the conversation. While we lean towards scholarly and academic works, we explore the fun and lighter sides of cities as well. We publish a wide variety of urban perspectives, from books by the experts about the city to personal stories and personal accounts of urbanites who live in the city.

urbanloftpublishers.com
@theurbanloft

Other Books by Urban Loft Publishers

The Communal Imagination
Finding a Way to Share Life Together
Mark Votava

Everyday life is often times not experienced as very relational anymore. The church has been co-opted by services and meetings detached from a relational expression within a particular place or parish in everyday life. We need to create the context to reimagine the body of Christ in everyday life as embodied through its proximity and shared life together. Without the value of inhabiting and listening to the place where we live, we will have very little expression of faith together in everyday life. There needs to be an embodied expression for our ecclesiology to make sense. If we do not have a local expression together, we will create a duality between our spirituality and our everyday lives in the ordinary. *The Communal Imagination* will draw out a new way of being for ourselves into this transition of embodied expression by stressing the importance of proximity and shared life within a particular neighborhood where we live, work and play. We need to embody practices as a way of life that are based on a spirituality of love, grace, humility and simplicity within the place where we share life together. This is how we will be able to get along and function in a healthy way over time that does not do damage to the cultural context we are in as we build on the particulars of our relationships together.

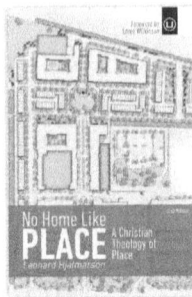

No Home Like Place
A Christian Theology of Place
Leonard Hjalmarson

"The sense of being lost, displaced, and homeless is pervasive in contemporary culture. The yearning to belong somewhere, to be in a safe place, is a deep and moving pursuit. Loss of place and yearning for place are dominant images ..." (Brueggemann, *The Land*)

Fragmentation, mobility, dualism—these forces work against our belonging, and work against our richly dwelling in the places we live. Add to these the rise of "virtual" place and relationships, and our sense of displacement only increases. It has been difficult to embrace a call to *life as mission* in this world under these conditions, and equally difficult to embrace a call to *place*.

Are there "sacred" places? If *every* place is sacred, does the word lose its meaning? What is it that God loves about place? Can architecture contribute to our ability to engage in a place? How do experiential human questions like "belonging" intersect with a theological lens? Does a biblical view of place imply an ecology and an ethic? How do pilgrimage (the journey) and place (stability) relate? Can the arts assist us in place-making?

This book addresses these questions and more, in a lively dialogue between theology and culture.

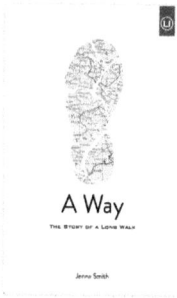

A Way
The Story of a Long Walk
Jenna Smith

But why? Why would a young urbanite leave the comforts of home and walk 65 days through rain and hail and scorching sun? So begins *A Way*, the recounting of a young woman's pilgrimage along the Camino di Santiago from France through Spain, with nothing more than the bag on her back and her husband by her side. It tells of the people met (the quirky ones, the lost ones, the kind and unforgettable ones), the physical discomforts endured (and oh, how many there were) and of the road travelled (all 1065 miles of it). It reveals how a sacred pilgrimage can bring about the most unsacred of experiences. It is a memoir, intertwined with reflections from the walking and lessons learned on the road about time, about the body, and about community. But most of all, it's a story. The story of a long walk.